Darkest Italy.

Darkest Italy.
The Nation and Stereotypes
of the Mezzogiorno, 1860–1900

John Dickie

St. Martin's Press
New York

ISBN 0-312-22168-1

Library of Congress Cataloging-in-Publication Data
Dickie, John, 1963-
    Darkest Italy : the nation and stereotypes of the Mezzogiorno, 1860–1900 / John Dickie.
        p.   cm.
    Includes bibliographical references and index.
    ISBN 0–312–22168–1
    1. Italy, Southern—Civilization—Public opinion.   2. Italy, Southern—Social conditions—19th century—Public opinion.
3. Italy, Southern—Politics and government—1861–1922—Public opinion.   4. Public opinion—Italy, Northern.   5. Stereotype (Psychology)—Italy.   6. Italy—Politics and government—1870–1914.
    I. Title.
DG825.D53   1999
945'.7—dc21   99–23083
                                                                                                         CIP

Design by Letra Libre, Inc.

First edition: November, 1999
10   9   8   7   6   5   4   3   2   1

Contents

Acknowledgments

The preparation and publication of this book has been so drawn out (through no fault of St. Martin's Press, it should be stressed) that a list of all the people who have played an important role in it would read like an index to my personal and academic autobiography over a decade. So many members of the community of scholars working on Italy have influenced and helped me that I am reluctant to offer individual thanks here lest I miss anyone out. I hope, therefore, that my friends and colleagues will not think my gratitude any less sincere for its being expressed to them collectively. Nevertheless, I owe a special debt to David Forgacs, the supervisor of the doctoral thesis on which this book is based; his meticulous and stimulating comments on my submissions were of inestimable value. I would never have been able to pursue my work without Anna Maria Nardini's friendship and hospitality during my time in Italy. My thanks are also due to the institutions that provided the time and money without which it would have been impossible to write this book: the British Academy; the Italian Cultural Institute; University of Wales, College of Cardiff; University College London. Finally, I would like to thank my parents for their love and support, and for never allowing even the suspicion of a doubt about the worth of my protracted studies to cross their minds. The book is dedicated to them and to the memory of Pat Jessop (1934–1966).

Introduction ❋

The South as a place of illiteracy, superstition, and magic; of corruption, brigandage, and cannibalism; of pastoral beauty and tranquility admixed with dirt and disease; a cradle of Italian and European civilization that is vaguely, dangerously, alluringly African or Oriental. The South as the theater of sweet idleness *(dolce far niente)* and of the "crime of honour"; of tragic courage and farcical cowardice; of abjection and arrogance; of indolence and frenzy. Southerners as a friendly people in whom lie dormant the seeds of *mafiosità* and atavistic violence; a "woman people" who practice an "Arabic" oppression of women[1]; a pathologically individualistic people who are nonetheless indistinguishable in their teeming masses or bound to the tribal logic of familism; a people both ungovernable and slavish. The South as a society verging on anomie that is resilient in its feudalism or clientelism; a society shot through with residues of a precapitalist past that is also the site of hopes for a national resurrection. "Here it is as if we were outside Italy"[2]; Italy's greatest problem; its anomalous lower third: a metaphor for the state of the country as a whole; the embodiment in extreme form of the whole nation's characteristic problems; the index of Italy's modernity and claims to nationhood.

The four essays that make up the bulk of this book are united by a single thesis: representations of the South from the centers of political and cultural power in Liberal Italy were informed by a repertoire of stock images and criteria akin to those I have just listed. The common element in those stereotypes was the situating of the South as Other to Italy and to totemic values considered all but synonymous with the Italian nation. For example, to define Italy as civilized, one has to have a sense, albeit perhaps implicit, of where that civilization fades at its boundaries into the barbarous. The South was one of nineteenth-century patriotic culture's most important funds of images of alterity. The barbarous, the primitive, the violent, the irrational, the feminine, the African: these and other values—often but by no means always negatively connoted—were repeatedly located in the Mezzogiorno as foils to definitions of Italy. My aim, therefore, is to study the role that representations of the South played in forming notions of an Italian national identity. The problem that stereotypes of the South address relates to whether southerners are "us" or "them"; the unease that such stereotypes express derives from the difficulty of defining who "we" might be.

One does not have to spend long in Italy to discover not only how frequent the incidence of stereotyping of the South and southerners is, but also how sensitive Italian public culture is to the intolerance that such stereotypes can evince. One does not have to read very far into the history of Italy to discover similar instances of prejudice and sensitivity. Yet until recently, stereotypes of the South have been the subject of strikingly little historical attention. What work exists is often marked by important limitations, chiefly of a theoretical nature.[3] As a way of engaging with some of the existing literature on the subject, and of preparing the ground for my four studies of different instances of stereotyping, I want to look briefly at one text that generated a fierce debate in its day and became the *locus classicus* of prejudice against Southern Italians: Alfredo Niceforo's *L'Italia barbara contemporanea* (Contemporary Barbarian Italy), published in 1898. Like many instances of prejudice against southerners, this book has previously been understood as evincing both regionalism and racism. This interpretation of Niceforo, it seems to me, is mistaken. Moreover, both of these terms bring with them a theoretical and historical baggage that has obstructed the study of representations of the South in general. Through a reading of Niceforo, I want to suggest that in the postunification period at least, stereotypes of the South are more fruitfully interpreted as a question of nationalism and ethnocentrism.

Alfredo Niceforo published *L'Italia barbara contemporanea* at the age of only twenty-two; it was to be the beginning of a distinguished academic career. Niceforo's hypothesis is that Sicily, Sardinia, and the southern mainland are stagnating at an inferior level of social evolution to the northern and central provinces. In support of his case, Niceforo invokes what he calls the "magical power" of statistical evidence in those fields (crime, education, birth rates, mortality, suicide, and the economy), which for the Italian school of positivist social anthropology were the key measures of the state of civilization of a society (Niceforo 15). For example, whereas the North is characterized by crimes of fraud, southern crime is predominantly violent, like brigandage; or, like the mafia, it is the result of an Arabic or medieval spirit of independence and rebellion against the principle of authority (Niceforo 45). Low literacy rates and the prevalence of superstitious practices, such as those surrounding the lottery, betray the "state of crass and primitive ignorance" in the population of Naples in particular (Niceforo 80).

Having set out the statistical basis of his contention, Niceforo proceeds to give a more detailed portrait of the "collective psyche" of the populations of Sardinia, Sicily, and the mainland Mezzogiorno (Niceforo 179, 184). In the Sicilian countryside, for example, he observes a "hatred for the spread of culture of a kind characteristic of societies that are not just inferior, but truly barbaric" (Niceforo 197). Outside of the cities, the Sicilian character "reminds one of the Orient and of out-and-out feudalism." In their "morbid conception of their own dignity" and their overbearing pride and love of pomp, the Sicilian aristocracy in particular present the scientific onlooker with "a stratification of the past which is still tenacious" (Niceforo 203–209). The wild lower orders of Sicily's urban population are capable of acts of "cannibalistic ferocity" and of scenes "that an African tribe would hardly have committed" (Niceforo 210–211). Sicilians in general display a love of weapons and aggression—"an essential characteristic of primitive and almost savage peoples," according to Niceforo (Niceforo 212).

L'Italia barbara contemporanea concludes that the backwardness of the South is in part determined by the fact that its population of "Mediterraneans" is a different race to the "Aryans" of the North (Niceforo 288ff). Niceforo follows Giuseppe Sergi in seeing the supposedly distinctive cranial form of Southern Italians as proof of this difference, which is the root cause of the greater individualism of the South and superior sense of social organization of the North. Niceforo maintains that Italy's hopes for the future rest on its becoming a federal state, since specific forms of government are necessary to deal with the distinct characteristics of each region. Government must be authoritarian in the South and liberal in the North (Niceforo 297).

The group of social anthropologists with which Niceforo was associated are conventionally regarded as having set northerners against southerners and sown discord between the Italian regions. Those who subscribe to this view of Niceforo as a *regionalist* tend to categorize *L'Italia barbara contemporanea* as an extreme manifestation of more widespread and enduring forms of a localist prejudice which constitutes one of many weaknesses in the fabric of the Italian nation. The existence of loyalties to village, town or region is indeed one of the deep continuities of Italian history.[4] Hence Massimo Salvadori argues that "The results of the denigratory campaign conducted by the 'anthropological school' constitute the major ideological factor which divided and still divides northern and southern Italians."[5] Yet if it is true that the sociobiological understanding of the southern question was simply a "work of defamation" (Salvadori 189) against Southern Italians, then it is difficult to account for the fact that its central text was written by a Sicilian: Niceforo refers to "my soul born at the foot of Etna" in the introduction to *L'Italia barbara contemporanea* (4); he also held a university post in Naples. Thus, even in the case of what Salvadori regards as the *ne plus ultra* of hatred towards southerners, ethnic prejudices do not necessarily pit the inhabitants of North and South against each other in a clear-cut way.[6] It is undoubtedly true that texts like Niceforo's were seen to speak to the mood of hostility toward Rome and the South in the Milan of the 1890s.[7] Strong provincial movements like those in Milan did indeed compete with and feed off of the centralizing tendencies of the state and often produced their own brand of bigotry.[8] The anti-southernism of the early Socialist Party is well known.[9] But Niceforo's ethnocentrism was essentially of an incorporative rather than an exclusive kind. Although he was a federalist, Niceforo did not want to divide North from South, but to create a more flexible and therefore stronger unity between them. He thus felt able to align himself with a tradition of patriotic social thinkers on the southern question. He firmly believed that, although racially different, northerners and southerners were as one in their "spirit of nationality" (Niceforo 292). Throughout *L'Italia barbara contemporanea* and the debate that followed, Niceforo and others saw their work on Southern Italy as the victory of science over two opposing taboos: a short-sighted regional pride on the part of those who refused to consider the problems of other areas of the country and attempted to conceal the defects of their own; and a cult of national unity, which sought dogmatically to fit all of Italy's diverse regions into one administrative model (a tendency whose most recent exponent had been Francesco Crispi).[10] Niceforo's book is also a response to the crisis of colonial expectations after the calamitous defeat of Italian troops by a native army at Adowa in 1896. Referring to the South, Niceforo says in his introduction: "Here modern Italy has a lofty mission to accomplish and a great colony to civilize" (Niceforo 6).[11] Niceforo writes not as a southerner or as a northerner, but as an Italian. The problems he describes are thought of as Italian problems. The agent to be responsible for their solution is Italy. The worrying thing about *L'Italia barbara contemporanea* is not its excessive regionalism, but the particular form of its nationalism. These observations about Niceforo can, I believe, be generalized. Stereotypes of the Mezzogiorno in Liberal Italy were most often *not* symptoms of Italy's failure to become a nation-state. It was rather discourses associated with the very project of nation building and modernization that produced those stereotypes in their predominant forms. The issues raised by stereotypical representations of the South in the Liberal period need to be relocated in the context of attempts to create or imagine a national culture.

L'Italia barbara contemporanea in particular, and stereotypes of the South in general, have been vilified more than understood. The blame for this historical failing lies as much with a certain notion of racism as it does with the idea of regionalism. The horrendous forms of oppression that have been legitimated by racism make it both an important and a difficult object of historical study. The study of racism is accompanied by a loose but interrelated set of analytical habits. Too often, perhaps, the need to disprove and condemn racial theories has left little room for historicization and analysis. The study of nineteenth-century racial theories also exposes historians to the risk of producing a teleology of Nazism. Some commentators on the race debate in *fine secolo* Italy have resorted to the kind of nonexplanation that attributes racism to ignorance (yet people are prejudiced because of the way they organize what they *do* know rather than because of what they do not).[12] There is also a tendency to ignore the variety and indeed vagueness of the use of the term "race," and thereby to reduce racism to a single and unchanging thesis according to which race is the *causa causarum* in human affairs. There is also the temptation to see bigotry only in those instances in which racial language is used, or to see racial chauvinism as the secret essence of all forms of ethnic prejudice. All of these tendencies are intermittently present in work that takes the problem of intolerance towards the South as one of racism.[13]

More recent studies have found a more fruitful line of interpretation by translating the problem of racism into the terms of ethnocentrism, if by ethnocentrism we understand the construction of essentialized differences between geographical entities or between socially and culturally defined groups. Whether those differences are between "races," between city and country, center and periphery, colonizer and colonized, believer and heathen, the essentializing effect is comparable. Racism, as a subset of ethnocentrism, can be redefined as a range of discourses (racisms) that produce many different concepts of race. Races do not exist, either as groups distinguished by hereditarily transmitted aggregates of characteristics, or in any other sense as far as human biology is concerned. The notion of race is biologically useless.[14] "Race" is thus not "an objective term of classification" denoting a physical reality that may or may not exert an influence on our behavior.[15] It is an analytical fiction, a trope that can be incorporated into and transformed by a variety of styles of argument. Just as ethnocentrism is not restricted to instances in which racial terms are used, so that concept, as well as being part of elaborate theories, can have ideological effects in "less formally structured assertions, stereotypical ascriptions and symbolic representations."[16]

Stereotypes are perhaps the most important feature of ethnocentric discourse. They make particular demands on the form and method of historical study. At the most fundamental level, in order to understand stereotypes, we must question some of the premises of an empiricist historiography that aims to get access to facts, events or ideas that it conceives of as prelinguistic. It was from the perspective of this empiricism that stereotypes were once dismissed as oversimplifications or errors, mere obstacles in the way of objective understanding. They have now come to be seen as having their own historical weight inasmuch they inform the languages through which real agents act out historical events.[17] When arguing against stereotypes, it might well be important to examine them on a cognitive plane, in terms of their degree of accuracy or truth. When studying them historically, it is better to do so on a pragmatic plane, in terms of their function in creating cultural identity.

The stereotype "Neapolitans are superstitious" provides a useful example. Depending on how and when it is uttered, and by whom, it may purport to be a statement of anthropological fact, an expression of disgust or a fond self-accusation. Yet, in each case, what that stereotype says is simply that Neapolitans are different. Thus its effect is not merely that of oversimplifying a complex reality. "Neapolitans are superstitious" has a certain probabilistic force, drawing as it does on images familiar to Italian culture, such as the scenes of Neapolitan crowds at the drawing of lottery numbers in the last century. But that vague plausibility itself in part derives from the way the stereotype establishes the (scientifically useless) category of superstition as the grounds on which a "we" and a "they" are constructed: either "Neapolitans are different from us," or "we Neapolitans are different from them." Stereotypes of this kind are about drawing boundaries; about differentially constructing the geographical and cultural concepts by which humans live; and about projecting a plausible picture of reality to fit a dualistic mind-set. Stereotypes are functions of social identities, including regional and national identities.[18]

Ethnocentrism towards the South is not limited to the sociobiological theories of Lombroso and his ilk, or to those moments when racial criteria are used; those moments do not constitute the "origin" or even the most extreme expression of that ethnocentrism.[19] For example, Niceforo's whole analysis has a single enabling presupposition that has nothing necessarily to do with racial theories, and that is shared by a great many far more credible writers. For Niceforo, all of the different aspects of his account—statistical, anecdotal, sociological, behavioral, racial—are interrelated simply because he thinks the South in a particular way, as "an organic whole" (Niceforo 17). Furthermore, Niceforo's text, controversial though it was, made sense to him as to his contemporaries partly because it was able to tap into a whole tradition of stereotypes of the South's Otherness across various cultural fields. In the following passage, Niceforo explains the origin of the title of his book and his formative encounters with the countryside of the South:

> those words [contemporary barbarian Italy] issued forth from my mind in
> sadness, certainly, but also with an immaculate spontaneity. They blossomed
> in my thought when my horse carried me up through the dangerous woods
> in the mountains of Sardinia, and when the train hauled me across the soli-
> tude of the Sicilian latifundia. Those words returned to my lips when I was
> lost amongst the villages of the Mezzogiorno, which were so rough, so prim-
> itive, and which I unconsciously compared to the completely civilized and

modern grace and courtesy which surrounds the little villages of Tuscany or Lombardy like a golden halo surrounds Giotto's madonnas (Niceforo 5–6).

Travel amidst solitude and barbarism, across landscapes unmarked by human activity: the same images recur seemingly endlessly in writing of all kinds on the South. The perceptions of the traveler in strange territory, it need hardly be said, are never wholly spontaneous or immaculate. Travel is a culturally saturated experience, structured through powerful precedents: the railway has a strong range of meanings in postunification Italy, for example.[20] The passage cannot be understood without reference to that broader culture; it invites further questions. Why should the sight of southern villages conjure up their counterparts in the North? Why, particularly, do Tuscany and Lombardy offer themselves as an image of the contrast with the Mezzogiorno? Why should the terms civilization and barbarism seem the most obvious articulation of that contrast? Why should Niceforo stress the modernity of the North, yet also associate it with an early Renaissance painter? As a critical tool, the model of racism can prevent us from even asking such questions.[21] Yet stereotypes inform the whole experience of the difference of the South in the postunification period, whether that difference is thought in racial terminology or through the conventions of travel literature.

But why should discourses of nationality have articulated such profound and varied forms of ethnocentrism toward fellow nationals, and toward an area of the national territory? What was it about the South, or about the national identity of the elites of Liberal Italy, that made such ethnocentrism possible? In the next three sections of this introduction, I will give preliminary answers to these questions by tackling three related issues: first, the situation of the South *vis-à-vis* the Italian state; second, the relationship between reality and representations of the Mezzogiorno; last, the functions of nationalist discourse in the culture of the elites and middle classes. The strength of ethnocentrism toward the South is explained not so much by the reality of the Mezzogiorno as by the interpretative models that were applied to that reality by the elites. The South could not help seeming backward or even deviant compared to certain templates of statehood, nationhood, and modernization.

The Mezzogiorno and the Italian state

It is evident, even from a brief outline of the history of the Mezzogiorno in the forty years after unification, that the question of intolerance towards the area does not derive from a simple relationship of political and economic subordination of South to North.[22]

The specific problems presented by the incorporation of the Kingdom of the Two Sicilies into Italy had not loomed large in the minds of the thinkers and statesmen of the Risorgimento in Northern and Central Italy.[23] If the construction of a single state including the South was considered at all, the assumption was that southerners, like all other Italians, would consent spontaneously to a liberal government that worked in the interests of the nation as a whole, allowing the natural wealth and energy of the region to be unlocked.[24] However, as Marta Petrusewicz has recently argued, many of the generation of intellectuals exiled from Naples to Piedmont and elsewhere after 1848 had become frustrated with the slow progress of the Kingdom of the Two Sicilies and had come to view its population as "almost biologically corrupted and therefore as beyond recuperation by any governmental or administrative activity."[25] As we shall see, the crisis of unification pushed the optimistic liberals and moderates toward views that resembled those of the pessimistic exiles.[26]

The Bourbon kingdom did not offer promising conditions for liberal progress. At unification, the ownership of southern agriculture was excessively concentrated in the hands of a landed elite that also dominated the governmental sphere and set lasting patterns for a political culture based on personal ties. The great estates or latifundia, based on extensive agriculture, did not encourage much-needed commercial innovation. Other areas of the economy were stronger: the cultivators of citrus fruits and olives could get access to rich markets; helped by a protectionist policy under the Bourbons, industries such as textiles, metalworking, and paper production had developed to a level smaller than that of the Northern Italian states but certainly of the same order of magnitude when compared to the industrial giants of Northern Europe.[27]

The crisis of unification certainly undermined some unrealistic expectations, but it did not pave the way for policies more responsive to the economic needs and social realities of the Mezzogiorno. There was widespread peasant revolt and administrative chaos after the fall of the Bourbon regime. The northern moderates aimed to establish order and construct a national state without making any concessions to other social groups in terms of political change.[28]

The politically subordinate role played by the South at unification meant that it was underrepresented in government for the first decade and a half of the state's existence. Liberal economic measures were implemented immediately without knowledge of the damaging effects they would have on sectors of southern manufacturing used to more protection. The abolition of government offices in Naples removed support from associated services and industries. However, the agricultural economy tended to respond well to free-trade policies, helped by an upward trend in grain prices and the expansion of markets for citrus fruit, almonds, and olive oil. The land that had belonged to the church and municipalities was distributed in the hope of creating a class of smallholding farmers. However the greater part of it had, by fair means or foul, finished up in the hands of large landowners or in those of a new rural bourgeoisie. Land continued to be seen as the safest and most socially prestigious place to put one's money. Thus a substantial proportion of the capital available for badly needed investment was soaked up.

A set of environmental and infrastructural difficulties beset the Mezzogiorno before and after unification: as a whole, it had a low proportion of easily arable flat land; hilly and mountainous areas had problems of soil erosion and water availability. The Mezzogiorno had a poor internal transport network, which hampered the development of an internal market for produce, products, and labor. It also suffered from inadequate links to the major markets of Northern and Central Europe. Over time, the unified state did improve communications between the South and the rest of peninsula. But the nineteenth century had ended before the erosion of the laissez-faire consensus allowed integrated programs of land improvement to be put into action.

In 1876, the Left, a diverse grouping of generally more interventionist interests in which southerners were numerically predominant, finally succeeded the moderates as the controlling influence in parliament. But the "parliamentary revolution" changed the problem of political representation in the South rather than solving it. The Mezzogiorno certainly became more of a national concern. And this more "southernized" state became more proactive in its nation-building initiatives. But the South lacked a politically experienced entrepreneurial cadre. Political struggle revolved around the control of local resources and the distribution of state money: it therefore tended to take the forms of clientelism and patronage that made the articulation of the interests of industrial development difficult at a time when industry was becoming increasingly investment-intensive and dependent on links to the state. When necessary, conservative agricultural interests could scupper attempts to shift the balance of ownership and encourage the creation of peasant smallholdings: this was the case with the response to the agrarian reforms proposed for Sicily by the government of Francesco Crispi in 1894.[29]

The condition of the peasantry remained desperate: so much is evinced by the mass emigration from the South (but by no means only from the South) that began toward the end of the century. The educational divide between the classes evident across Italy tended to be widest in the Mezzogiorno. Truancy in southern elementary schools was often well over 80 percent. Yet, without a substantial economic need for further education, it had a higher percentage of its population at secondary schools and universities than the North and center. Most of these students would subsequently number among an "intellectual proletariat" that competed for jobs in administration and the state-controlled utilities.[30]

Other problems came to characterize the Mezzogiorno. Malaria was responsible for 20 to 30 percent of the deaths in parts of the region.[31] Cholera killed at least 7,000 people in Naples alone in 1884. In parts of Sicily the mafia represented a constant challenge to the state's claim to the monopoly of legitimate violence, as did the camorra in Naples. Finding itself either unwilling or unable to tackle the mafia in anything other than a perfunctory way, the state ended up falling into a kind of *modus vivendi* with it. Banditry consistently reappeared to embarrass official claims that it had been eradicated.

The crisis of European agriculture and the depression in prices from the 1880s hit the Mezzogiorno particularly hard. Other problems arrived, such as a trade war with France and the increase of Spanish competition in the area of citrus fruit. At the turn of the century, two main factors began radically to change the terms of the southern question: mass emigration, which pushed up the price of labor and made money earned abroad available to many peasant families; and the concentration of Italy's growing industries in the Northwest.

At no point during the Liberal period did a significant group of interests in the Mezzogiorno mobilize by identifying with the banner of a neglected or oppressed "South." The notion that a conservative group of southern landowners formed a protectionist "historic bloc" with northern industrialists from the 1880s has been undermined by recent scholarship, which has, by contrast, "repeatedly underscored the failure of the southern élites to establish greater autonomy."[32] Indeed, as John Davis has argued, at the fall of the Bourbon kingdom, "the South became increasingly fragmented and diversified in its outward orientation, as well as in its internal structures" as the former provinces of Naples sought a more independent commercial and administrative environment (Davis, "Changing Perspectives" 55). The South was thus a region defined by certain economic and social problems rather than by the collective identity of an actual or potential political agent. As we shall see in chapter 3, prominent politicians were often reluctant explicitly to claim a southern identity in the national arena.

The Mezzogiorno was not the victim of a colonial type of exploitation by the North for which racism might have provided a legitimation. Nor was the relationship between North and South one in which two cultures led separate, hierarchical existences: they clearly interacted and fused at many levels. The southern elites and middle classes were not a marginal group: in many ways they were central to the Italian state. Indeed identification with a strong state was, if anything, more prevalent among southern intellectuals than those of other regions.[33]

So this book is *not* an account of an "Italian counterpoint," of a North-South dialogue fraught with hypocrisy, oversimplification, and misunderstanding.[34] The reasons for this, in addition to the socially and politically fragmentary nature of the South, lie with the weakness of the North as a power container, or pole of attraction for collective political identities. Northern Italy had nothing like the long common history of the Kingdom of the Two Sicilies. It is certainly the case that, in the decade before 1859, northern moderates had come to coalesce around the project of winning a liberal constitution and independence from Austria under the umbrella of the Savoyard monarchy—a kingdom of Upper Italy that would, nevertheless, leave a wide margin of autonomy for local notables. A northern state actually existed for no longer than the few months before Garibaldi's expedition to Sicily. But even if it had existed for longer it would have had a considerable task to mold and homogenize the territory in its own image. And although, in the century before unification, much of Northern Italy had had a common experience of administrative modernization on the periphery of systems based in Vienna and Paris, this process of constructing the regions had also fostered intense local rivalries, such as that between Turin and Genoa. Moreover, the map of power in the North, which had been redrawn many times since the French invasion, was still highly pluricentric and showed great internal diversity: the Milanese bourgeoisie did not share the dynastic and martial ethos of their Turinese counterparts, for example.[35] The northern elites, for much of the period that is my concern here, were as agrarian in outlook, and almost as tied to the specific interests of their locality, as their southern and central co-nationals. There were undoubtedly differences between North and South: in terms of economic and commercial development, and particularly in terms of infrastructure and the spread of a liberal-capitalist culture. But these were never the basis for collective political demands made in the name of the North as a whole *against* the national state or the South. The "North" was never one of the vehicles of political exchange between the locality and the central state that characterized the workings of government in Liberal Italy, from the Alps to the Mediterranean. The relationship between the elites and the state is the key to understanding why Niceforo, as a southerner who spread stereotypes of the South, is an extreme but by no means isolated instance: the names of southerners will recur throughout this book. But before tackling this issue in depth, we need to look at exactly what is meant by the "South" or the "Mezzogiorno."

The Mezzogiorno as a concept

My study of representations of the Mezzogiorno arrives, to some extent, in the wake of recent work carried out by many historians, notably those grouped around the *Istituto meridionale di storia e scienze sociali* and its journal *Meridiana*.[36] Whilst the range of this work is too broad to summarize adequately here, it can be handily characterized as a challenging of many received ideas about the South. For example, the latifundia have been shown to have been more than merely irrational and oppressive feudal residues, but to have worked and survived with a relatively flexible economic logic in a very unfavorable economic situation.[37] The middle classes of the South were, in the past, the object more of vilification than of analysis. Now the activities of groups such as entrepreneurs, lawyers, political brokers, landowners, and *mafiosi* are seen in their relative rationality and complexity. The reduction of the southern economy to its rural dimension, and the reduction in turn of the rural economy to subsistence methods, have been questioned. The differences and relationships between the economies of North and South have been rethought and reperiodized. The idea of a distinctive model of southern family has been exposed as a myth.

Reduced to its common denominator, the new southern history can be seen as an attempt to liberate the history of the South from the "southern question." Since the 1870s, some of Italy's leading intellectuals have sought to denounce the state's failure to address a range of problems associated with the South, from the peasant poverty of the Liberal period, to the unemployment and drug trafficking of the present day.[38] Despite the variety both of these problems, and of the political perspectives from which they have been viewed, the "southern question" has tended to be formulated as a question of the South's "backward" or "anomalous" nature. The extent to which the Mezzogiorno was backward or anomalous tended to be measured against Italian or European norms, such as an archetype of modernization according to which the nation-state, political liberalism, an entrepreneurial middle class, an organized working class, the nuclear family, and industrialization advance together. The idea of a "dualism" between North and South, whether it suggests a relationship of subordination or the separate existence of two social worlds, has also been called into question to the extent that it underplays the irreducible internal diversity of both North and South: that diversity has long been recognized without ever becoming a founding analytical principle. Reflecting polemically on Giustino Fortunato's evocation of the "great geographical whole" constituted by the South, and on the "different and almost opposite physiognomies" presented by the two halves of the peninsula, Carmine Donzelli remarks, in an essay that is something of a manifesto for the new southern historiography,

> But one has to ask oneself . . . in Fortunato's time, what degree of homogeneity, or even of identity there could be, let us say, between the Naples of the engineering industry, and sheep and goat rearing in the Abruzzi; or be-

tween agriculture in the gardens of Palermo or Campania Felice, and the grain latifundia of the Catania area. And if we put ourselves on the other side of the divide, would it not be an idle question to wonder what relationship there could be, let us say, between cosmopolitan Milan and the wretched villages of the Rovigo area; or between the textile industry concentrations of Piedmont, and the rural Veneto which was destined to pour forth almost 2 million people—the largest share of any Italian region—during the great wave of transatlantic emigration between the end of the nineteenth century and the beginning of the twentieth. . . . If we really want to undertake the scientific task of explaining southern difference in a way which is adequate to today's sensibilities, then there is no other way than to dilute that difference and produce an analysis based on a series of historical objectives, of linked responses to particular problems, of specific approaches to characteristic functions. In such an analysis, there must be a continuous adaptation of the scale of analysis and measurement. After all, this is how all the other bits of the world are studied.[39]

Historians of Italy can no longer take as given either the Mezzogiorno's existence as an integrated social, economic, or cultural totality, or its utility as a plane of analysis across all the permutations of time, space, and social relations. The South, like all such geographical spaces, is a concept. As soon as the Mezzogiorno is thought, as soon as it becomes an area of political intervention, the place of a history or of characteristic political structures, the object of loyalties, the bearer of certain psychological traits, the sum or average of the diverse social realities within it, it becomes a concept. To say this is most emphatically not to throw some blanket of skepticism over the possibility of knowing the realities that "the Mezzogiorno" names. Nor is it even to deny that it might be possible or desirable, in certain circumstances and for certain purposes, to represent the South as a *relatively* unitary reality. It is simply to point out that studying the Mezzogiorno inevitably involves taking decisions, implicitly or explicitly, about what the Mezzogiorno is, about how and where to apply the concept "Mezzogiorno." That concept can be used well or badly, but it never stops being a concept.

Moreover, that concept has a history of its own. The new southern historiography has done much to puncture stereotypes of the South. But it has yet to address systematically the historical task of analyzing the various ideas of the South produced at various times. To put it in philosophical terms, historians of the South have shown us the gap between stereotypical utterances about the Mezzogiorno and their referent, but they have not shown us the relationship between those utterances and their context.

At least at this introductory stage, I am concerned to include as much material as possible in my definition of stereotypes. This means that the kind of theoretical errors that Donzelli and others have identified must be part of the subject matter of a history of ethnocentric stereotypes of the South as I have defined it. Two important theoretical weaknesses are common to many studies: the South is constructed as an organic totality; and it is seen dualistically as a failed version of some scarcely defined idea of the North, Italy, Europe or civilization. Just as importantly for my purposes, these weaknesses can also be read as a theoretical elaboration of the underlying assumptions of many of the most widespread commonplaces in literature, art, journalism, and other registers: the Mezzogiorno is conceived of as a single, simple reality that is Other. In other words, theoretically speaking, there is no absolute divide between ethnocentric stereotypes of the South and the idea of the South as a geographical totality. Historically speaking, the idea of the South as a distinct part of the Italian nation, and the stereotype of the South as Other to Italy, are born at the same time.

It hardly needs pointing out that these stereotypical representations have had concrete effects: in the name of the Mezzogiorno policies have been formulated, resources have been distributed. One of my aims in each of the four chapters in this book is to relate representations of the South to the real historical forces by which they were shaped and that they shaped in their turn. But the power of such representations resides, in the first instance, in their ability to create the *impression* of truth or accuracy, to essentialize or reify the Mezzogiorno and locate the observer in relation to it:

> Everyone who writes about the [South] must locate himself [*sic*] vis-à-vis the [South]; translated into his text, this location includes the kind of narrative voice he adopts, the type of structure he builds, the kinds of images, themes, motifs that circulate in his text—all of which add up to deliberate ways of addressing the reader, containing the [South], and finally, representing it or speaking [o]n its behalf.[40]

Thus the first task I set myself is a textual one. It is to establish, for example, how the "South" is textually constructed as an object of knowledge, and what position is created in the text for the subject of that knowledge. It is to analyze how both subject and object are built into narratives, rhetorical structures, fantasy scenarios, or implicit logics.

Nation, state, and class in Italy after 1860

In its predominant forms, stereotyping of the South after unification cannot be considered a symptom of residual, subnational impulses. If anything, it was the desires and fears associated with the effort to bring the nation up to the standards of modernity putatively embodied by the rest of Europe that produced stereotypical definitions of the Mezzogiorno. The problematic of "nation building" constitutes the proper frame of reference for a history of stereotypes of the South. I have isolated the approximate period from 1860 to 1900 for my analyses of stereotypical discourse because of the relative consistency displayed by the nation-building problematic over those years: before 1860, the governing elite was not united in a single state; after 1900, the state adopted a much more open attitude to previously excluded social groups as socialists and Catholics became legitimate interlocutors for government for the first time. The history of the South can also justifiably be seen as undergoing an important shift at the start of the twentieth century: Prime Minister Zanardelli's journey to Basilicata in 1902 symbolized the Italian state's first programmatic recognition of the existence of a southern question; mass emigration from the South in the years before the First World War changed social relations in the countryside for good; the rapid industrialization of the northwestern triangle radically altered the economic balance of the whole country.

After 1860, the Liberal elites had good reason to be concerned about nation building. The much-quoted statistics for the areas of education, industrialization, and political participation, which are often taken as privileged indicators of the kind of socialization associated with mass nationalism, remain impressive.[41] Compared to France, Italy had one quarter of the number of pupils at elementary schools in 1861. The government's literacy statistics, based on criteria now generally agreed to be optimistic, showed that some 75 percent of Italians were illiterate. This figure reached the high eighties for the South and islands, indicating a well-nigh total illiteracy among the rural population. In large parts of the country, primary education remained ineffective: local government was often reluctant to fund schools properly, and schooling had a very limited practical relevance to peasant life.[42] At unification, 70 percent of the working population (not including women involved in family work) were occupied in agriculture, many of them day laborers or tied to the land.[43] Communications were poor, especially in rural areas. In 1860, Italy had 2,404 km of railway compared to 9,167 in France, and 14,603 in Great Britain. Sicily, Sardinia, Calabria, Basilicata, Puglia, and the Abruzzi had no railways at all (Candeloro 36). Those entitled to vote in parliamentary elections in Italy numbered less than one in fifty. Until the reform act of 1882, the country had the lowest percentage of enfranchised citizens in Europe. The proportion of people allowed to vote in general elections never reached over 9.5 percent in the nineteenth century.

What these figures demonstrate is that the divide between the state and the lower classes is an unavoidable and determinative fact of the history of Liberal Italy. The process of unification had been a diplomatic and military one that was marked by a paucity of popular involvement. After unification, the state represented a force that was at best distant and at worst hostile toward the masses of the peninsula. The damaging split between church and state greatly weakened the capacity of the institutions to build consensual links with the populace. Nevertheless, Liberal Italy was far from being a static society. From the 1880s, new social forces began to make their influence felt. Industrialization began in the Northwest. Illiteracy was slowly eroded at something like 0.5 percent per year (Vigo 47). By the end of the century, the processes of politicization and "nationalization" of the masses were well under way, albeit in geographically and socially uneven patterns. The country saw patriotic rallies, marksmanship contests, and the like, despite the nervousness with which such events were often regarded by the press and policed by the authorities.[44] The "social question" drew both state and church into greater intervention in society. The growth of the population and its increasing concentration in towns continued, with a consequent intensification of the organizational demands on the state.

Nationalism, at least when understood as something like "the cultural sensibility of sovereignty," can only have been irrelevant to the majority in the newly unified Italy.[45] Nevertheless, to call that majority Italians is not entirely anachronistic or mistaken in that it is consonant with the terms of reference of the country's governing class in the second half of the nineteenth century. Their use of terms like the "Italians," or the "Italian people" involved a great deal of historically significant wishful thinking and disavowal. The discourse of nationhood was a fundamental and complex component of the mentality of all of the social groups who were represented in the country's institutions.

A mixture of dividing and unifying factors can be seen as defining the profile of the country's middle classes and elites. The divisions have been well documented. The Risorgimento had witnessed a struggle between very different visions of what Italy should look like. No simple economic logic dictated the necessity of a single state to the middle classes of the preunification states.[46] After unification, each locality maintained its own pattern of conflict and alliance between the landed elite, the commercial and petty bourgeoisie, and the professional classes. To the end of the century and beyond, local elites jealously guarded their networks of patronage and structures of paternalism against intrusions from Rome.[47] Land ownership remained the most important marker of social status in Liberal Italy, and land tied its owners to a locality and to the particular geographical and social features of that locality in a country that had a huge variety of types of agriculture (Banti 65–97). There were strong lines of division in the political sphere on issues such as the spread of the franchise, church-state relations, taxes and tariffs, state intervention in the economy, and the social question. Commentators often lamented the lack of an impersonal public sphere and a culture of the common interest: newspapers were predominantly local in their coverage and circulation, and cliquish in their appeal; political power worked through the management of relationships and resources by groups of notables.[48] A distaste for parliamentary politics was one of the defining cultural characteristics of the bourgeoisie in this period (Banti 237–270).

Yet there were also factors that provided a certain cohesion between key sections of Italy's upper strata. They had a language in common and a common point of reference in the literary and scientific culture in that language. Literature was important both as a propagator of patriotic values and as a basis on which to claim continuity with a distant past. The monarchy came to symbolize unity for many groups. But most importantly, the middle and upper classes were held together throughout the postunification period by the system of patronage and power which was the state. Francesco Saverio Nitti famously called Italy's bureaucracy "the civil list of the bourgeoisie" (quoted in Banti 65). The elites and their allies competed for influence by allocating public works, managing the redistribution of public land, and appointing politicians, railway employees, mayors, doctors, teachers, and administrators.[49] The Italianization of the middle class spread fairly rapidly. After a slow start, the demand for secondary and university education increased greatly (Barbagli 108). Although the North had dominated the process of unification, by the 1870s a national political class was being formed. Italy's middle class has been defined as a "state bourgeoisie."[50] In the political sphere, the professional and administrative cadres came to predominate as the century went on: at the end of the 1870s Italy had 170 lawyers in parliament; during the same period France had 48, Britain had 30, and Germany had 10. In 1901 Italy had six times as many lawyers per capita as did Germany.[51] The army was another major employer and inculcator of patriotic values among the upper and middle classes, as well as being the force upon which legal Italy regularly relied for its protection. The industrial bourgeoisie, whilst gaining in power and influence as the century wore on, remained politically tied to the socially defensive nature of the Liberal order. Many sectors of the capitalist class, such as those benefiting from the huge military budget, were also economically dependent on state expenditure. Government bonds were a staple of bourgeois incomes. And when the ramshackle mechanisms of patronage and clientelism failed and economic crisis threatened, what held the bourgeoisie together were fears of the masses outside the state.[52]

The state therefore bestowed a paradoxical unity on Italy's bourgeoisie: the management of limited resources through patronage and clientelism is an unstable basis for hegemony. Yet the Liberal bourgeoisie was also extremely patriotic. The ideology which signified allegiance to the state, the language in which its affairs were conducted, was patriotism. The term "patriotic classes" gets closer to capturing the way Italy's rulers understood themselves than does the term "bourgeoisie." It is in order to understand this patriotism that we must move beyond the terms in which nation building is often understood. Nationhood is frequently equated, in the historiography on Italy, with social and political *integration*. Nation building is considered to involve spreading a sense of political and cultural belonging, inculcating of a sense of allegiance and a democratic "competence" into the masses, and integrating the modern state in an industrialized society.[53] This is a model not all that far removed from the criteria used by the elites of Liberal Italy when they themselves posed the question of how to "make Italians." Nevertheless, the "integration" theory of nationhood has a number of serious limitations, notably its failure to consider the discursive aspects of nationhood. My research draws on an understanding of nations as discursive constructs or social fictions. This is an approach that originates in Benedict Anderson's well-known definition of nations as "imagined communities." There seems little need systematically to treat the strengths and weaknesses of Anderson's case here.[54] But as far as this project is concerned, the main limitation of *Imagined Communities* is its failure to grasp the importance of the enormous variety of ways in which a nation can be imagined; of the vagueness of the term "nation" in both academic and everyday usage; and of the seemingly limitless variety of uses to which it is put. In addition to its community-creating functions, the idea of the nation also has the properties of what Walter Gallie terms "essentially contested concepts": there is endless disagreement in a given society about what the concept "nation" means, about whom it includes and excludes and what values it represents, but no modern society seems to be able to do without it.[55]

As Alberto Banti has observed, Italians consistently managed to invoke the national interest over decidedly local or selfish concerns, to be both patriotic and clientelistic (Banti 213–225). There is nothing paradoxical or peculiarly Italian about this; nor are we dealing with a strange kind of "psychological duality" (Banti 225). Patriotism has always and everywhere been "the last refuge of a scoundrel."[56] Less cynically and more precisely, we might say that one of the secrets of the nation's success as a concept is that it allows people to express entirely different meanings when it seems that they are talking about the same thing.[57] Patriotic discourses can express any number of political ideas. Public debate in the Liberal period saw often incompatible definitions of the nation competing against each other.

Nationalism had a great political, social, and cultural importance as the language in which relations between the groups operating on the terrain of the state were acted out. And just as the "nation" provided the patois of "paese legale" ("legal Italy"), so it offered the terms in which a faltering dialogue with "paese reale" ("real Italy") was begun.[58] There was an insistent political and cultural concern about the solidity of the state, and about the classes beyond the institutions. That concern found its expression in the language of nationhood: D'Azeglio's famous formulation of the need to "make Italians" is the most obvious example, but the same fundamental issue produced myriad inflections of "Italy" in response to different circumstances. Stereotypical representations of the South belong to this wider field of the perceptions and imaginings generated by the patriotic classes.

The meanings of "Italy" and "nationhood" that were involved in representations of the Mezzogiorno are too varied to be summarized at this introductory stage; one of the central concerns of the chapters that follow will be to tease out those meanings. But they all have at least one quality in common, a quality that is found, at some level, in all forms of nationalism: they are normative. As Giulio Bollati argues, in the context of an essay on national character which is more quoted than it is acted upon in historical analysis,

> every discourse on a people's make-up, nature or character seems to be an ambiguous combination of knowledge and prescription, of science and decree. What a people *is* (or believes itself to be) cannot be distinguished from what it is thought that it *must* be, except insofar as there are variable proportions of each.[59]

Bollati's point applies to any use of the concept of "nation" in that it pretends to a certain inclusiveness or unanimity, yet as such it is also the most powerful tool in gestures of social distinction. This normative dimension is obvious enough in those models of national modernization that, perhaps taking Britain or Germany as an example, sought to find a path for Italy's future development and, in doing so, to isolate those social phenomena that were holding it back. But even in less prescriptive discourses of nationhood, the imagined national space is defined contrastively by the exclusion of the alien or the unpatriotic, by the projection of Others.[60] Nations, inasmuch as they can be considered imaginative constructs, are made at their mobile conceptual frontiers.[61] The nation defines itself against impurities and weaknesses, traces of the foreign, which can be projected onto phenomena both inside and outside of the real boundaries of the state. Hence the imaginary power of defining "enemies within," of distinguishing the good citizen and the bad influence. The imagined nation is defined not only in a contrastive field of other nations but in the differentiation of any motif that the nationalist, the citizen, holds to be associated with it.

Stereotypes are thus important to nationalist discourse: they produce the kind of essentialized differentiation which is necessary for the idea of the nation to take hold in our minds, for it to seem like an obvious, objective reality.[62] For postunification Italy the South was one of the most important sources of the stereotypical images against which Italian culture defined itself. The different studies that comprise the body of the book each examine ways in which the essentialized South was situated in relation to projections of Italy.

Stereotypes of the Mezzogiorno and discourses of the nation spread far into the cultural and personal lives of Italy's middle and upper classes. Their diffuseness as objects of study constitutes a challenge to the historian. In the final section of this introduction, I will sketch out the shape of the book to follow and explain the influence that the nature of nationalism and stereotypes has had on my methods.

Stereotypes and history

Toward the end of Emilio De Marchi's novel *Demetrio Pianelli* of 1888, Melchisedecco Pardi, a factory-owner, wanders with a frantic aimlessness through the streets of Milan. Tortured by the discovery of his wife's infidelity with an opera singer, he finds himself before the walls of the jail:

> Locked inside, and almost embraced by that iron-set building, there are thieves, counterfeiters, knifers and murderers waiting for prison. When Pardi added all of this evil together, it still seemed small when compared to the harm done to him by that woman. A knife-wielding thief almost seemed like a gentleman compared to that man, that perfumed seducer. He had not felt even one jot of love for her. Yet, with the power of his voluptuous music and Roman accent, merely for the sake of some theatrical vanity or to pass the time between writing one thing and the next, he had come and sunk a poisoned knife into the heart of a hardworking gentleman whose efforts sustained a hundred honest workers. If some poor woman took four buttons from the factory, or a little skein of silk, the judges find that, according to the criminal law, she deserves at least six months or a year in prison. But these murderers of people's honour, these stealers of other men's women, these burglars of family tranquility go about in triumph after their conquests, like Zulus and redskins who go about boasting about the scalps they have torn from their enemies.[63]

The ethnocentrism here is obvious, on one level. The reference to the wife's lover's Roman accent is enough to set off a sequence of stereotypes of a vague, "colonial" South (the boundaries of the South were more than flexible enough to include or exclude Rome at different times). In De Marchi's text, honest industry is contraposed to sybaritic indolence and deception; civilized legal rationality, together with social and familial order, is contraposed to a ritual tribal ferocity. But it would be a crass misreading of the novel that imputed these attitudes directly to the author, or made of them the message to be extracted from the text. The above words are in free indirect style; they are the ventriloquized opinions of a man who is about to commit a crime of passion, that hoary cliché of the subjugation of reason to emotion. The text presents the passage as symptomatic of the febrile state of mind of a cuckold and in doing so places it in a kind of sanitary isolation. Nevertheless, the very isolation of Pardi's internal monologue from the rest of the novel is arguably part of an ethnocentric effect that is procured vicariously, pruriently, in wriggling past a disapproval of blatant prejudice against fellow Italians.

Whilst they clearly draw from a well of stereotypical discourse, Pardi's ravings demonstrate how difficult it is to reconstruct ethnocentrism toward the South exclusively in the form of systematic propositions or themes. Ethnocentrism expresses itself in apparently casual similes calculated to remain within the bounds of respectability, in jokes, or in fantasies that cannot always be predicted or read off from a set of propositions, an unambiguous psychological or political motive, or a calculated collective interest. Stereotypes are often tied into a dynamic of taboo and transgression in this way. In the Liberal period, any expression deemed to be "regionalist" was frowned upon as unpatriotic. For this reason, any historical analysis of stereotypical texts needs to remain alert to their complexity, to the specific texture of their effects.

Stereotypes are an elusive object of analysis. It is for that reason that this book does not take the form of a monograph but comprises studies based on four relatively distinct contexts. Stereotypes cannot, for example, be restricted to any genre or safely be assumed to happen outside the bounds of academic or scientific discourse. Ultimately, indeed, there is no marker we might use scientifically to distinguish stereotypical discourse from normal discourses. Moreover, there is only so much we can learn about stereotypes when we study them by tracing their origins and development.[64] Such a diachronic frame of reference may well disguise the fact that stereotypes very often operate synchronically, in contrasting pairs of good and bad images. Stereotypes work in this way as instructions in how to behave, or in how to expect people to behave: *either* one will be confronted by a happy Neapolitan mandolin player, *or* by a violent and duplicitous *camorrista*. Finally, and most importantly, to study stereotypes within the framework of a linear narrative would be to ignore the context-specific way in which they function: stereotypes take on meaning within local fields of social and semantic influence. The stereotypes used to pose the problem of the Mezzogiorno after 1860 were undoubtedly borrowed from a long line of ethnocentric representations prior to unification by both Italians and foreigners.[65] Democratic patriots tended to view the South, and Sicily in particular, as the powder keg of the national revolution.[66] A particularly strong condemnation of the Kingdom of the South's "primitiveness" was articulated by exiles from Naples after the failure of the 1848 revolutions.[67] We should also remember that the stereotypical polarity between a North (considered industrious, civilized, and freedom-loving) and a South (considered idle, backward, and dependent) was far more likely to be mapped over the opposition between Northern Europe and a Mediterranean area that was deemed, even by Northern Italians themselves, to include the whole of the peninsula.[68] And the pocket teleologies involved in labeling a society as backward are everywhere a part of the rhetoric used to galvanize support for modernization. Soon after unification, some new themes, such as the mafia, were added to the old repertoire of representations of the South.[69] But what is important from my point of view here is that these different Souths, these fragments of discourse, were reworked in a different social conjuncture as part of the processes of delineating a national space after 1860.

The fact that stereotypes do not respond best to a narrative analysis also means that I would not claim that the four chapters of this book are representative of all of the very many *mises en scène* of stereotypical discourse on the Mezzogiorno; they are inevitably a selection rather than an overview.[70] The interdisciplinary range of the analyses and the diversity of source materials are intended chiefly to exemplify the variety, flexibility, complexity, and power of stereotypical representations of the Mezzogiorno. In analyzing these representations, and in making assumptions about what readers from different disciplinary backgrounds already know about, say, the history of postunification Italy or methods of textual analysis, I have tried to err on the side of expository clarity. In the first chapter, on the Italian army's campaign against brigandage in the South in the 1860s, the material includes personal letters, eyewitness accounts, and military documents. In the war against brigandage, the representation of the South as Other was related to the confused and violent circumstances in which it was integrated into the Italian state. Chapter 2 analyzes the birth of the southern question. At the waning of the parliamentary rule of the Right, which had been the dominant force in the foundation of the Italian state, two of the leading figures of early *meridionalismo*, Pasquale Villari and Leopoldo Franchetti, investigated the conditions of a Mezzogiorno that they conceptualized in tendentially ethnocentric terms. The *Illustrazione Italiana*, a popular middle-class magazine, is the subject of the third chapter. Like other magazines of its kind, the *Illustrazione Italiana* was an important factor in the Italianization of the middle classes, but the ideas of Italian culture it promoted were harnessed to representations of the South as picturesque. Chapter 4 examines literary material together with political analyses, biographies, journalism, and diaries in order to assess the changing conceptions of the nation and the South in the political domain towards the end of the century, with particular reference to perceptions of Francesco Crispi, the first southerner to become prime minister. One of my hopes is that different as they are, these four chapters can shed new light on some of the fundamental questions about Italian society after unification by focusing chiefly on how that society perceived itself.

Chapter 1 ✸

A Word at War:
The Italian Army and *Brigandage*

What was brigandage?

In the years following the unification of Italy, no phenomenon evoked the South more powerfully in the imaginary of the middle and upper classes than brigandage. This was a stereotype that owed its force in large measure to the war fought by the Italian army against southern brigandage after the annexation of the Kingdom of the Two Sicilies. This chapter aims to analyze that campaign through the stereotypes, both of brigandage and of the South, that were an essential moment of the army's activities. Without having a declared beginning or end, the war continued for almost a decade, cost more lives than all the other battles of unification put together, and at its peak in 1863 necessitated the deployment of about two-fifths of the effective strength of the Italian army.[1] In the period from 1861 to 1864 large bands, which often comprised hundreds of members and had varying degrees of legitimist support and motivation, attempted to spark popular uprisings.[2] In 1861 particularly, some towns were briefly taken over and troops and national guard units directly confronted. As the brutally repressive military campaign to combat banditry was stepped up, the size of the bands began to shrink, and their political affiliation became less marked. The more spectacular activities of the bands took place "against a wider background of food and tax riots, land occupations, attacks on public offices and officers, cattle rustling, reprisals against property and stock, selective murder and kidnapping."[3] Brigandage brought to an exasperating, bathetic end the Risorgimento "epic" whose protagonists had been Cavour, Victor Emmanuel and Garibaldi. It exposed the weakness of legal Italy and the profound and tendentially violent social divisions in the real country, occasioning as it did the first dismayed formulations of a North-South "divide." The war did much to shape perceptions of the South as the nation's backward, unstable, and violent underside for years to come.

As an object of historical study, brigandage itself raises the issue of the relationship between representations and realities in a particularly complex form. What was brigandage? What does it tell us about southern Italian society? These apparently simple questions are actually pitched in a way that can be misleading. So much is evident from the way that the tradition of answers to such questions has itself produced a number of stereotypes. In analyzing some of this historiography, I want to highlight the difficulties that the study of brigandage presents, and to suggest that these two questions are better preceded by two slightly different questions: what did brigandage mean? what was the image of Southern Italy that the idea of brigandage was involved in constructing? In other words, it is more illuminating to approach brigandage in terms of *representation* rather than *reference*. We can learn a great deal about how evasive an object brigandage is by examining the historiography on the subject, for we cannot get direct access to the reality of brigandage from the historical sources. It is always already the product of a labor of interpretation. Indeed, it is often the case that this body of historical writing has reproduced, albeit in distant echoes, some of the presuppositions and commonplaces that were an essential part of the way in which the idea of brigandage was constructed in the nineteenth century.

The first salient feature of much historical work on banditry is that it views its object as a failed, incomplete, or primitive version of an ideal (but unelaborated) form of political mobilization. According to Franco Molfese's pioneering 1960s study of postunification brigandage, it is "the extreme, armed manifestation of a protest movement, based on certain demands, which rose to the level of crude forms of class struggle."[4] This is a theme echoed in some studies of brigandage not limited to Italy. In his *Bandits,* Eric Hobsbawm also evokes the difficulty of explaining the "pathological aberrations" and "ultra-violence" displayed by banditry.[5] He offers tentative explanations of brigand violence, leaving a fuller account to social psychology, about which he admits to knowing very little (he calls it "a jungle into which only a fool ventures carelessly" [64]). For Molfese and Hobsbawm, the attempt to pin down what brigandage actually was, and even more notably the attempt to give reasons for its ferocity, ultimately place it beyond the bounds of explanation. Brigandage, in the last analysis, is irrational, violent, primitive: it either has something missing (strategy, or the Party) or it is "excessive." It is the point at which the rational ends and the irrational begins; the point at which one stops writing history and starts writing psychology.

The kind of teleology and ethnocentrism implicit in labeling brigandage as "primitive" can also be seen in some attempts to place the phenomenon in postunification Italy in its social context. According to Giorgio Candeloro,

> In order to construct a historical evaluation of the "great brigandage" which raged in the continental Mezzogiorno from 1861 to 1865, one needs first to remember that brigandage happened in a backward, depressed country where individual banditry and the creation of brigand bands had for centuries been the normal form taken by the anarchoid rebellion of the poorest peasants.[6]

Brigandage, it would seem, is the inevitable consequence of a society's failure to keep up with the historical timetable. It reveals a lost world where the links of cause and effect between poverty and violence have a harsh simplicity.

Brigandage, in all its manifestations, has been the focus of a huge variety of interpretations. Towards the end of the last century, positivist criminologists of the school of Cesare Lombroso even attempted to isolate a pattern of physiognomically identifiable hereditary defects in brigands.[7] Brigandage has been represented as the demonic legacy of an elemental folk culture, a perversion of religion, a conspiracy, an atavistic monstrosity, a jacquerie, a protorevolution and an outburst of blind animal rage. Students of brigandage seem to find it impossible to talk about it without resorting to colorful metaphors: brigandage is an infestation, a delirium, a cancer, a sore, a plague, a hydra, an inverted society eating away at the foundations of order, a scourge, a poisonous weed.

It is virtually a convention of histories of Italian brigandage in the 1860s to distinguish "a strictly historical point of view" from the myths perpetuated by the mass of unscholarly popular works. In an essay from the 1930s, the Neapolitan journalist and critic Gino Doria argues that the subject is of most interest to the "devourers of those unhealthy books which are the best and most sought-after ornaments of station newspaper kiosks."[8] The problem with this analytical commonplace is that such unwholesome narratives and pseudohistories are an important part of the very events a historian would seek to isolate. The brigand myth organizes perception in compelling ways. The campaign against banditry in the 1860s did not take place in a cognitive vacuum. All sides entered the conflict with a repertoire of expectations gleaned from the very texts Doria abhors. The brigand is a figure prominent in genres ranging from the oral narratives of the peasantry to the novels and plays of the bourgeoisie. People acted according to preconceptions handed down from previous episodes of banditry: the memoirs of the French general Manhès, who had fought a very similar campaign against bandits under Napoleonic rule, were reprinted and repeatedly invoked in debates; the bandits who resisted the French were well-known figures in popular culture; and the fight against "primitive" brigandage was a major law and order theme in many of the preunification states.

These recurrent features of much of the historical literature on brigandage do more than simply obscure the phenomenon's real complexity. In their faith that reality is what we find when myth or metaphor are stripped away, and particularly in their underlying confidence in history's progress toward a rational modernity, they share some of the fundamental ideological assumptions of the elite groups who conducted campaigns against brigandage in the late eighteenth and nineteenth centuries, and who viewed obstacles to the state-building process in comparably teleological and ethnocentric terms. Historians of brigandage in general, and of this period in particular, have tended to share a number of lacunae in their representations of brigandage: in the way that they register the slipperiness of the notion itself, for example. Toward the end of his military history published in 1868, one of the first historians of brigandage in postunification Italy, Armando Guarnieri, exclaims:

> Brigandage! This is a sad word in the annals of our country; it is a sore whose meaning has as yet only been badly defined, and whose causes were not even tracked down.[9]

Guarnieri's remarks constitute a rather striking admission: he was himself an army officer who had fought against the brigands. (Indeed, most of the first historians of southern Italian brigandage in the 1860s were soldiers.) Other features of the text show that its author's unease is combined with a certain assertiveness: he uses a powerful metaphor ("a sore") for a word whose meaning he does not know, and goes on to argue that despite all the argument surrounding brigandage, its existence is not to be doubted. Guarnieri's admission is more than a statement of the problems with which brigandage presents the historian, it is closely related to the war against brigandage in which the author himself was involved. As we shall see, the word "brigandage," and the skein of logics, narratives, and lurid stereotypes that accompanied it, informed the conduct of the ferocious campaign at every level: the anxious self-justifications of the officers, the legal measures adopted, and even the way brigands were executed. The image of brigandage constructed by much historical study overlaps in a number of important respects with the image constructed by the brigands' opponents.

Whether in this particular historical context or in any other, brigandage is a label, in the first instance, rather than a thing or a condition.[10] To treat it as being equivalent to the activities of those whom the law regarded as brigands is fundamentally to oversimplify the issue. Brigandage is a many-sided phenomenon, constructed in different ways at different moments in the relationship between various social actors. Paradigmatically, we could say that brigandage is formed in the interplay of practices and discourses between the central state, the local elites, and the peasantry. The word "brigandage" had a hand in shaping the reality it presumed merely to reflect, particularly when, as in the Mezzogiorno after unification, it became the premise of a whole military campaign and the focus of debate in public opinion and within the political class. The search to understand the relationship between brigandage and southern society requires a similar caution, for it is accompanied not only by the risk of reifying brigandage, but also by the risk of taking for granted what the South was. As we shall see, in the 1860s, the idea of brigandage influenced the construction of a barbaric, irrational South of which this form of criminal activity was taken to be a representative or typical phenomenon. But before looking more closely at the army's constructions of brigandage, we need to set the phenomenon in the context of society and the state before and after unification.

Brigandage, society, and the state: from the Kingdom of the Two Sicilies to the Southern Provinces

In their exasperation at the persistent unrest in the Mezzogiorno, some Italian soldiers and politicians claimed that the area was in the grip of an autochthonous tradition of violence, and that brigandage was a sign of the region's isolation and backwardness. Yet brigandage was an ordinary law-and-order issue in many of the states of the peninsula before unification.[11] And in the Kingdom of the Two Sicilies as elsewhere it was a product not of stasis but of the profound social upheaval that accompanied the transition from feudalism. Banditry was a function of the transformation of feudal patterns of land use and the accompanying legal, administrative, and policing reforms that had begun in the later years of the eighteenth century and accelerated in the Napoleonic era. The privatization and enclosure of lands, the ending of traditional rights of usage, and the introduction of commercial pressures into farming meant an increasingly casualized peasant workforce from among whose number bands of poverty-stricken desperados would arise in times of particularly acute hardship. Yet this was neither the only nor even the most characteristic activity to come under the heading of brigandage in the Kingdom of the Two Sicilies. The land question and the increase in the powers of local and central administration created new arenas in which new and old elites struggled for wealth, power, and status by establishing clienteles that reached down through the middle and lower orders. The losers in those struggles might well resort to violent crime, or indeed be branded as criminals by those able to establish private control over law enforcement. The winners might well use violence directly or indirectly to achieve and maintain dominance. Threats, smuggling, vandalism, armed robbery, hostage-taking, livestock-rustling, and murder were an extension of normal power-relations in some areas. At certain times, the relationship between the bands and their protectors might break down, and the bandits would operate in their own interests. The central state was an important factor in these conflicts: brigandage, which everywhere in preunification Italy was taken to connote barbarism and backwardness, provided a good pretext for the extension of central control. Yet, at the same time, by signaling their loyalty to the state through their cooperation in its fight against "lawlessness," factions in the countryside would attempt to enlist the help of the authorities in tipping the local balance of power their way.[12]

The fall of the Bourbon regime saw an increase in both the violence and the stakes in social and political conflict on all fronts. The chief factors behind peasant unrest were an economic slump, the reopening of the land question, and the fear of conscription. As at other times, the crisis of authority opened new avenues for collective action and individual social ambition.

From the point of view of the Italian state, however, the new season of conflict between local cliques was just as serious an indicator of the problem of hegemony presented by the South. The northern moderates who directed the establishment of the regime had done so with the aim of avoiding the kind of social change that the democrats and republicans had hoped might come in a package with the new Italy. But the moderates' very vision of what an Italian nation should look like was not adequate to the specific complexities of the situation in the Mezzogiorno. In the face of mounting evidence from its own representatives, Turin persisted in its belief that the region's natural wealth would be unlocked by free trade, sound administration, and railways.[13] The moderates looked in vain in the Mezzogiorno for a ruling class that subscribed to their own masthead values of order, progress, liberalism, and *italianità*. The old landowners seemed too feudal and, like the bureaucrats and magistrates, too compromised by their association with the Bourbon monarchy. The clergy were a powerful local force that was hostile to the new state.[14] Rome and its surrounding territory remained in papal hands. The new middle classes seemed untrustworthy, either because they were too radical or because whatever political values they held appeared merely to be a cloak for clientelism. The very political geography of the South, traditionally centered on Naples, did not fit with the moderates' initial project of a state built in harmony with the paternalistic authority of enlightened local notables. The extension of free trade legislation to the South severely harmed the local economy. In addition, the new state's limited financial resources made it difficult to implement what plans there were for job-creating infrastructural programs. The state failed to display the will to solve the key problem of demesne and communal land distribution, allowing it to become bogged down in the murky world of local disputes over ownership and usurpation. In January 1861, the government proclaimed its intention to conscript elements of the old Bourbon army at a time when the lack of Italian troops on the ground in the Mezzogiorno made that policy impossible to implement, thus fostering desertion and crime; the same mistake was repeated in the spring. The politically motivated disbanding of Garibaldi's southern army removed a force that could potentially have been a powerful weapon against disorder. Instead, the remains of two disbanded armies roamed the countryside; the Bourbon troops in particular swelled the numbers of the bands and tended to give them a legitimist political coloring.

The political priorities that shaped government policy, the confusion to which it was subject, and the objective difficulties of the situation left the moderates with little option but to try and follow the well-established practice of using the crisis of order to legitimate and consolidate their authority. But this was a risky path to take: failure to impose law and order would severely undermine the state's credibility. The means of repression, at least in the early stages, proved unable to meet the demands for energetic measures which came from some local notables and the government's men on the ground. Apart from the initial lack of regular troops, who were needed to defend Italy against a potential Austrian attack, the means of repression were inadequate in other ways. The locally recruited national guard, where it was not the instrument of local factions, was underequipped and quickly worn out by a struggle against lawlessness that would have proved difficult even for a large army. Reform of the police and magistrature proved slow and politically controversial. Unauthorized, brutal measures such as mass arrests, summary executions, and reprisals had been used from the start by the Piedmontese army against lawbreakers and rebels. Reports of such excesses also harmed Italy's standing abroad at a time when urgent democratic aspirations to conquer Rome threatened the delicate international equilibrium that had permitted unification.[15]

The theory that brigandage was the work of a clerical, reactionary cabal and of subversion emanating from papal territory suited both the moderates and their political opponents. From the moderates' point of view, it shifted the blame away from the current administration; for the radicals, the same theory fuelled their drive to complete unification by taking Rome and supported the case for giving more power to former *garibaldini*. But little evidence of a widespread conspiracy was discovered. And the disorder, which had reached dramatic levels in the spring and summer of 1861, reappeared

the following year after a lull. The conspiracy theory looked increasingly im-
plausible and blame for brigandage began to be directed at southern society
itself.

It remains difficult to gauge the exact mixture of social protest, faction-
alism, political struggle, criminal activity, and state oppression or confusion
that shaped the situation in the 1860s. It is only localized studies that can
provide a definitive answer. Yet it seems to me that such studies are necessarily incomplete unless they take account of one feature of the antibrigand
campaign that was relatively systematic across the whole of the South, and
that is my central concern here. Brigandage was the object of a structure of
representation; there was a regime of concepts of brigandage and of the
South that were produced by the army but also by the government and public opinion throughout the conflict. It is to the analysis of those concepts
that I now turn.

The army, the nation, and brigandage

Armies are not simply fighting machines. Order is maintained within an
army by a mixture of coercion and consent. Rituals and traditions help to
maintain official and unofficial behavioral norms. Moreover, among many
other things, an army must necessarily be able to conceptualize its enemy
and perceive it as worth fighting. Thus the historical events of the antibrig-
and campaign involved the army in reconstituting the concept of brigandage. All of the different fields of signification associated with brigandage,
including the myths and lurid metaphors, played a role in the tactically important discourses through which the army made banditry make sense.

In the antibrigand campaign, army officers and the government understood their opponent predominantly by means of a series of hierarchical binary oppositions, such as between civilization and barbarism, reason and
violence, social order and crime. In his report to parliament on behalf of the
Commission of Inquiry into brigandage in May 1863, the southern moderate Giuseppe Massari argued that "Brigandage . . . is the struggle between
barbarism and civilization; it is robbery and murder raising the standard of
rebellion against society."[16]

Animality, to give just one more example, is a constant theme of writers
on brigandage. Alessandro Bianco di Saint Jorioz, an army officer and author of a full-scale study of brigandage in 1864, wrote that brigands, "kill
and rape like beasts thirsting for blood and booty, and not men created in
God's image."[17]

Yet a persistent cognitive uncertainty also surrounds what a member of
the parliamentary commission set up to inquire into the problem called the
"funereal mystery" of banditry.[18] In the field, the bandits, using guerrilla tac-

tics, seemed to possess a dark and perfidious quality. Gaetano Negri, a young officer who was later to become the moderate mayor of Milan, quotes Da Ponte's libretto to *Così fan tutte* as he writes to his father in November 1861:

> The brigands are like the Arabian phoenix: everyone says it exists, but no one knows where it is; and I am beginning to believe that their existence is the product of the over-active imagination of the local population.[19]

Bianco di Saint Jorioz calls it an "eternal" question:

> it is occult, mysterious, absolutely vast, extremely widespread and intangible. It is invisible, almost imponderable, something like a fluid, but a noxious, hydrogenated, carbonic, murderous fluid.

He compares the labor of the historian of brigandage to the explorers of the virgin forests of America and says they are seeking the historical truth through "a maze of booklets, memoirs, reports, news-sheets, almanacs, pamphlets, writings of every size and style."[20] Brigandage is a hidden and omnipresent threat; it is threatening to the degree that it is unknown. In the struggle to understand it the most powerful contemporary paradigms of knowledge are evoked and deployed. Bianco di Saint Jorioz attempts to face the difficulties presented by a study of brigandage "with the patience of the doctor in the analysis of a putrefying body" (Bianco di Saint Jorioz 165).

A commonsensical myth-reality epistemology is also used in many texts from the 1860s, in which it is the peasantry who are duped by the legends surrounding the figure of the bandit, while the army sees through to the squalid reality.[21] The many grisly "hunting-trophy" photographs of the condemned or executed taken by officers bear witness to a drive to capture and define. The same need informs the actions of Colonel Bernardino Milon, a Sicilian veteran of both the Bourbon army and Garibaldi's *esercito meridionale,* who kept the head of a dead brigand leader preserved in alcohol in a glass jar like some biological specimen: "a rather distinguished figure," he comments, "resembling and English brewer."[22]

Banditry has the entire repertoire of ethnocentric imagery deployed against it by the officers of the Italian army: bandits are black, animal, feminine, primitive, deceitful, evil, perverse, irrational. Manichaean thinking of this sort attempts to explain brigandage away, and yet in doing so places it beyond explanation in an imaginatively and emotively charged realm of monstrosity. Brigandage becomes both horrific and fascinating, subjected to hard-headed sociological assessment and colorful, highly charged evocation. It is an empty stage on which to act out both the wildest of ethnocentric fantasies and the seemingly most rational of investigations.

The imaginative work surrounding brigandage is part of a discourse that influences both the perceptions of individuals and the tactics adopted during the campaign itself. Forms of knowledge and representation are generated by the army's operations and are a crucial part of them. The texts of the antibrigand campaign do not only construct the object of which they speak, banditry: in the process the imaginary space of the nation is differentiated and tested.

The army's privileged relationship to the new nation had its roots in pre-unification Piedmont. In the decade that followed the military reverses of 1848 to 1849, Cavour and his close allies in the military had to cope with a number of developments in strategy and ideology as the dominant aristocratic and monarchical ethos of early nineteenth century warfare faced the challenge of constant technological and social change.[23] A series of political issues was also involved in the task of military reform: the army had to be made less dynastic and more Italian, while still maintaining its status as a royal force. The Piedmontese army was therefore to be legitimated and motivated by a monarchistic Italian nationalism rather than by an aristocratic and parochial praetorian ethos, a bourgeois careerism, or a Mazzinian ardor. In the military sphere as elsewhere, the national cause provided the ground on which the interests of Piedmontese dynastic expansion and administrative modernization could be reconciled. That General La Marmora's reforms in 1854 were meant to stress the *italianità* of the military is evinced by the inclusion of some 500 non-Piedmontese officers like Manfredo Fanti and Enrico Cialdini.[24] For the ideologues of the Piedmontese ruling class, the army found its military and ideological raison d'être in a dynastic vision of the nation to come, as Italy was to find its incarnation and expression in the army.

After unification, the success which the politically disruptive *garibaldini* had enjoyed in the field and, seemingly, in the popular imagination made the need for a strong ideological role for the regulars particularly urgent.[25] The army, if it had not quite lived up to its heroic billing, at least presented a more unified facade than any other aspect of the new country: General Fanti's assimilation of the forces of the rest of the peninsula along Piedmontese lines was organizationally fairly successful, and carried out some three years before the country had proper administrative legislation.[26] For Luigi Settembrini, a literary scholar from Naples who had just spent eight years in a Bourbon jail, the army was "the iron thread that has sewn Italy together and keeps it united." According to General Lanza unity should be maintained, "with the army and in the army."[27] The military was the instrument of geographical unity and a bulwark against sedition and reaction; but it was also seen as the symbol of the resurgent nation and the principle means of Italianizing its citizens:

Let foreign writers say that Italy is the land of the dead. Yes, but the dead have at last risen from their tombs in the shape of 350,000 armed men, and of 200 battalions of mobilized National Guards.[28]

The officers involved in the antibrigand campaign were fully aware of the army's nation-building role. During the civil war in the ex-Kingdom of the Two Sicilies, the army was virtually a surrogate state, and its supposed role in "moralizing" the local population and spreading the gospel of national unity was often invoked: the army had to "make the southern peoples understand the National Idea."[29] But the campaign in the mountains and forests of Southern Italy presented enormous practical difficulties for an army designed for field warfare. The war asked awkward questions about the real and ideological task of nation building to an organization that was weakened by typhus and malaria, dispersed in small units over wide areas amongst a frequently hostile or resentful population, with bad supply lines, little or no leave, and poor communications. The unanimous verdict of contemporary commentators, both civilian and military, was that the task of fighting bandits was an inglorious and even dishonorable one.[30] There is evidence that one of the few compromises made by commanders to the unusual demands of the conflict, allowing officers to go into action without epaulets, was conceded not in a practical spirit but for reasons of decorum, "that is, so as not to give the character of a national campaign to a guerrilla war."[31] The new Italian force had its nationalistic *esprit de corps* severely tested. Gaetano Negri declared himself "revolted by this atrocious and base war, where betrayal and intrigue are the only way to make progress, and where we shed the character of soldiers to take on that of common cops."[32]

The army's conceptualization of brigandage as an Other is set in the broader frame of an imaginative geography in which the Italian nation is constructed as the opposite of its South. Perhaps the most frequently employed of the many ethnocentric parallels for Italy and the ex-Kingdom of the Two Sicilies is the familiar spatial and cultural opposition between Europe and Africa or the East. A government envoy writes to Cavour from Teano in 1860: "What barbarism! Some Italy! This is Africa: the Bedouin are the flower of civil virtue compared to these peasants."[33] Nino Bixio, writing to his wife while working with the parliamentary commission of inquiry into brigandage, exclaims: "in short, this is a country that should be destroyed or at least depopulated and its inhabitants sent to Africa to get themselves civilized!"[34] One officer compares the function of the army to that of the British in the Punjab.[35] Although the relationship between North and South in this period is not helpfully described as a colonial one, for the army itself colonialism provided a close imaginary analogue for the campaign. Gaetano Negri refers to himself as being in exile and describes a town in which his troops are billeted as "lodgings fit for the Kaffirs and Hottentots" (Scherillo 42–43). But transposing the opposition of Europe to Africa or the Orient onto the Italian situation begs an obvious question: if Italy is supposed to be one country, how can it be formed by such vast cultural differences? Permeating the writing of officers on the brigand campaign is a sense of the fragility of the national identity. One young officer, Enea Pasolini, sees Italy's spatial self-definition as being in crisis:

> The state of our country is enough to make one blush. Ah! Calabria is not the only place where there are powerful scoundrels! It's the same the whole world over. And morally the world is a very nasty place.[36]

Bianco di Saint Jorioz restates the problem: "Here we are amongst a population which, although in Italy and born Italian, seems to belong to the primitive tribes of Africa" (Bianco di Saint Jorioz 12). He sees the repression involved in combating brigandage as a spiraling waste of the nation's moral and financial substance, leading to a national debt crisis that threatens its very existence. In an apocalyptic conclusion he exclaims: "And who are we? A Nation and not a Nation: united and disunited: drawn, sooner or later, into a long and terrible war."[37]

Italy is constructed both as the opposite of the South and as an agent that knows, or ought to know, its mystery. That knowledge function can be performed in a number of registers; one of the most powerful, and most closely associated with the nationalism of the educated elites, is literature. One member of the parliamentary commission of inquiry quotes Dante emerging from hell to evoke his feelings on leaving Basilicata.[38] Enea Pasolini's letters from Calabria are peppered with literary allusion and include the kind of amateur ethnography typical of colonialist travel books. "If you ever write," he tells his brother, "a fanciful novel about savage peoples, don't put any of these facts in it because everyone would think them impossible in human nature" (Pasolini dall'Onda 239). Pasolini portrays the experience of fighting in the antibrigand campaign as an invigorating, character-forming confrontation with nature, a "one man against the elements" adventure story.

Reading the accounts of officers of varying ranks one is struck by the frequency with which social reasons are given for the turmoil in the area: even the infamous General Govone blames the problem on the poverty of the peasants, and sees it as, at root, a class struggle.[39] Gaetano Negri reaches similar conclusions: "[brigandage] has its origins in the enormous inequalities in social position. . . . Here brigandage, which is very strong, is a true civil war waged by the poor against the rich, and there is indeed a great imbalance in social position of this kind" (Scherillo 235, 251). Yet an understanding of the origins of the conflict in rural class antagonism is not incompatible with the army's overall regime of representation. The army's understanding presupposes that the area in which they operate is an analyzable entity, a totality whose parts are interrelated and about which one can legitimately generalize. Just as the army represents and embodies Italy, so brigandage is seen to be symptomatic of a diametrically opposed Mezzogiorno: it comes to typify the South, to become a metonym of it. Images of brigandage, without a fixed referent or meaning, are inserted into an imaginative geography, where they can be applied to a host of situations and where any number of things can be read as somehow part of this mysterious phenomenon: "Southern Italy naturally produces wheat on the plains, oil in the valleys, brigands in the mountains."[40] A lieutenant in the carabinieri, Giuseppe Bourelly, wrote a history of banditry in 1865, which in addition to details of the history, the economy, the class structure, the mores, the hygiene, and housing of the area concerned, includes analyses of the weather, geology, and natural history as background factors in the emergence of the problem. Despite this thoroughness, he is not averse to using the most extreme of binaristic descriptions of brigands: "this rabble of fearsome beasts whose only human characteristic is their bodily form." He can also refer to "the occult, invisible, secret, powerful brigandage which lurks and skulks about mysteriously in the cities, villages and hamlets."[41] If everything in this reified South is related to brigandage, then brigandage becomes that through which one may know the South as a whole, the target and vehicle for the surveillance of everyone and everything in wide areas of the country. If banditry is "occult, invisible, secret" as Bourelly maintains (69), and if it extends throughout the social fabric and even into the "instincts of these people" (Bianco di Saint Jorioz 15), then to combat it the army must have an unrestricted reach. More than anything the South needs to be watched. Most of the numerous pamphlets and histories of the time recommend that the Italian government and army should tackle the problem by supervising all public employees and suspicious characters and rapidly building a modern road and rail network—tasks that were quite beyond their capacities. The measures proposed are often little short of fantastic: one pamphleteer recommends, in order to deprive the brigands of cover, "that all the undergrowth in flat areas should be cut down."[42] Whilst the national space is demarcated by dint of its diametrical difference from the South and brigandage, the state is imagined and identified with as the powerful but insecure subject of a knowledge of this Other.

Brigandage and the law

The Mezzogiorno spent the first five years after incorporation into the new Italy under different forms of what was essentially a military regime. The state's fight against brigandage can be divided into several stages; at each, the government had to balance the army's impatience with the civilian legal machinery against fears about the impression that the use of illegal measures would have on European public opinion. For a year after the plebiscites of October 1860, which sanctioned union with the Savoyard state, the southern provinces were under a governorship. Initially, establishing law and order in the countryside seemed less important than administrative and political questions. The national guard and those few regular troops who could be spared to combat lawlessness had frequent recourse on their own initiative to illegal and brutal tactics. A very difficult situation developed into one of near anarchy in the Spring of 1861: Turin then even gave General Enrico Cialdini the go-ahead to bolster national guard units by recruiting from the former *garibaldini* and to authorize illegal tactics such as shootings and the arrest of suspects' relatives. The situation improved, although Cialdini's differences with central government led to his resignation in August. The lieutenancy was replaced with a centralized system in which the commander of the army in the Mezzogiorno, General Alfonso La Marmora, doubled as the prefect of Naples and was given a supervisory role over other prefectures. The "state of siege" proclaimed to counter Garibaldi's expedition in Calabria in August 1862 was extended to deal with the situation in the South until November. As the situation worsened, despite these exceptional powers, brigandage moved to the top of the political agenda. In December it was decided to set up a parliamentary commission of inquiry into brigandage. Following the recommendations of the commission, the infamous Pica law explicitly dealing with brigandage was passed in August 1863 and remained in force, in different forms, for over two years. As the repressive measures took hold, and the local elites began to converge around the desire for a return to normality, brigandage died down, although there were serious sporadic outbreaks until the end of the decade.

There is little doubt that the military regime deemed necessary to tackle the situation in the South, involving tactics such as special tribunals and the widespread use of the death penalty, was clearly in contravention of a constitution that expressly forbade such courts and set strict limits on capital punishment. The principal terms of the way measures such as the Pica law were discussed can be isolated quite easily.[43] They tend to pivot on the following type of question: does the way in which brigandage seems to refuse to obey normal juridical rules and categories permit the forces of order to do the same in order to combat it? An extreme meditation on the legitimacy of exceptional measures comes from the prefect of Avellino in October 1862:

> our attempts to tame the ferocity of these murders with the word of the law
> are in vain. The law is strong and authoritative only in societies which have

undertaken to respect it, but is weak and ineffective against declared enemies of society itself.[44]

The further brigandage could be located outside the juridical space, the easier it was to legitimate the exceptional legislation formed to suppress it. Indeed, if brigandage was constructed as the very antithesis of law, civilization, and reason, then the use of unconstitutional measures to combat it becomes not only justifiable but ethically imperative. The political effects of this type of representation of brigandage is evident from an article which appeared during the summer of 1863 (during the debate over what was to be the Pica law) in *Il Pungolo,* a Neapolitan newspaper that generally adopted a mediating position between _____ serts that "everyone" is convinced of the _____ on, but condemns those who do not h_____ t with "decidedly extraordinary means _____ ____age as the worst nightmare of a hypostatized law or society makes it the pivotal point of legitimate political dialogue. Its demonization creates and polices a consensual boundary beyond which one may not go without becoming guilty—a bandit by association. The more enthusiastically one abominates the enemy, pushing further the Manichaean logic of antibrigandage, the closer one is felt to be to the center of the differentially constituted social space. Although the fight against banditry was often a lower priority for the government than keeping its political enemies in check, brigandage loomed large in the collective imaginary of the ruling elite. The very epideictic ferocity of the persecution of an enemy located beyond the pale of civilized society was seen to be the best way to guarantee a basis for the values of nation, law, and civility around which the moderates hoped that a socially conservative consensus might be formed.

Yet to embrace illegal, extraordinary means to fight a phenomenon that the report of the parliamentary commission of inquiry into banditry called "the bloody violation of every natural and written law" would also seem to place one on the side of banditry, or at least to make one an imitator of it:

> between enemies of such a diametrically opposed nature the rules of the art of war are not practicable. To combat the brigand effectively one must use his own methods.[46]

For the author of the report, Giuseppe Massari, the language of violence comes purportedly from outside the imaginary space occupied by the state, from outside the social body, but it is a language the state is forced to mimic. Brigandage, as the antithesis of the law, draws the forces repressing it into a borderline area where they can remain legitimate only by claiming to be replying in kind to the reviled methods of banditry.

The sense of having to go beyond the law in order to protect it perme-
ates the reflections of many officers in the South. The ideology of extraordinary measures also works in the most intimate self-justifications of the
individuals involved in the fighting. One particular style of argument recurs
with a striking frequency. In Canto XX of the *Inferno*, Dante weeps as he
sees the fraudulent twisted around, "between the chin and the beginning of
the chest," so that their heads face backwards.[47] The human body is de-
formed in a grotesque parody of the sin committed. Virgil's remarks to
Dante are famous for their harshness:

> mi disse: "ancor se' tu delli altri sciocchi?
> Qui vive la pietà quand'è ben morta;
> chi è più scellerato che colui
> che al giudicio divin passion comporta?"

Are you even yet among the other fools? Here pity lives when it is altogether
dead. Who is more impious than he who sorrows at God's judgement?[48]

To show any sign of pity to such sinners would be pitiless. To be humane to
the damned is the worst sort of inhumanity. In June 1868 Enea Pasolini
writes to his father:

> The commander here is a certain Milon . . . ; he is a resolute and decisive
> man, and he has already done a great deal of good for the area, but he has a
> great amount still to do. He must keep Dante's maxim well in mind: "Here
> pity lives when it ▮▮▮▮▮▮▮▮▮▮▮▮▮▮▮▮▮▮▮▮▮▮▮▮▮-established knowl-
> edge that people ▮▮▮▮▮▮▮▮▮▮▮▮▮▮▮▮▮▮▮▮▮▮e shot without pity
> and without a tr▮▮▮

A month later he writes to his old teacher: "'Here pity lives when it is altogether dead.' If we give in for just a moment, we will be back to the horrors
we had before" (Pasolini dall'Onda 251). That Dante should be invoked has
a multiple significance. Quoting from the *Inferno* makes an implicit comment on the way the South of Italy and its inhabitants were imagined.
Dante's eschatological themes and status as the poet to whom (literary) nationalism traced its origins also endow Negri's brutal sophistry with a
grandeur bizarrely at odds with the reality of the antibrigand campaign.
Dante, the most sacred totem of legitimacy and nationhood, is invoked precisely at a point at which the integrity of the imaginative space defined by
the law and Italy is put into question.

Massari uses a logic similar to Dante's in his report to parliament: "the severe punishment meted out to the few was an act of mercy to the many and

to the *patria,* as mercy shown to the few would have been cruelty to the many and to the *patria.*[49] One anonymous officer writes that those deputies who spoke up against the granting of extraordinary powers to the army on humanitarian grounds, "should resign themselves to being, or passing for, inhuman and ferocious."[50] The argument seems to have been a favorite of General Macedonio Pinelli's: "Against enemies of this kind, pity is a crime."[51] One contemporary writer approves of fierce repression in all cases of brigandage: "compassion towards such men would have been little short of a crime."[52] The dualistic categories constructing the relationship to the enemy prove dangerously unstable, their poles virtually interchangeable. The fear that the division between human and inhuman might disintegrate, or that in dealing with the barbaric one might actually be contaminated by it, seems to haunt the military imagination. One of the most infamous instances of pitilessness was the razing of the town of Pontelandolfo whose inhabitants had deceived and butchered a column of troops. On hearing the news of the army's retribution in August 1861, Gaetano Negri writes to his father: "The punishment inflicted on it, although deserved, was nonetheless barbaric" (Scherillo 18).

Brigandage seems to stretch the law beyond the boundaries of legality and even make it parade itself as brute power. Running through the discussions of the time there is a repeated emphasis on the operation of justice by visible example. The correspondence between 1861 and 1862 in which Prime Minister Ricasoli and General La Marmora discuss the situation in the South reveals that their plans were informed by stereotypical notions of the impressionability of southerners:

> One must give the example of a strong Government and impartial administration to the southern peoples. . . . You recognize the nature of the southern peoples and know how little it takes to win their affection. One must satisfy their imagination and, at the same time, their expansive character.

> Your Excellency well knows how impressionable this population is; to believe, it has to be able to see.[53]

The Pica law grafted transportation onto the system of punishments for the first time, an unusual move legitimated by the invocation of the responsiveness of the population of the South to deterrence:

> The effectiveness of this punishment was commended to us by almost all the honourable magistrates and jurists we interviewed. They all made us reflect on the fact that, in addition to this punishment's intrinsic effectiveness, there is also the advantage that derives in this special case from the nature of the southerners, who are extremely fond of their own land, infatuated with their

own sky, and unbelievably averse to the thought of leaving the house where they were born. Even just the announcement of this new punishment would bring about a salutary and useful fear.[54]

Some of the many pamphlets produced on brigandage at the time are unequivocal about the pretence of legitimacy required of special legislation. One Fabio Carcani argues that a special law is needed to establish military jurisdiction, "thus giving every military execution the guarantees deriving from some sort of judgement, and the appearance of legality."[55]

By watching a powerful judicial and military apparatus in operation, southerners are to have instilled in them a sense of legality that they have somehow lost. According to this authoritarian spatial logic, the South is outside the law as its spectator, the brigands are outside as its object; the forces of order should therefore exceed legal limits to deal with them both, working no longer by its impartiality in individual cases but by putting itself on display, by striking a pose of legitimacy. Thus when the law is invoked in such arguments it is both the space defined by the "normal" legal contract and an agency that goes beyond that space as a demonstration of its power and consistency.

Yet it was not only the monstrosity, the Otherness, of brigandage that fed into its imaginary relation to the constitution. The ambiguity of the term was also built into the structures designed to attack it. The commission of inquiry proposed legislation including the new "crime of brigandage," which remained only very loosely defined and which incurred the strongest penalties. In effect, any band of three or more people caught in the countryside with arms of any kind (including agricultural tools) could be accused of brigandage.[56] Tabling an amendment to the proposed law that would have introduced a more graduated scale of punishments, a deputy from the Left expressed the mechanism as follows:

> According to the article proposed by the [Parliamentary] Commission [of Inquiry into Brigandage], since the words "attack" and "resistance" are not in it, the brigand would be shot for resistance alone, even if he had not yet committed any crimes. If he had committed a misdemeanour he would be shot, and if he had committed a crime he would be shot; in short, shooting would be the punishment for the name *brigand,* and not for his misdeeds according to their severity.[57]

Many circulars and clarifying notes were sent to local military authorities on the application of the Pica law. A letter from the advocate general in Turin late in 1863 gives a definition of brigandage that is vague and tautological:

> The crime of brigandage ... is a continuous crime with an indeterminate character inclusive of all those crimes and misdemeanours which are commit-

ted by those who go around the countryside in groups of three with this objective in mind.[58]

A circular dated September 8, 1863 from the commander of the Chieti area is also revealingly phrased:

> The law on brigandage which has just been published entrusts the Military Authorities with a difficult task. A distressing set of circumstances has impelled the government to adopt this law. Since it is impossible more precisely to define the limits within which it has to operate, those called to implement it are left with a field in which they could get lost if they were not guided at every step by political acumen and an extremely conscientious sense of justice.[59]

The crime of *manutengolismo,* or aiding and abetting brigands, was an even more elastic category and incurred very heavy penalties.[60] The high turnover of arrests in the military tribunals in the South indicates that the army cast its net very wide as part of a systematic harassment of the peasant population.[61] It became regular practice to arrest the relatives of suspected brigands.[62] The army often relied on little more than rumor in cases of complicity in brigandage, and as a consequence the military tribunals were frequently the instrument of local struggles.[63] Undoubtedly many peasants took to the hills for fear of the heavy hand of justice. The power to stop all economic activity in an area declared "infested" with brigandage must also have driven many to take up arms. A wide field of suspicion and half-guilt was set up; it encompassed opposition of all kinds but centered on the catch-all category of brigandage. The army's criminalizing tactics, which forced many diverse activities to fit the conceptual grid provided by brigandage-*manutengolismo,* depended upon a large amount of "play" in the system, upon the very vagueness of the terms involved. The different logics at work in the army's repressive activity dovetail to provide both a legitimation and a practical epistemology for the army. The discourse of the antibrigand campaign is an integral and organizing moment of the practice of repression. Without a relatively stable regime of truth, there could be no reign of terror.

How to shoot a brigand

The army fighting brigandage saw itself as operating on the imaginary frontiers of the nation. The officer class had a profound sense of the fragility of such boundaries and lived the constant crisis and redefinition of the national space and of values considered to be coterminous with it. In such a situation, the most minute rituals of military life can become more than usually redolent with national meaning. The differential construction of nationality is played out in routines like marching, wearing a uniform, quoting Dante, and indeed, executing an enemy.

During the civil war, execution by firing squad became the emblematic method of dealing with brigands: the thuggish General Pinelli announced that it was the penalty for insulting the House of Savoy, the king's picture or the Italian flag. Vast numbers of peasants seem to have met their end this way. For the protagonists of the repression, in a situation where the local judicial apparatus was seen to be either in chaos or in cahoots with the reactionaries, the firing-squad was viewed as an efficient, portable, and quick means of meting out justice, a laconic contrast to the long-winded civilian legal process.[64]

The regulations for cavalry and artillery troops in force at the time provide a very detailed account of how the shooting of a soldier should be carried out. They specify the precise distance the firing party should be from the victim; who should bind his eyes; the role of the priest; how to give the order to fire; and how the assembled troops should file past the corpse of their dead colleague. The aspects of the process that might offer a spectacle to the onlooker are reduced to a minimum: the culprit's death is to be an example rather than a show in which the ranks participate in any active way. By decreeing the exact formation and movements of the troops present, and through a set speech to be made by the presiding officer, the instructions rigorously control the public interpretation of the punishment:

> The sentence will soon be carried out. Let it serve as an example. . . . The patient asks forgiveness from God for his sins, from the Sovereign for the offence he has given, and from his fellows for the outrage to their honour: let us pray for him.[65]

When employed within the army, the firing squad distributes carefully measured doses of salutary intimidation. It assures that no one person administers the law, but rather a panoptic machine, functioning with an almost clinical order. The violence used is minimized and applied with exactitude (the firing party is instructed where to aim) from a calculated, sanitary distance. It is, as Foucault would have it, an execution aimed at the life rather than at the body of the offender.[66]

Outside the parade ground, the firing squad admits of a number of variations on the regulation model. Like many standardized forms of punishment, it requires a minimum of cooperation from the victim in order to function smoothly. In return he is allowed ritual expressions of bravery, contrition, or consent: refusing or taking a blindfold, or giving the order to fire himself. A Bourbon officer smuggled into Italy to lend expertise to the brigands chose to be shot in a kneeling position as he intoned his final prayers.[67]

Both the proclamation at a parade-ground shooting and the small courtesies of the execution in the field involve a ritual accord between the offender and the law, a minimum demonstration of the victim's legally recognizable subjective coherence. It is almost as if the victim were normalized and moralized in the instant of annihilation.

The following newspaper report from 1865 deals with the execution of two brigands at which there was an "immense" crowd:

> Pinnolo and Bellusci were not walking, but running, and the priests in attendance were struggling to keep up. . . . Bellusci looked at the Church and said to the priest, "Father, I would like to be shot near the walls of that Church." "That can't be done." "But at least they could let me kneel first." "It's not up to me." "Then commend me to God." These were his last words. Twelve rifles fired at Pinnolo and Bellusci's backs. . . . Some surly characters could not understand why the people ran to collect the bullets, and thought they were doing it in the hope of gain. This is not true. It is a popular superstition in Calabria that a bullet which has pierced the chest of someone condemned to death is an infallible cure for colic when hung over the stomach.[68]

Some of the differences between this execution and the regulation model merit exploration: the denial of the usual expressions of repentance, for example. Such features can tell us a great deal about the symbolic role played by the bandit and the way the army's practices were influenced by imaginary constructions.

Peasant brigands were considered to be motivated by a pagan fanaticism instead of bravery.[69] They were seemingly incapable of genuine participation in their own punishment, unfit for any kind of formal complicity between law and victim. As a result it became a widespread convention to execute bandits by shooting them in the back. There is a basis for this practice in the military penal code of the time.[70] Article 8 of the code specifies that whereas shooting in the chest does not change the status of the soldier, shooting in the back is always preceded by reducing to the ranks.[71] Offenses such as betraying the army to an enemy or the violent rape of a minor were punished in this way—offenses, in other words, that were deemed to situate the perpetrator beyond the pale of nationhood or humanity. To be shot in the back one has to be below the symbolic threshold of citizenship, unfit to wear Italian uniform.

The regulations for cavalry and artillery regiments give some idea of the significance of this variation on the firing squad.[72] When a soldier is sentenced to an "ignominious death," the execution takes place in a rigorously enforced silence, with the victim sitting in a chair with his back to the firing party. The troops are not made to file past the dead body, which is pointedly ignored. The entire ceremony is designed publicly to break off any traces of a "dialogue" with the victim, denying any of the ritual expressions of assent which made him a legal individual rather than a subsoldier. The execution dramatically reactivates these distinctions that help define the army's collective sense of self.

Other changes in the army's violent practices were brought about by the way in which justice was felt to have to function as an example for a large watching public. It was thought more effective to display brigand heads on posts or leave bodies unburied than to issue written proclamations of execution, as was the normal practice.[73] As in the above example, executions by firing squad habitually had many spectators and were frequently carried out in the town square. By imitating the atrocities of the brigands, or rather by justifying their own brutality as an unavoidable response to those atrocities, it seemed to the army that it would be speaking a language the southern public would understand. Military judicial procedures began to operate theatrically, as an event rather than according to a code, publicly punishing the body rather than correcting the soul behind closed doors. But in doing so they found themselves having to respond to the expectations of an audience who could not be regulated, an audience that seemed to be well-equipped to make its own meanings from the display (by using bullets for amulets, for instance). Each execution involves just such a grisly contest for cultural meanings, fought out over the body of the brigand. The army saw itself as caught up in a war of signification conducted in terms alien to those in which it normally expressed its patriotism.

On occasion women were members of brigand bands, and their gender seems to have caused disruptions in the way in which the army discussed and legitimated punishment: should the army shoot brigands when they were women? The capture of Maria Oliviero, the widow of the band leader Pietro Monaco, provoked just this discussion amongst the authorities in May 1864. The advocate general wrote to the war minister listing her crimes, which included arson, murder, cutting off ears, and complicity in rape; he calls her "a tigress in a woman's form." But to carry out the sentence of execution by firing squad passed against her would be repugnant to the "feelings of noble pride" and "generosity of character" that animate the Italian army.[74]

Another individual incident gives some idea of the conflicting arguments even involved in the execution of a male brigand. In May 1865 near Potenza, Vito Francolino, condemned to be shot in the back, seems to have broken the rules of decorum attached to the firing squad. On hearing the order to fire, he ducked and, although wounded, made off across the countryside pursued by the firing party who sustained a number of injuries before the fugitive was captured and bayoneted on the spot (Riviello 370–371). The case drew the attention of the minister of war, concerned about the conduct of Captain Bertagni, who had been in charge of the execution. The commander of the local military tribunal wrote to the ministry about the case.[75] More than Bertagni's incompetence in letting Francolino escape, it was the irregularity of the brigand's death that provoked the "indignation" of the commander and necessitated his judgment over the legal issues involved. Bertagni has clearly overstepped the mark between (civilized) execution and (barbaric) murder:

> much more than for the failure to take the necessary precautions, Captain Bertagni should be called to account for the subsequent inhuman killing of the fugitive. This is an episode which dishonours the army, and for which there is no corresponding sanction in the Code . . . The brigand Francolino had been condemned to be shot and not to be barbarically slaughtered with sabre and bayonet blows.

An important factor in the commander's concern about the case is the bad publicity that would accrue to the army. While operating in the public eye as a representative of the Italian nation, the military must also respond to the desires of its audience, whose tacit consent seals the propriety of the execution. The letter mentions that if the escapee had been recaptured alive, as should have been the case, a second shooting would probably not have been ordered,

> this being precisely one of those cases in which the Sovereign's mercy would have been opportune and would have been greeted with the unanimous approval of the local population.

The determination of justice as a spectacle in this way is at odds with a regime focused on reforming the individual wrongdoer and operating not in dialogue with a public but according to a coherent impartiality.

At another point in the local commander's letter, the inhumanity of the executioner is denounced in the name of the humanity of the criminal. The death penalty, it would seem, has already served its moralizing purpose for the victim whose actual death is no longer required. Francolino's escape is perhaps evidence of his residual humanity:

> at that point Francolino was no longer a brigand but a patient who had already suffered the final pangs of death. Feelings of humanity and the generous pride of the Italian Soldier spoke eloquently in his favour.

Yet in a later communication to the war ministry on the same subject, the status of the brigand is distinctly different: "But I thought and I still think that an Officer who soils his sabre in the blood of a man condemned to death is no longer fit to wear that sabre."[76] Here it is as if the officer's "inhumanity" were contracted by a form of contamination from the criminal's taboo-laden body. The hygienic, impersonal distance that the regulations prescribe between executor and victim, law and criminal, has been closed. The metaphors of dirt that apply to the victim here are the flip side of the humanitarian rhetoric quoted above. The authorities show alternately concern and contempt for the brigand, and his death is at the same time a breach of the rules of decency, a blot on the army's conscience, and a failed propaganda ceremony. The brigand, here as elsewhere, is the pivotal point of ambivalent representations of the relationship between the social space and crime.

Reflections in conclusion

In the political domain in the 1860s there was a matrix of possible constructions of banditry that was common to both Left and Right, despite their very different political priorities. The representations of brigandage and the Mezzogiorno on which I have focused here also circulated between the public arena and the specific sphere of military activity. Within the army, the discursive construction of brigandage informed the conduct of the campaign and the way it was experienced by officers. One can only speculate about how profound was the long-term influence of the view of the South relayed to the homes and public arenas of northern and central Italy by veterans.

It seems to me that other episodes of bri[gandage could] be studied in comparable ways. Brigandage should be trea[ted not as a] constant but as a construct produced in fields of practices [and represent]ations. The "reality" of brigandage is not something that c[an be separat]ed, even for heuristic purposes, from representations of it. [In this conte]xt, brigandage involves a different combination of practice[s and represen]tations from many sides.

But what contribution m[ight an und]erstanding of brigandage as a discursive construct make to [the broader si]gnificance of banditry within southern agrarian society? And m[ore spe]cifically, what can brigandage tell us about the lives and mentalities of the peasantry? While an anthropologically based study of brigandage is beyond the scope of this chapter, the conclusions reached here in relation to the bandits' opponents do provide the space for some hypothesizing.

We owe the revival in interest in banditry to Eric Hobsbawm. His *Bandits* is a rewarding survey that has often been reduced to a caricature of itself by subsequent criticisms. All the same, Hobsbawm's contention that brigands were primitive rebels is now largely and rightly discredited. Many studies, including John Davis's *Conflict and Control,* have argued that banditry had social features but these are not to be found in the generalised symbolism of revolt that could always be read into the act of banditry, but rather in the particular circumstances of the social and economic environments in which banditry developed and was sustained. (73)

Yet in refuting the case put forward by Hobsbawm, we should not overlook the fact that brigandage was also a cultural phenomenon. In the longer term, it was encountered more through fable, song, and rumor than through the bandit's real activities, and its cultural importance cannot be reduced to a function or side-product of those activities. In his review essay on *Bandits,* Anton Blok makes the point that the "social bandit" whom Hobsbawm seeks to identify tells us more about the psychology of the peasantry, about their desperate "craving for a different society," than about the reality of brigandage.[77] The bandit-hero, in other words, is more significant as myth than as fact. But despite this insight, Blok underestimates the range of possible meanings of brigandage. His assumption seems to be that the bandit imagined by the peasantry was exclusively that exemplified by legends of the Robin Hood type. For Blok, those sordid aspects of rural crime that "did not provide attractive ingredients for myths and ballads" implicitly belong to an ugly and therefore, one assumes, culture-free reality.[78] In his reply to Blok, Hobsbawm senses that reality and representation should somehow be reintegrated, yet seems unable to get very far beyond empiricist premises in attempting to do so.[79] I think Hobsbawm's suggestive but underelaborated references to social banditry as a *role,* which was ascribed to brigands by the peasantry and which some outlaws tried to play, can be used to re-read *Bandits* as an attempt to understand the cultural significance of brigandage as seen from below.

Hobsbawm implies that we can measure brigandage in different times and places against a paradigmatic "pure" or "classical" "social banditry" (*Bandits* 72–73):

> The point about social bandits is that they are peasant outlaws whom the lord and state regard as criminals, but who remain within peasant society, and are considered by their people as heroes (*Bandits* 17).

According to Hobsbawm, the violence of brigandage grows in proportion to the alienation of the protagonist from his peasant origins and the seriousness of the breakdown in "customary devices of social control" (*Bandits* 66). The more violent the bandit, it would seem, the less likely are the peasantry to identify with him. Like Blok, therefore, Hobsbawm assumes that the bandit only echoes themes in the folklore of the peasantry when perceived to be acting in their interests. But if the social bandit is a role waiting to be assumed, then why, one wonders, should peasants not also perform other parts hallowed by tradition such as "defender of the true king" and "bloodthirsty instrument of a landed clique"? Furthermore, Hobsbawm reduces the cultural aspects of banditry to an identification between peasant and brigand. In focusing too exclusively on perceptions of actual brigands, Hobsbawm does not take account of the fact that brigandage exists in the collective memory as a skein of fables, anecdotes, and associations that offers more than mere role models and can be richly significant without being projected onto real examples. For Hobsbawm, the bad, violent side of brigandage is without determinants and effects in the peasant world-view. His theory renders that vi‐ it as a deviation from an ideal: "such elong to the central image of brigandage"

If we are not to dismiss violence as something akin to an unchaining of primitive instincts, it must, at least heuristically, be treated as a relatively organized system. This is all the more important given the notoriously widespread hearsay about cannibalism, blood-drinking, and other practices.[80] How, then, might the historian read accounts of bandit activity such as the following?

> he ripped out his intestines (people said) and forced him, half alive, to walk round the trunk of an oak tree, thus barbarically making him wind his innards round it, and then, having hung him by his feet from a branch, burned him slowly amongst the flames (Riviello 383).

It would probably be futile, as well as misleading, to attempt to sift out the true incidence and style of brigand violence from the myths that surrounded it. Both real and imagined violence served the same function and drew on the same culture. The most important of the type of mutilation that characterizes brigand treatment of enemies would have been as a means of information. The report cities obviously suited the ideological purposes of the authorities Hobsbawm implies elsewhere in *Bandits,* in a guerrilla war amid the population a brutalized body would relay the fame and fear of gands also relied more effectively than any other channel of com . The power spelled out by dismemberment would operate as a generic patrimony of expectations and phobias that enabled spread and grow along familiar lines. Even ferocity has conven bandits' actions were fed back into the popular language of brigandage with its narratives of bravery and brutality, honor, and inexorable vengeance: "on the body of one of them, riddled by 11 stab wounds, there as a piece of writing: after 11 days I caught up with you—Donato Tortora."[81]

Bianco di Saint Jorioz gives the following account, supposedly gleaned from an arrested brigand:

> Canon Bianchi and Altieri were made to suffer horrible torment: they had stiletto and bayonet wounds, and were frightfully mutilated, and all of this carried out amidst the laughing and mockery of the group. At last their heads were cut off just by using a stiletto, so that they bore the marks of the Roman state's revenge! The other man had his head cut off with a hatchet (Bianco di Saint Jorioz 301).

The text goes on to say that the heads were placed on posts "symmetrically," with a sign reading, "killed for being enemies of religion and the legitimate king." The content of the sign is not what is important here; loyalty to the king or to the old order was often a mobilizing theme of brigandage. What the sign itself makes manifest is the fact that there is a signifying practice that informs these murders. The symmetrical arrangement of the heads betrays clearly enough their function of proclaiming brigand fame and power. The mutilation is carried out according to a retributive, almost poetic principle of justice to be represented by and acted out upon the body. Yet we can detect a degree of linguistic interference in Bianco di Saint Jorioz's treatment of the events. There is a barely submerged modern category of the criminal at work as an explanation of the deed: hence the perpetrators *enjoy* their work. Whether they are fictional or not, and whoever might have been responsible for their creation, there is a strange inventiveness about the perpetration of such acts, which play out endless variations on the theme of a graphic violence.

Blok rightly criticizes Hobsbawm for failing fully to exploit his own observations on the ambiguity of the bandit's position, caught as he (or she) was between the peasantry and the powerful. The point might also be extended to the brigand as cultural artifact, formed in what could loosely be called a dialogu_____ge" drew its significance from its positio_____eres; it was the point at which the lang_____nd the peasantry intersected. It could well be that it is the very ambivalence of brigandage, its combination of the heroic and the horrific, the rebellious and the repressive, that makes it an evocative concept in peasant culture, "good to think with," as Lévi-Strauss would have it.[82] In other words, brigandage would seem to have exercised analogous kinds of fascination over both the peasantry and the bourgeoisie. For the patriotic classes, banditry was a powerful stereotype of the South because its combination of romanticism and brutality, of exoticism and squalor, encapsulated the Mezzogiorno's own ambivalent position between the Italian national space and the badlands beyond.

Chapter 2 ✖

The Birth of the Southern Question

Introduction

The southern question, which a small group of intellectuals first sought to pose to the ruling class of Italy from the mid–1870s, was a national question. It was national not in the sense that it preoccupied broad sections of the population or even of the governing elite. The first *meridionalisti* ("southernists") emphatically failed to set their concern for the plight of the peasantry at the center of Italian politics: their diagnosis of the Mezzogiorno's problems entailed too radical a rethinking of the social basis of the post-Risorgimento state. The southern question was a national question because it was thought entirely as a subset of another group of issues which concerned nation building, how regional and national cultures were related and how Italy might progress and compete with other countries.[1] It was also "national" in that the first *meridionalisti* were strongly motivated by patriotism. It seems to me that we cannot understand the picture of the South which emerged from the writings of Pasquale Villari and others without reconstructing the concepts of the nation which formed the intellectual and emotional framework within which they worked.

The southern question was born in March 1875 with the publication in the moderate Rome newspaper *L'Opinione* of Pasquale Villari's four "southern letters." The letters were more than an isolated polemical intervention, or even a newly penetrating analysis of key problems in the South. For at least a decade, the central aim of Villari's work had been the same: it was to infuse a new sense of a national mission into his bourgeois readers. In the first "southern letter," Villari deals with the camorra, describing it as the natural and inevitable consequence of the depressed state of Neapolitan society (he focuses particularly on housing).[2] Writing on the mafia in the second letter, Villari argues that it is not a secret organization but has been "spontaneously generated" by the social conflicts on the island. Paradoxically, however, as Villari observes, the mafia is strong in the wealthier, coastal areas of western Sicily where commercial forms of agriculture based on citrus fruit have taken root, rather than in the desolate inland domain of the latifundia.[3] In the third letter, Villari argues that the condition of the southern economy inevitably produces a society divided between a tiny class of landowners and a mass of brutalized peasants who are often forced by their desperate circumstances into brigandage.[4] Villari's final letter makes an impassioned plea for government intervention aimed at fostering the growth of a class of smallholding peasants: upon such preventative reforms depends the very moral and economic future of the nation. In each of the letters he lambastes those who complacently believe that liberty, charity and progress alone will cure the country's ills. He repeatedly urges people to abandon theories and to go and see with their own eyes. The social question is to reawaken in Italy "that moral life without which a nation has no purpose and does not exist."[5]

Villari's call galvanized a whole generation of scholars, writers and reformers, including Leopoldo Franchetti, Sidney Sonnino, Giustino Fortunato, Jessie White-Mario, Renato Fucini, and Pasquale Turiello. Later intellectuals also took up the cause, particularly in the 1950s with the period of state intervention in the southern economy. Indeed, to this day the Mezzogiorno has continued to be perceived in a way we could call Villarian, as the testing-ground of Italy's modernity, the measure of its claims to civility, and the focus of national solidarity. In other respects, however, the early *meridionalisti* have been the subject of criticism by recent historians who have seen them as producing a simplistic picture, an undifferentiated South of anonymous peasant masses and feudal landlords.[6] My own aim, as distinct from this revisionist historiography, is to understand how and why that particular "South" was constructed at that particular time. In the first part of this chapter, I look at Villari's work in the decade after 1866 and show how his "South" was the product of a far-reaching project to reform the national character. The second part is devoted to a close analysis of the text that is without doubt the greatest achievement of the first *meridionalisti:* Leopoldo Franchetti's famous study of law and order in Sicily, first published in 1876. I will argue that the image of Sicily created in that study is substantially an inversion of an ideal liberal bourgeois nation, and that the image of the mafia is an inversion of an ideal liberal bourgeois class.

To those who are already familiar with Villari and Franchetti's writings, it may well seem willfully perverse to place a study of their work in a history of stereotypes of the Mezzogiorno. Early *meridionalismo* is conventionally seen as a *vox clamantis in deserto,* its "modern" concern for scientific truth in contrast with the small-mindedness of the political class. Villari and Franchetti are often viewed, from both left and right, as the origin of a long and honourable tradition of social analysis anchored in objectivity. Alberto Asor Rosa argues that

> From the cultural point of view, by taking the unbiased analysis of real problems as their starting point, the conservative *meridionalisti* showed what it meant for scholars to be able to tell the whole "truth" even to their own social class, and imparted a great lesson in moral and scientific seriousness.[7]

Historians have continued to read the early *meridionalisti* in something like this way, as if the nature and meaning of objectivity and social-scientific seriousness had not changed since the 1870s, or as if their work could neatly be sorted into a part that is factual and a part that is the product of politically motivated distortion. Greater care is needed in uncovering the historically specific conceptions of objectivity and factual enquiry structuring those findings that later readers have been keen to view as almost timeless in their scientificity. Thus, by embracing Villari and Franchetti within my history of stereotypes, I am most certainly not trying to suggest that their picture of the South was simply biased, artificial, or worthless. The constructions of the Mezzogiorno produced in the early southern question are stereotypical in that they were integral to the way a set of values and a cultural identity were articulated: they emerged within specific discourses of "moralism," patriotism, liberalism, and positivist social analysis. If we are to read Villari and Franchetti better, not just in the context of their intellectual culture but also for what they can tell us about the reality of the South that they studied, we should be aware of how their findings are woven into a specific discursive fabric.

"Moral danger":
the Mezzogiorno in the work of Pasquale Villari

Pasquale Villari did more than anyone to set in place the terms of the southern question in the years of the Right. He had been attempting to bring the problems of the South into public view since the seven letters he sent from Naples to the Milanese newspaper *La Perseveranza* in 1861 and that were later published as *Le prime lettere meridionali*.[8] Beyond his importance in stimulating study of the South, Villari was a figure of influence in a number of spheres. Following the events of 1848, he moved at the age of 22 from his native Naples whence his mentor, Italy's foremost literary critic, Francesco De Sanctis, had been exiled.[9] Villari gained a post at Pisa University in 1859. He lectured in history at various institutions in Tuscany for over half a century, publishing famous works on Machiavelli and Savonarola, amongst other topics. He reorganized the Scuola Normale in Pisa and was its first director between 1862 and 1865; thereafter he became president of the philosophy and philology section of the Istituto di studi superiori pratici e di perfezionamento in Florence. A widely respected political commentator and educationalist, he was general secretary of the ministry of education between May 1869 and March 1870, and was himself minister of education from February 1891 to May 1892.

Massimo Salvadori has remarked on the significance of the fact that the southern question was first posed not by a politician or an economist, but by a moralist.[10] Yet Salvadori and many other historians of the southern question have failed properly to explain Villari's "moralism" and its influence on the way the South was represented. Many evaluations of Villari's thought as a whole display a comparable blind-spot. Villari was one of the pioneers of positivism in Italy. The climate of reaction against positivism at the end of the last century has left us a legacy of interpretations of Villari that has tended to obscure his powerful cultural influence and distort the true character of his thought.[11] The notion of "moralism" has been applied to Villari pejoratively rather than descriptively: his interest in civic virtues has been dismissed as if it were merely a by-product of the shallowness of his historical analyses and the sloppiness of his conceptual thought. Recent reappraisals of Villari have done a great deal to uncover the true profile of his work, and to place the notion of the "moral" at its center.[12] That concept, rather than constituting the limit of Villari's thought, is actually his chief object and instrument of analysis, both as a historian and as a social commentator; the notion of "la morale" is the pivotal term in a discourse that regulates a domain of expertise, an identity and role for the intellectual, particular habits of thought, rhetorical strategies, and cultural reference points. The label "moralist" is one Villari would not have felt uncomfortable wearing. As a moralist, Villari's concerns went beyond ethics; his object was the national character and its relation to liberalism and capitalism. In displaying a specific concepti[on] character, and of the Italian nation's moral attributes, Villari [...] f assumption and disquiet that produced the de[...] servation of southern society for which the m[...] n.

Villari was a leading figure amo[ng ...] cial and economic sciences who, whilst remaining liberals, were beg[innin]g to question the holy writ of laissez-faire. Faced with the social question across Europe, and with the economic backwardness, geographical diversity, and institutional weakness of Italy, conservative liberals began to rethink the role of the state, which they saw as the potential agent of educative, corrective, or preventative policy rather than merely as a necessary evil. At the same time, it was increasingly thought to be important to study the variety of cultural contexts in which the liberal economic and political system had to operate. Villari is perhaps best known for being the first to place positivism at the center of Italian intellectual life with his "La filosofia positiva ed il metodo storico" ("Positive philosophy and historical method") of January 1866.[13] The essay was written as an introduction to his history lecture course at the Istituto Superiore in Florence for 1865 to 1866 and it provides a useful means of access to his thought. In it, he explicitly argues for the application of methods drawn from the natural sciences to various branches of the social and moral sciences. Villari's intervention was conceived in a practical spirit: he saw positivism as a method and not just one more philosophical system. Why speculate about the essence of steam, he wondered, when we can analyze its properties and learn how to power trains? By extension, the historian's proper territory was the facts and laws of human society and therefore the human spirit. History should be harnessed to psychology in an effort to provide a better understanding of contemporary man, who was, after all, the inheritor of the traits of previous generations. History constituted a gallery of the human spirit's possibilities and a laboratory in which to test our hypotheses about ourselves. By studying it, intellectuals could provide the information needed to improve the practice of government.

It need hardly be said that Villari's positivism, for all that it earnestly eschewed metaphysical philosophizing, was in fact fraught with premises that merit analysis. For my purposes here, the most significant of those premises is the substantial homology Villari posits between the individual and the collective character.[14] These assumptions are made more explicit in Villari's 1883 review article on the work of Henry Thomas Buckle, whose *History of Civilization in England* (1857) had generated much discussion about the nature of civilization, as about the methods most appropriate to evaluating cultures.[15] Villari argues against Buckle's overreliance on statistics and his resultant failure to grasp the significance of individual facts, both as they exemplify greater realities and as they act in themselves to change the course of events: "When is it that we may truly say that a fact is historical? When it reveals to us the character, the moral strength of a man, of a people; and when it becomes the cause of other important facts" (239–240). The moral denotes a pattern of behavior common to individuals and the whole of a people at any given time. It derives in part from social conditions; it is in part handed down by heredity and in part cultivated through upbringing and education; but it is also the seat of our autonomy of action and a causal factor in the historical process: like John Stuart Mill, Villari argued against determinism on the grounds that the human character was in part self-made.[16] The exercise of reason enabled us to shape our moral character and to transmit it in such a way that it manifested itself in "men of limited intelligence" (258). Thus Villari's conception of national character attributes a dominant role to intelligent elites across history.

Villari goes on to argue against Buckle's method of isolating the components of a society and judging them separately (a technique, he says, akin to breaking down a great painting into its constituent colors as a means of explaining its beauty). In a revealing passage, Villari states his belief in a kind of sociological anthropomorphism, which he considers a natural and spontaneous mental process:

> Buckle was never able to conceive of society as being a living organism, with a personality, a consciousness, a character of its own. Yet we cannot construct a clear concept of a people, a century or a society for ourselves unless we represent them in a human form. (256)

When Villari turns his attention to contemporary society (and, as he implied in "La filosofia positiva e il metodo storico," the historian must always have one eye on the present), each of these discursive traits help shape the meaning of the social question. Indeed, the South itself is constructed for Villari within the terms of a problematic of the national moral character. Villari wrote "Di chi è la colpa?" ("Who is to blame?") in 1866 and "La scuola e la questione sociale in Italia" ("Schools and the social question in Italy") in 1872: these two essays give the clearest image of the coalescing of the many political and cultural elements that characterized the first formulations of the southern question. "Di chi è la colpa?" has been seen as the first self-critique of Risorgimento liberalism. It was occasioned by the recriminations following the military disasters of Custoza and Lissa in 1866. Far from affirming itself in a national feat of arms as many had hoped, Italy exposed its military weakness and diplomatic dependence on France. For some, what Carlo Cattaneo called this "simulacrum of a war" revealed Italy's backwardness at every social level. Hopes that a renewed Italian primacy in Europe would follow quickly on from unification were dashed.[17] The public reaction to Villari's essay was such that he was offered the chance to stand for parliament against Marco Minghetti (an offer he declined) (Urbinati 23). The second essay, published in *Nuova Antologia,* takes stock at the completion of Italian unification and the affirmation of German power in Europe.[18] Both essays measure the spirit of the nation, diagnose complacency and self-delusion, and recommend a strong dose of honest self-analysis.

The enabling assumption of the moralist's discourse is, as we have seen, a homology between the properties of the individual and the nation:

> A civil nation is one which has schools which, as they impart instruction, also fortify the individual intelligence, multiply the national intelligence, shape the character, bestow moral and civil discipline, and improve the whole man. ("Di chi è la colpa?" 296–297)

The homology is expressible in corporeal terms, as is demonstrated by the way in which Villari habitually resorts to a familiar trope of political writing by using medical analogies for national problems: in "Di chi è la colpa?" critiques are considered the "grave symptoms of a moral illness" (287). Villari's occasional use of racial vocabulary within a Lamarckian framework fits in with the same system of assumptions: "Man not only has the power to improve animal races, but also his own race through hygiene, gymnastics, hunting, riding, target-shooting, fencing, etc., etc." (297). The national character manifests itself in the conduct of waiters and shopkeepers and interrelates with historical events on the grand scale.[19] It is formed by the most minute practices of education and upbringing as it is in the national experience of war, yet without it the successful functioning of military and educational machinery is impossible. It is regulated from above by the state, and in turn it informs and controls the state in its manifestation as public opinion:

> We will never get beyond a situation where the government is in the hands of the few until the country begins seriously to discuss its own business, to determine its own opinion and then impose it on ministers by legal means. . . . In Italy there is one person who is very much to blame, who has done more harm and committed more errors than the generals, the ministers, the radicals, the timid conservatives, the cliques; that person is all of us. (288–289)

The moralist is an authoritative dispenser of ethnic stereotypes and of exhortations to the nation in the first person plural. Villari's favorite such exhortation, and the one that informs the entire ideological project of the *questione meridionale,* is that Italy must find a new sense of its identity through the social question:

> A new ideal would rise up before us if we were to accomplish a great social duty. Such an achievement would re-ignite in the Italian spirit the same enthusiasm that, at the beginning of our revolution, gave reason to hope that we might do great things. Examining the problems which encompass national life in its entirety could help us to give a new and more powerful boost to our culture; it could help us, through study and a clearer awareness of ourselves, to rediscover the ancient originality of the Italian mind.[20]

Self-understanding is the central pillar of Villari's planned moral-national architecture: Italy must rediscover its true character by knowing itself. Villari's own work can be seen as an effort to begin the task of building an Italian knowledge of Italy. Both "Di chi è la colpa?" and "La scuola e la questione sociale" place repeated stress on the need for self-examination:

> One thing that has always amazed me, and that seems to me to be unworthy of our culture today, is seeing how little we study ourselves, and how little work is done in precisely those areas of study which would have immediate practical applications here and which offer an enormous field of observations. ("La scuola e la questione sociale" 166)

Hence the first stage of putting new backbone into the enervated national body "is the one in which we ourselves lay bare our sores, and destroy national illusions or prejudices" ("Di chi è la colpa?" 290).

With whom or what does Villari identify the Italy that knows as opposed to that which is known? the Italy with a social duty as opposed to the Italy with social problems? Just as Villari's historiography attributes a leading role in the formation of moral character to intelligent elites, his social thought attributes a paternalistic role to the bourgeoisie. Nadia Urbinati reads Villari's paternalism as a conservative translation of Mill's idea of an educated elite that rises above sectional interests and educates people towards liberty, justice and progress (Urbinati 3–9). Villari uses the concept of the nation to conflate the interests of the bourgeoisie with those of society at large: the needs of the propertyless are collapsed into those of the state in the name of the *patria.* _____ is also a notion that excludes certain group_____, inhabit a closed world of illiteracy, cut _____ t is the public terrain of the bourgeoisie. Hence the final stage of the civilizing process is an education that will "at last, with the letters of the alphabet, open their minds to that moral world which still seems closed for them" ("Di chi è la colpa?" 301). Thus, as well as denoting a national character, the moral implies both a civil competence, which one must achieve through such skills as literacy and the capacity to reason impartially, and a social sphere from which one may be excluded. The moralist's concepts police the lines between the "people" and the "plebs" as between civilization and the primitive.

Villari also associates the subject of his reforming zeal with the army. The military is mythologized as a kind of super-nation, an ideal of corporate belonging and corporeal discipline: "the army has united all Italians under the honour of the same flag, and of all the moral, unifying and civilizing forces in the country, it has become the most effective" (ibid., 258). Villari's well-known admiration for the army is less important in this regard than his use of war as a paradigm for the kind of collective action that can reinvigorate the national self.[21] Since, as "Di chi è la colpa?" avers, war is the greatest test of a civilization, Italy must prove itself by a self-examination akin to combat. The conclusion to Villari's 1866 essay uses a striking analogy:

> The moment has come to carry out a mass call-up of all men of good will, and to conduct this new expedition into the interior. The country is convinced, and it is prepared for any sacrifice, as long as it can feel truly itself. (304)

The southern question as imagined by Villari is the central thrust of such a campaign. His concern for the Mezzogiorno is, in some respects, a continuation in the imagination of the military expedition conducted in the South during the 1860s. Those who fought in the antibrigand war are seen by Villari as the source of a redemptive wisdom. When, in April 1876, Villari addressed the chamber of deputies on the agrarian question, he chose to quote the memoirs of an army officer, whose views he took to represent those of an entire "order of citizens"—views that were grounded in experience and shot through with patriotic meaning.[22] The association of social reform and war is made clear in "Le lettere meridionali" themselves:

> Italy is unified, free and independent. We do not want to make any conquests, nor are we up to making them. A defensive war is impossible because no one is attacking us. So what [   ] turn all of our attention inwards, t[   ]t to animate us, a new ideal to shine [   ] rimedii," 67)

Villari's other model for a specifically Italian cognition is his view of language. Long passages in "Di chi è la colpa?" are directed against the "bureaucratic formalism" of Italian society (274). The country is compared to a writer enmeshed in rhetoric, unable to distinguish sign and sense.[23] "La scuola e la questione sociale" goes even further: writing itself is dismissed as a "fictitious" obstruction preventing a character-forming confrontation with reality:

> If the hour of sacrifice does not start, the hour of true liberty cannot chime. And we can only have an ephemeral and fictitious shadow of liberty: we can only have laws, codes and regulations, everything that is written on paper, and nothing that is in the spirit, and which alone can redeem us. . . . Morality is taught with facts and not words. (203–204)

Empirical observation has a function that is as much moral, in Villari's sense, as it is cognitive. The social question has as much to do with bolstering the solidity of the nation as it does with concrete reforms.

Naples is the place in which the quintessentially patriotic act of knowing Italy is carried out. In "Di chi è la colpa?" Villari calls on his readers to penetrate into the heart of Naples for the sake of Italy's moral being:

So is it nature that has made us so inferior? Or is it not rather our upbringing and education, which have been received and handed down from generation to generation? Is it not, that is, the very things that in other countries have improved every habit and faculty in all of the social classes, and honed the whole man?

Therefore, do not only think of reading and writing. Enter the city of Naples, and leave the streets where the educated and well-to-do live, where the opulent, splendid carriages run. Instead, penetrate the most remote quarters, where the alleyways and the din are so confused and intertwined, and the houses so tall and close to each other, that they form a labyrinth in which not even the air, let alone anything else, can circulate freely. (300)

Naples and the South are, for Villari as for the *meridionalisti* who followed his lead, the paradigmatic theater of a moralizing empirical knowledge. Even before any practical measures are implemented, the description and proclamation of the squalor of Naples can bolster Italy's dangerously weak claim to the status of civility and nationhood. If the country cannot solve its problems, it must at least face up to them, declare its own responsibility for them, and by doing so transform itself into the potential subject of remedial action:

If it is true that Negro slavery prevented the general progress of the Southern States, and that it harmed the White slave-owners themselves more than anyone else, then I think it will be impossible to achieve a genuine improvement in the moral and civil conduct of a people as long as it tolerates this kind of disgrace in its very bosom. We need some kind and noble soul to go there, to make a description in minute detail, to depict the way those people live and their moral _____ denounce it to the civilized world as an *Italian* crime. ("La scuola _____ ne sociale," 173, my emphasis)

As Nadia U_____ argued, the paradox of empirical social analysis in Villari's schem_____ while it reinforced the paternalistic role of the moral elite an_____ e of their appeal to patriotically connoted civic virtues, it also _____ impressions of Italy's fragility and immaturity as a nation, its un_____ for liberty (Urbinati 9). The ambivalence of Villari's South can_____ n one level, as a function of that paradox. Colonial or oriental _____ or the South appear intermittently in his texts, suggesting a cor_____ en his attempts to define the South and its problems as a nation_____ concern, and a tendency to grasp the South as beyond Italy, or even as its antithesis. The peasants to be moralized are *almost* Indians or cannibals:

[The peasant] could kneel before his master with the same feeling that an Indian has when he adores a storm or a bolt of lightning. If the day came when this spell were broken, the peasant would rise up to avenge himself with ferocity, long-repressed hatred and brutal passions. Indeed, on occasion, these hordes of slaves have been seen to change suddenly into hordes of cannibals. ("I rimedii," 57)

To be Italianized, Villari argues, the South must be studied. Yet his understanding of what it means to study different cultures is heavily influenced by a positivist teleology of science and by the way he conceives of a conception of history as a progression through levels of civilization. Both of these features of his thought make study itself into an affirmation of superiority over the society one is attempting to understand. Thus, although Villari argues a case for the South's not being barbaric, the binary opposition between civility and barbarism and the social-evolutionary model of history that often accompanied it inform his whole understanding of the southern question and its relation to the national culture. The words Villari puts into the mouth of the southern poor in the "Lettere meridionali" show the Mezzogiorno to be locked into a death-struggle with Italy, a fight between opposing ends of the evolutionary scale: "Either you manage to make us civilized, or we will manage to make you barbaric" ("I rimedii," 70). Elsewhere in Villari, it would seem that to be fully Italian, all the country has to do is to recognize the fleeting, authentic, unself-conscious *italianità* in the objects of its attention: "in questions of taste, Italy does not need to struggle to have cause for pride; it only needs to know itself, and to spread the treasures that it always keeps hidden."[24] Villari's *meridionalismo* needs to make the South both into an Other *and* into the raw stuff of the nation, the promise of the country's rise to the moral uplands. Villari's discourse of the moral invests an otherness in Naples that Italy can investigate and, by doing so, know and moralize itself. Villari's fragile Italy can then even aspire to giving itself an existence beyond language, in the concrete reality of the poverty that preoccupies it. Throughout Villari's work, Italy is to constitute its identity by finding in the South both its Other and its most intimate self; its greatest "moral danger" and its ultimate salvation ("La scuola e la questione sociale," 173). In Villari's thought, the difference between Italy and the South can be that between civilization and the primitive. It can also be the difference between the superficial and the essential, or between the rhetorical and the real, or the actual and potential. As a matter of both public policy and personal ethics, the South is both "us" and "them"; it is situated both reassuringly inside Italy and tantalizingly beyond it; the site of a secret, mute, precultural self, and of an as yet untamed alterity. If the *meridionalisti* could set out to confront isolation, squalor, and danger on the moral stage of the Mezzogiorno, it was in part because Pasquale Villari had penned this motivational and intellectual script for them.

"The moral value of violence":
The mafia and Sicilian Society in
Leopoldo Franchetti's *Condizioni
politiche e amministrative della Sicilia*

Introduction: Franchetti and His Readers

In the early weeks of 1876, three wealthy young Tuscans, one of them a future prime minister, set out with their manservant to assess the state of Sicilian society. The task undertaken by Enea Cavalieri, Sidney Sonnino, and Leopoldo Franchetti (the manservant's name is not recorded) presented considerable stresses and dangers: amongst the equipment they took were repeating rifles and l[...].[25] Choosing their routes and guides at the latest possible [...] they traveled on horseback across a ter[...] or nonexistent and among the vas[...] e a dialect incomprehensible to them. Sicily was still "a half legend[...] d perilous world" for the university and salon milieu that they had left behind.[26] The three were motivated by a strongly patriotic pioneering spirit. Franchetti, one of Villari's university students and the veteran of a similar journey to the mainland South, had described his earlier mission as follows:

> This I affirm with confidence: in Italy today, whoever wants to learn how to understand the country's condition, which, unfortunately, is so little known, should not content himself with studying political economy, administration or constitutional law from books, most of which are foreign. Rather, when he has finished his theoretical studies, he should get up, gird his loins and go and see things with his own eyes, hear things with his own ears; he should go and ascertain the facts, and verify whether they justify these writers' theories. Only then will we have a science, and an economic, administrative and political tradition which is Italian. Only then will we no longer be so many schoolboys repeating from memory the lessons we have learned from foreigners.[27]

The Sicilian expedition was to be a model of the hands-on patriotism inspired by Villari; it was to be concrete and all but corporeal in its efforts to establish an Italian cognitive dominion over the country's marches.

The report that resulted from the expedition was published in two parts (due to other travel commitments, Cavalieri withdrew from the task of writing up the findings). Sonnino analyzed the social and economic conditions of the island's landless peasants, who were exploited by land managers acting in the stead of absentee owners. Despite his own economic liberalism, he argued that the state had a right to intervene and regulate patterns of land ownership when, as in Sicily, they were not working in the interests of all.

The state should encourage the evolution of more dynamic forms of agriculture and, in particular, of a class of peasant smallholders.[28]

However, my interest here centers on Franchetti's half of the inquiry, *Condizioni politiche e amministrative della Sicilia* (hereafter *Condizioni*), which deals with public order, local government, and administration.[29] Franchetti's book has a stature that is rare if not unique: it is a work of social analysis from the nineteenth century that is certain to be considered an authority on its subject in the twenty-first. It is cited in virtually all of the literature on organized crime in Sicily, a fact even more noteworthy given the great diversity of interpretations that the mafia has generated.[30] Diego Gambetta refers to *Condizioni* as "arguably the best [study] on the Sicilian mafia to date."[31] Paolo Pezzino argues that its "value transcends the contingent circumstances which produced it" and admires the "modernity of the analytical categories employed."[32] *Condizioni* has even acquired the status of a touchstone, a guarantor of timeless scientificity; for Carlo Tullio-Altan, it is "a text of an exemplary modernity and a permanent validity."[33] I want to suggest that this is a status that is not entirely deserved. Indeed, my aim is to counter what I think are unhistorical readings of *Condizioni* produced by those who have turned Franchetti into a hero of science, modernity, and nation building, and a historian of the origins of the mafia. Such readings have too rarely been sufficiently sensitive to the specific meanings of a number of Franchetti's concepts, including not only "science," "modernity," and "nation," but also "Sicily," "mafia," and "violence." When we unpack these notions what we find is that Franchetti understands Sicily as an inverted mirror image of the model of liberal, paternalistic capitalism that provides both his social ideal and his analytical protocols. For that reason, Franchetti's utility as a source for the history of the mafia needs to be reexamined.

Franchetti's argument is that the origins of the parlous state of law and order in Sicily lay in a failed transition from feudalism to capitalism. Because of the backward state of agriculture, society was divided overwhelmingly between landowners and landless peasants. Thus, when feudalism was abolished in 1812, the reforms were not backed up by a numerous middle class inclined by their very makeup to champion the cause of impersonal, impartial legality. As a result, the public domain remained dominated by private interests, and private force remained the ultimate determinant of social relations. All that had changed was that the institution of violence, like that of propertied wealth, was now accessible to groups other than the aristocracy. An "industry of violence" came to be conducted by an independent class of criminals, the best organized of whom were called the mafia. Sicilians were entirely deprived of a sense of the law's being above all and equal for all. The violent pursuit of private interests was the norm in all walks of public life; it commanded the kind of consensus that the law commands in the public opinion of normal societies. Different areas of Sicily displayed different versions of the same syndrome. The provinces of the east of the island were more tranquil, but only because the landowners had managed to maintain their monopoly over the use of violence, and criminals were less organized. The interior was dominated by brigands: even the landlords were often subject to attack. Brigands had wide networks of contacts for the pursuit of crimes such as cattle-rustling; they levied what amounted to taxes on the rural population; they create   stures of generosity. In Palermo and i   had elevated themselves to the status   tal, it was perceived as legitimate to use   egemony of criminal interests in Palermo created a culture of *omertà* that prevented any recourse to the law at all. Violence was openly practiced. Organized criminal bands intervened in various commercial spheres to guarantee monopolies. Middle-class *mafiosi* acted exactly like capitalists in their control of the violence industry and its workforce.

A number of problems in this analysis have been pointed out. As Gambetta has argued, the much-quoted definition of "the violence industry" is potentially misleading because "violence is a means, not an end; a resource, not the final product."[34] For some, Franchetti's picture of an island entirely in the sway of private violence is too sweeping. Salvatore Lupo, one of Franchetti's sternest critics, has taken issue with the view expressed in *Condizioni* that a Sicilian culture of force and *omertà* accounts for the population's solidarity with the criminals against the state. This is an argument that makes *Condizioni*, according to Lupo, a founding text of the socioanthropological tradition according to which the mafia is virtually indistinguishable from Sicilian culture per se.[35] Others have pointed to Franchetti's failure to attribute enough blame to the political strategy of central government under the Right, whose concern for order was too often distorted by a desire to defeat the democrats.[36]

Now, these are all criticisms of Franchetti with which I broadly agree. But I think that the critique needs to be taken a stage further, and the origins of these and other weaknesses in *Condizioni* need to be traced back to the logic of Franchetti's sociological method. Franchetti's failings have too often been almost dismissed as lapses into ideology or short-term political bias; they are treated as uncharacteristic slips that can be discarded from the scientific body of the text. This is particularly true of the harshest criticisms of *Condizioni*, which have been reserved for the draconian and impractical measures Franchetti suggests should be taken to establish the rule of law on the island. A brief look at these measures, at the way they have tended to be interpreted by historians, and at the political and intellectual context of the inquiry is enough, it seems to me, to justify re-examining one of the most cited sociological texts of its era.

What *Condizioni* advocates is the surgical removal of an entire class of criminals to allow a true middle class to grow in its place (155). Franchetti envisages a newly organized police force, judiciary, and administration, staffed entirely from outside the island by a young, moral, energetic, intelligent, and courageous elite. A pyramid of rapid communications would build up a detailed knowledge of the complexities of the island's criminality. After several months' careful and secretive preparation, most of the island's dangerous criminals would be arrested in one swoop. Tried in courts without juries due to the untrustworthiness of the local population, the first wave of arrestees would be taken to prisons in Northern and Central Italy to break their contacts with Sicilian society (170–175). Franchetti asserts on many occasions that "arbitrary" police measures would do more harm than good, showing the state to be just one more force bidding for domination within society rather than being above it (the failings of the Right's rule in Sicily in this regard had been exposed in a fiery law-and-order debate in parliament in 1875). Nevertheless, in the event that the first strike fails, Franchetti advocates the use of an exceptional regime (without military tribunals, but including detention without trial for unlimited periods) "in order to clean and prepare the ground" (232): "being inexorable, cruel, is a virtue and a duty; compassion is a crime, because half measures produce immense harm" (234). The state, by demonstrating in two or three major trials that it had greater "material force" than the criminals, would break the spell of terror and *omertà* binding the population to the criminal element (174). Franchetti himself acknowledges that the government and public opinion, "the Nation excluding the Sicilians" (223), would have to be unanimous and determined to carry through the task of normalizing conditions on the island: "unhappily, for now, this is but a beautiful dream" (230). In other words, Franchetti's solution to the law and order problem in Sicily presupposes a wholesale reconstitution, not only of the government of the island but also of Italian society as a whole.

Salvatore Lupo sees this "reactionary utopia" as revealing the "evident political motivation" of *Condizioni,* its "instrumentalization" of the crime issue (Lupo 37). Strong circumstantial reasons for Franchetti's limitations do indeed seem readily to offer themselves when we consider the political context of the 1876 investigation, a context dominated by the aftermath of the 1874 election in which some 44 out of 48 seats in Sicily went to opposition candidates.[37] The election gave dramatic evidence of the breakup of the hegemony of the Right. The South in general, and Sicily in particular, had palpably failed to respond with the predicted gratitude to the removal of the Bourbon yoke. Signs that the South was turning to the Left were often read with ethnocentric puzzlement by the moderate press of the North and by many politicians: in the spring before the election, the Milanese conservative newspaper *La Perseveranza* had argued that southerners "are less fit to govern Italy and feel less of a calling to do so because they have a worse understanding than anyone of the Italian conception of politics." In his interpretation of the election results published in the *Nuova Antologia,* Diomede Pantaleoni explained the fact that the northern and central provinces had voted for the government by the fact that they were "incontestably the most intelligent and illuminated."[38] Since unification, the Right had regarded Sicily as a constant source of potential rebellion.[39] Without political allies it trusted, and faced with a genuine crisis of authority, the Right had attempted to criminalize opposition.[40] In short, after 1874 there was likely to be a ready audience for a study discrediting the social groups that had supported the Left by portraying them as medieval or criminal, thus legitimating the Right's practice of using law and order as a political instrument: this, after all, had been Marco Minghetti's aim when he set up the *parliamentary* inquiry into the state of the island in August 1875.[41]

However, while we do need to take into account this political context of Sonnino and Franchetti's investigation, there are a number of reasons why political bias does not seem to me to offer a comprehensive explanation of the problems in *Condizioni,* let alone its strengths.

The first set of reasons are biographical: Franchetti's patriotism cannot plausibly be dismissed as mendacious puff, a smoke screen for party interests. After all, according to Umberto Zanotti-Bianco, this is the man who had, to an unhealthy degree, "transferred the need for adoration which lies deep in every heart onto something earthly, and this something was the *patria*"; the man who fell into such a depression after the Italian defeat at Caporetto in 1917 that he committed suicide.[42] As I hope to demonstrate, the concepts of "nation" and "national interest" operative in *Condizioni* shape Franchetti's findings, and they do so in a way that is far more subtle than political bias.

Secondly, to read *Condizioni* as an apologia for the rule of the Right in the South is to oversimplify both Franchetti's own position and a political situation in which the Right was already beginning to undergo the kind of fragmentation that would continue in the following years. It is also worth remembering the mixed reception that Franchetti and Sonnino's work received even from newspapers associated with the Right: *La Perseveranza* accused them of "Jacobin extremism."[43] Furthermore, the investigation was motivated by criticisms of the post-Risorgimento state that had a much longer-term scope. Early *meridionalismo* represented a bold attempt to enlist developments in liberal political economy and positivist analysis to a revision of the laissez-faire consensus and to placing the Italian state on sounder foundations by undertaking a more proactive nation-building strategy than the Right had done. By transcending the interests of cliques, Villari and others hoped that new constituencies for moderate liberalism might be carved out from the rural population. For Franchetti and Sonnino as for Villari, the defeats of 1866 had laid bare Italy's backwardness. Yet the Paris Commune had darkened the landscape of ruling-class Italy with the threat of popular disorder and seemed to urge a more sheltered path to economic development. Sonnino in particular saw the paternalistic Tuscan sharecropping system as a good model for a rural capitalism that would avoid the dangerous proletarianization of the country's peasants: Zeffiro Ciuffoletti describes Franchetti and Sonnino's social ideal as a mixture of Tuscan paternalism and English liberalism.[44] Antonio Jannazzo argues that Franchetti was attempting to launch a kind of "Gladstonian" project in Italy.[45] So rather than short-term political issues, it is these strategic problems and principles that inform the investigation, and went on to inform Franchetti and Sonnino's journal, *La Rassegna Settiminale,* founded in 1878.[46] If the polemic against the clientelism of elements of the Left was certainly a catalyst for Franchetti, the southern question had more fundamental political and intellectual origins.[47]

Other readers of *Condizioni* tend to have a different reaction when faced with Franchetti's authoritarian wish-list. Where Lupo suspects a political interest, they assume, less plausibly, that there is a "hiatus" between his analysis, which is good and scientific, and his proposals for change, which are bad and ideological.[48] Yet Franchetti himself posits a close parallel between the problems of knowing Sicily and those of governing it, which are separated in such readings. The text attributes a striking, almost Benthamite, importance to knowledge gained through surveillance: observation is not only the key to Franchetti's remedies, it is the state's central role as he perceives it. Indeed, the members of his new judiciary would have to be astute sociologists, "men capable of analyzing complex social facts, and of going to track down their causes" (226). Thus the inquiry not only argues the case for better government of Sicily; it is on one level a rehearsal for that government in the way that it attains a systematic knowledge and contributes to the consolidation of the nation. This close relationship between analysis and governmental practice, and more generally the rigor with which Franchetti's solutions follow from the internal logic of his study, seem to me to make it very difficult to hold onto the image of Franchetti as a "coldly scientific" reformer.[49]

From this review of previous readings of *Condizioni* I derive several simple premises for my own analysis. We need a more subtle appreciation of the conceptual nervure of *Condizioni* than can be derived from a rather cumbersome Marxist idea of ideology, from imputing a calculated political bias to its author, or from the assumption that the meaning of "objectivity" has not changed since 1876. Rather than timeless scientific norms, Franchetti was actually obeying a historically specific code better described as a form of *impartiality*. The meaning of this notion, and of the other key concepts in *Condizioni,* is not dependent, in the first instance, on the social reality of the island or the truth of the inquiry's findings, but on the conceptual and rhetorical economy of the text in general, and on certain normative discourses of nationhood in particular.

The meaning of impartiality: class, nation, civilization

The analytic honesty and accuracy of the first *meridionalisti* were to serve a political purpose in reminding the ruling class that the social order ultimately rested on the passive consent of the masses. Franchetti, Sonnino, Villari, and others envisaged an Italy where public life would be organized around a bourgeoisie dedicated to a truthful assessment of the reality of the country and not to rhetoric and clientelism. A modern public sphere had not evolved naturally in Italy and would therefore have to be created heroically, by an enlightened elite of reformers. Social analysis therefore served a *moral* role as well as a cognitive one. What gives impartiality in *Condizioni* a very different meaning to the scientificity that some modern historians have read into it is the way that Franchetti's particular understanding of the social function of knowledge shapes its cognitive procedures.

For Franchetti, the language of nationality and citizenship acts to translate class values into universal ones through the demarcation of an imaginary boundary. Outside of this boundary, people become ineligible to participate in the political process because they are presumed to be unable to articulate their interests in terms of those of the nation and the public interest as a whole: "in its current economic, moral and intellectual conditions, the great mass of the population is absolutely incapable of judging a measure of relevance to the public interest either well or badly" (222). Yet, at the same time, *Condizioni* is unapologetic about the universality it attributes to bourgeois values. In theory, for Franchetti, the majority in a constitutional government represents the majority of the middle class who in turn represent the desires of the majority of the entire population. Public opinion is, by definition, middle-class opinion.[50] Franchetti's conception of the moral is less distinctive than Villari's; it is closer to the classic liberal idea and reflects none of the "ethological" or corporeal concerns of his mentor. Nevertheless, for Franchetti as for Villari, morality denoted a code of public behavior rather than an individual ethics. For Franchetti, therefore, impartiality is the central tenet of a code of conduct for public life, the criterion one must fulfill in order to be admitted into the national political sphere. Crucially, then, Franchetti understands his work as conforming as much to the moral demands of civic duty and the national interest as to methodological standards of scientificity.

Another facet of Franchetti's impartiality derives from the vision of history which accompanies it. As Corrado Vivanti has argued, in the minds of the Tuscan reformers, the capitalist social order and civilization were one and the same thing: they represented the highest point reached on the scale of social progress.[51] Franchetti and Sonnino wrote in the name of impartial national values that were simply unthinkable before the development of capitalism. The same applies for the liberal concepts of legality which Franchetti takes as his norm: before the bourgeois order, during the Middle Ages, social existence was seemingly dominated by individual and group interests backed by force. But Franchetti's Middle Ages turn out to be largely the product of a back-projection of nineteenth-century bourgeois values. In *Condizioni*, medieval society is characterized by a *lack* of industry, commerce, and a responsible middle class; its law is determined by "private material force" and not by socially agreed codes (73); life is cheap and violence absolute. In other words, Franchetti's historicism is a covert binarism: history progresses from violence to order, from cruelty to humanity, from the rule of force to the rule of reason.[52]

In several passages Franchetti describes Sicily as backward, as being at an earlier stage in a linear journey that different societies undertake on the way from barbarity to civilization (237). Sicilian social conditions are, "those proper to a different stage of civilization" (84):

> those who want the same criteria of order and disorder, of right and wrong to apply in a medieval Society as are in force in a modern society are using an inadmissible premise; their demand is unjustifiable and their judgement absurd. (135)[53]

These assertions actually contradict the central and more sophisticated thesis of *Condizioni*, which is that Sicily has undergone a delayed and perverse form of the transition from feudalism to capitalism. They nonetheless exemplify Franchetti's teleological view of history. Indeed, a powerful aspect of Franchetti's discourse of impartiality is the confidence gained from knowing the direction in which the society he studies must develop, and from the dualistic moral and historical schema that underlies that confidence.[54] His ideal citizen was equipped *both* with a code of impartiality *and* with an ability to judge how advanced or rational a society was.

There is one final aspect of the impartiality of *Condizioni* that needs to be set out at this stage. Franchetti has a totalizing understanding of the way a society works. Every aspect of a given civilization is a direct expression of its central principles. We are constantly told, for example, that seemingly strange features of Sicilian life are only the "inevitable" or "natural" product of its socioeconomic base. The job of impartial social analysis, in Franchetti's text, is to trace such laws of social causality.

The traveler and the scientist

Franchetti's concept of "impartiality" is put to work in *Condizioni* within a specific rhetorical structure. Large parts of the text, particularly early on, stage a development between two sets of attitudes: those imputed to the visitor to [...] ange between the following two passage [...] on between voices we can call those o [...] "impartial analyst":

> Without distinction between the different provinces, the sight of the conditions of the whole island inspires a profound dejection. The mind alternately feels disdain and pity towards the various elements that blindly crash into one another in that desperate confusion. All of those criteria and concepts of good government, that universities and books taught one to believe were secure, become bewildered and confused. And one feels the painful doubt that all of those principles of justice and freedom in which one had grown used to believing in an almost religious manner, might just amount to nothing more than well-planned speeches to disguise ailments that Italy is incapable of curing, a layer of gloss to make the dead bodies gleam. . . .
>
> Such is the first impression of someone who has come from the Continent to visit Sicily. However, once his initial surprise has been calmed, if he goes back over the things he has seen and heard in his mind, and searches for the thread to lead him through that infinity of confused facts, and if he seeks their origins in the past and present, and looks for the reasons that make them persist, he will see them gradually take on an order. Every fact takes its place, and at last a picture unfolds in front of him. It may not be beautiful, but it is at least clear, distinct and ordered, and it gives hope that remedies can be found to these evils, whose causes now appear so manifest. (56–57)

The traveler's assumed cultural background is clearly identifiable with that of the enlightened liberal man at whom Franchetti directs *Condizioni*. His perspective is closely related to the framework of expectations of Franchetti himself, arriving in Sicily from the continent. The traveler's perplexity also resembles Pasquale Villari's reaction to the lawlessness in the Conca d'Oro: "I did not want to believe this news, which seemed to subvert every single principle of political economy and moral science" (Villari, "La mafia," 24). The visitor is lost and confused, prey to emotions such as pity and disdain, and frustrated by the limits of his own understanding.

The traveler voice also corresponds to a position in the text for the reader, drawn towards a close involvement with the difficulties of examining Sicily.

Through the use of impersonal structures ("the sight," "the mind," "in which one had grown used to believing") the point of view is generalized, projected as that of a wider group. Throughout *Condizioni* a confident rapport with the reader is implied through a number of appeals to a reservoir of assumptions purportedly shared by author and readership. The use of phrases such as "everyone can imagine" is habitual (39). We are assumed both to have an easy familiarity with the principles of the modern liberal order ("it is easy to imagine what the effects can be" [194]); and to be absolute strangers to Sicilian society and mores ("nothing can give an idea of" [134]). Between these two points of reference are located the values of a rational, impartial, socially aware "cultivated class of the nation" to whom *Condizioni* is addressed and that is the repository of the national interest that Franchetti invokes (238).

By contrast, the impartial analyst is both a doctor and an observer detached emotionally and physically from the flat, self-contained world he contemplates. Through the relationship between the registers of traveler and analyst, *Condizioni* reconstructs the expedition and certain problems of cultural perspective associated with it as an adventure, a journey into the badlands on the edges of civili___ ___ ___ national space. Yet a rhetoric of impartiality is also reinforced. The ___ ___ ___ ___torial pronouncements emerges by way of a con___ ___ ___ ___ ___ages such as the following account of th___ ___ ___ ___and:

> The train sets off again and, without knowing it, the traveler is overrun by the sensation experienced by people who find themselves amongst mysterious and unknown things . . . He experiences a kind of moral mirage. . . . the mind involuntarily goes back to the days when the Sicilian countryside was cultivated by crowds of slaves, and to the horrors of the slave wars in Sicily under Roman domination. . . .
>
> The new traveller feels himself overcome by a profound sense of isolation. It seems to him as if something akin to the nightmare of a mysterious, evil force is weighing down on this naked, monotonous land. He has no help or defence against this force, apart from himself and the companions who have come with him from over the sea. And he suddenly feels overcome by a profound tenderness towards the rifle he is carrying across his saddle. (20–22)

From the language of the traveler voice in *Condizioni*, it is evident that the spectacle of Sicily does more than challenge the courage and intellect of the Italian/European visitor: it provokes a profound crisis in the values of liberalism, threatens the legitimacy of the unified state, and even afflicts the Italian soul. Some of the most powerful passages in the text refer to the acute cognitive and judgmental problems that Sicilian society presents to the onlooker: "the mind struggles in vain" to distinguish good and bad (33); there is no thread to lead one through this "labyrinth of truth and falsity, of intertwined wrongs," and the mind is "tormented" by the question of who is to blame, which "weighs constantly on it like a nightmare" (52).

Thus the change from traveler to author, and with it the achievement of impartiality, is presented as a narrative in which a kind of identity crisis is overcome. The solution that *Condizioni* implicitly proposes to this crisis of patriotic liberal identity is a shift in the way the onlooker's descriptive and judgmental capacities are applied to Sicily. For the traveler, judging and knowing Sicily and its inhabitants are part of the same process, as is evinced by a constant slippage in Franchetti's prose between ethical and cognitive categories: he writes, for example, that "it is impossible to appreciate these relationships using the moral criteria which are in force in other countries" (131). The transition from traveler voice to impartial analyst is equivalent to a radical adaptation of these civilized European norms, to the loss of the pretension that liberal ethical values can be applied universally. Franchetti frequently asserts that Sicilians are not better or worse than people on the Continent, but that their moral sensibilities are attuned to the most powerful forces in that society, those of criminality: for Franchetti, *omertà* is on the island what a sense of social responsibility is in other countries. In other words, Franchetti opts to take a limited dose of what we might today call cultural relativism in his approach to Sicilian society: he attempts to grasp phenomena like the mafia as the product of a different code of mores and not the absence of such a code.[55]

Yet although Franchetti's findings in *Condizioni* are enabled by a relativizing the criteria that inform the perspective of the traveler, he is ultimately not able to think sociologically without those normative aspects of his idea of impartiality, which is, I repeat, not so much an analytical method as a code that inheres in the public life of the elites of advanced societies. Thus, rather than abandoning judgmental terms such as "immoral" and "abnormal" in the study of Sicily, *Condizioni* changes their level of application: "the state of public safety, considered from the point of view of a modern society, is abnormal" (111). Sicilian society as a whole is a deviation from the standard of modern "central Europe" (82). The answer to the question "who is to blame?" is not any individual or group but Sicilian society:

> But if Sicily is to be governed according to the same criteria as the rest of Italy, the persistence, even for a short time, indeed the very existence of this state of affairs must be considered as a pathological phenomenon, as a disorder. And as a consequence, Italy has the duty to suppress it in as short a time as possible. . . . the Sicilians, considered in general, are not fit to contribute to this

task, because it is precisely their way of hearing and seeing that constitutes the illness to be treated. Sicilians' opinions, judgements and suggestions ... should be thought of as phenomena, as symptoms which are of capital importance for anyone wishing to discover the nature and progress of the illness, but not as instructions on how to obtain a cure. (220–221)

The social and legal uniformity of the nation is here self-evidently desirable: a disunited nation would be a contradiction in terms for Franchetti. From that assumption it is only a short step to the hypostatization of Italy itself ("Italy has the duty"), and thence to the pathologization of Sicily, which is no longer seen to be a society organized on different principles, but a "disease" or a "dis-order." According to Franchetti's totalizing model of societies or civilizations, everything within a culture is bound firmly and directly to its dominant principles—even, as in this case, the mentalities of its people. Modern principles of law and the common good are rendered "unintelligible" for Sicilians by their surroundings (83). The possessing classes are utterly untrustworthy since they are incapable of having disinterested middle-class opinions, "being incapable of withdrawing their minds from the social state which absorbs those minds on all sides" (133). The Sicily produced by *Condizioni* is both a sealed totality and an Other to Franchetti's ideal model of a European nation.

Franchetti's medical metaphor for objective knowledge encapsulates the implications of this reasoning and once again highlights the logical link between Franchetti's analysis and his proposed solutions. The power of Italy over Sicily is to be the total, unidirectional power of doctor over patient. The doctor engages in no dialogue with the patient and treats her utterances as lies or symptoms. The doctor knows the patient better than she does herself. (The gendering of Sicily as female is also in Franchetti's text: Sicilians are later referred to as the "little sisters" of the Italians [238]). Franchetti also concludes by placing an underdeveloped Sicily within a vision of a struggle for survival between civilizations. Sicily is in direct and deadly competition with the Italian nation:

The coexistence within the same nation of the civilizations of Sicily and of middle and upper Italy is incompatible with the prosperity of this nation and, in the long term, with its very existence. This is because it produces a weakness which makes the nation vulnerable to falling to pieces at the slightest jolt it receives from outside. One of these two civilizations must disappear, therefore, to the extent that parts of it are incompatible with the other one. (237)

In a way similar to that in which Franchetti uses nation to mean the imagined community of all Italians and exclusively the group determining the agenda in the political sphere, Italy both embraces Sicily and is fundamentally opposed to it. If   Sicily is the life-threatening disease that it both harbors and

"Violence" and the "mafia"

The notions of violence and force are pivotal to Franchetti's understanding of Sicily, and particularly of the mafia. To understand the function of violence in those pages of *Condizioni* in which Franchetti gives his most sustained and coherent description of the laws of motion of Sicilian crime, it helps to make explicit the only partially elaborated model of a normal, modern society which underlies his work.

Franchetti's benchmark society is hierarchical but harmonious. It is premised on certain agreed principles of liberty, property ownership, and the rule of law. The keystone of the social order is a class of aristocratic landowners. But agriculture is not in stasis: it is increasingly capitalized and the laborers are no longer in a state of semi-serfdom but contract out their services in a free market. The bourgeoisie control an increasing amount of the alienable and productive capital of the society; this is justified by their energetic use of it, their moral and material leadership of society along the path of progress. They create wealth and constitute public opinion. Between the upper echelons of the social order and the propertyless is a rampart of smallholding peasants. Protected from the worst effects of the market by their relative self-sufficiency, these peasants have an interest in property relations as they stand. To ensure that the rules of the economic game are respected and property ownership guaranteed, the state is endowed by the citizenry with a monopoly o   ence. Force is no longer exercised by individuals in pursuit of t   ts, but is extracted from the economic life of the country. Crim   ntisocial elements find themselves isolated by this general ac   on property and progress. In this model of society, violence be   plicable as well as illegal. When the legal and social accord is b   issue is reduced to one of punishing or reforming the offenders.

The meaning of violence in *Condizioni* d   rt from the senselessness it has within this version of the classic   -century liberal vision of the system of legality. As we shall see,   the way Franchetti mixes normative and analytical criteria togethe   talizing view of society, Sicily comes to be seen as essentially v   nchetti argues that since the abolition of feudalism on the island, the aristocracy have lost their total control of the means of violence (although they still sponsor and protect the culprits). Force has become "democratized" and accessible to members of nearly every class (91). Liberated from the restrictions placed upon it by feudal custom that did allow an approximate sense of when force was legitimate and when it was not (84), violence becomes the basis of social life and the norm according to which that society's codes of acceptable behavior are determined; it is "the foundation of social relations," accepted by the "juridical sense of the population" (90). In Franchetti's Sicily, while there may be disagreements between individual criminals, there is no disagreement across the whole society on what he terms the "moral value of violence" (128). In other words, in Franchetti's scheme of things, where civility means capitalist legality, Sicily is a society based upon a contradiction in terms.

The group to have emerged to profit from the democratization of violence is an independent class of criminals, brigands, and *mafiosi*. The composition and homogeneity of this class in the Palermo area and in the rest of the island vary slightly, but they seem closely to mirror the middle classes and smallholders cherished by Franchetti's vision of a perfectly ordered and increasingly capitalist society. They do not yet hold the bulk of the property, but they determine the values of the collective. They are like the middle classes in a healthy society in that their values have become hegemonic: in and around Palermo they determine a public code of private power and of *omertà,* creating a "false public opinion" (216), a vast system of complicity in which the values of illegality are the law. In other words, private force and violence play in Franchetti's Sicily a role uncannily like that of private property and capital in what he posits as a normal culture. If it is property that underarches the law in Franchetti's ideal society, then it is violence that determines the nature of Sicilian juridical relations. Paradoxically, in Sicily, the law is that "it is forbidden to resort to the law against violence" (99). Violence is excluded from society in Franchetti's ideal, reappearing only as an inexplicable aberration. It is law that has an almost nonexistent effect in Sicily, which is unintelligible to its citizens, and appears only from outside it, from the Continent, to disrupt a homeostatic system of force. It is for this reason, according to Franchetti, that any initiative for change in Sicily must come entirely from outside the island because "society is too perfectly organized in its current form" (107).

Criminal interest groups compete under this umbrella of shared norms in exactly the same way as businesses within the terms of capitalist legal and social values:

> The criminals always preserve their interest in the free and safe exercise of their industry, common and identical for all, even when their short-term interests are in conflict. For this reason, the sense of preservation has induced the class of violent criminals in Palermo and its surrounding countryside to promote this interest which we could refer to as social, and which is abstracted from the individual and short-term interests of its members. (99)

The criminal class of Sicily emerges from Franchetti's text as a twisted version of a normal European bourgeoisie. The language used to describe this "class" is striking:

> in that industry, the *capo mafia* . . . acts as capitalist, impresario and manager. He determines the unity in the management of the crimes committed . . . he regulates the way labour and duties are divided out, and controls discipline amongst the workers (and this discipline is indispensable in this as in any other industry if one wants to obtain abundant and constant profits). It is his job to judge from the circumstances whether the acts of violence should be suspended for a w   fiercer character. He has to adapt to mark   s are to be carried out, which peopl   nce is best used to obtain the desire

At first glance, passages like the above display an uncanny consonance with recent interpretations of the mafia as a business, like Diego Gambetta's. Yet it seems to me that such an impression is to some extent the product of a historical optical illusion, a back-projection. For Franchetti, the mafia was not a business or a set of businesses, but a hegemonic social *class*. This fact should not be obscured by Franchetti's economistic definition of the middle class, which he assumes is entirely composed of capitalists.[56] Franchetti uses an ideal model of capitalist enterprise within a society governed by bourgeois legality as an analogue for violent cliques within a society governed by a code of illegality. What Franchetti is trying to describe is a set of relationships among the economic, political, and criminal spheres of Sicilian society, yet he does so by using a metaphor that posits an inverted homology between a liberal capitalist nation and Sicilian society as a whole.

How much of Franchetti's analysis of the mafia is correct? There are some aspects of it that seem to me to be definitely wrong. Firstly, the mafia was not equivalent to a social class, and it is not convincing to label the whole of the middle class in and around Palermo as *mafiosa* in the way Franchetti does. To do so is to ignore what is specific to the activities of violent *mafiosi* within the middle class. Secondly, competition between violent cliques cannot be based on any sort of accord on basic rules analogous to the relationship between the interests of the property-owning classes and the law. The homology Franchetti posits between them is simply too neat. Thirdly, Franchetti's model of capitalism is normative and mechanistic and has had any notion of social conflict deleted from it entirely. Anyone hoping to use Franchetti to explain Sicilian society in the 1870s would have to substitute a differentiated model of entrepreneurial activity and situate the Sicilian economy in a wider geoeconomic context.[57] The specific role of mafia-like practices within Sicily's criminal, commercial, and political markets would need to be studied in its different phases within the overall development of the Italian economy, society, and state.

Franchetti's much quoted references to the "industry of violence" perhaps encapsulate both the strengths and weaknesses of *Condizioni*. As Gambetta has remarked, that phrase can involve a confusion between the means and ends of mafia power: violence is a means, not an end; the mafia's core business is protection. Indeed, the way Franchetti uses the analogy between violence and entrepreneurship at times comes close to implying that force has *replaced* economic activity rather than having a relationship to it. I do not see this as a localized error in *Condizioni*: it is the necessary result of the way Franchetti attributes to violence in Sicilian society the same function that capital and property have in a "normal" society. Nevertheless, the phrase "violence industry" is also potentially very apt. As Salvatore Lupo has shown regarding the citrus-fruit industry around Palermo, the capacity to use force can become a resource to be deployed in unstable, highly risky, but highly profitable commercial sectors.[58]

The current state of historical research on the mafia does not allow us to draw up a final balance-sheet on Franchetti. It is nevertheless instructive to evaluate *Condizioni* in the light of one recent study which draws on it heavily. Diego Gambetta's *The Sicilian Mafia* is also comparable to *Condizioni* in that it sees an economic rationale underlying mafia activity. Gambetta's account, which seems to me the most suggestive of the sociological approaches to the topic, describes mafia as the "brand-name" of a cluster of organized, exclusive groups or "families" specializing in, and holding a virtual monopoly of, a specific core business—that of providing protection guaranteed by violence or the threat of violence. If one wants to operate in a given business, whether it involves lemons, concrete, or drugs, and even more if one wants to dominate that business, one has to pay for mafia protection and intervention. *Mafiosi,* according to Gambetta, are not principally criminal entrepreneurs, paralegal enforcers, extortionists, or the heads of clienteles. They regulate, intervene in, and profit from a range of markets, legal and illegal, by turning into a commodity those guarantees that the state fails to provide.[59]

Despite Gambetta's sophisticated hypothesis on the origins of the "business of private protection," it is not clear whether a mafia in precisely this sense existed in Franchetti's time.[60] Lupo has suggested that a recognizably modern mafia can be detected from the 1870s onwards in the relationship between *mafiosi,* the heads of brigand bands, land managers, and noble landowners. The first records of mafia rituals borrowed from Masonic models also date from the 1870s. The spread of this style of organization into different provinces, which can be attributed to the way in which prisons acted to disseminate strategies and forms of behavior among inmates linked to the families, seems to date from the 1880s.[61] But these facts do not necessarily back up either Franchetti or Gambetta. The answer to the question of whether the mafia existed in a modern form in Franchetti's time obviously depends on what idea of the mafia one happens to have. And Lupo is at pains to distinguish his own looser definition and more empirically oriented approach from both Franchetti and Gambetta's strong, sociological model of the mafia as a business.[62]

Nevertheless, even assuming that Gambetta's theory is correct, we are left with a number of open historical questions. We do not know, for example, where and when the protection market reached the level of specialization Gambetta envisages, or when Cosa nostra adopted its current form and achieved a tendentially monopolistic control over that market. It seems often to have been the case in Franchetti's time, for example, that entrepreneurs resorted to arming themselves to protect their own interests. What is more, in many cases we do not have a complete picture of how the protection market related to other specific markets. And we do not know the precise extent to which the organization of private protection was based territorially, or whether it cut across geographical space and followed commercial channels. The mafia's characteristics vary to a degree according to the specific nature of the economic activity onto which private protection is parasitically grafted, as on the specific social hierarchies with which the protection industry has to coexist. It is certain that in the 1870s, western Sicily produced factions, clienteles, and associations whose domain was the interlinked spheres of commerce, crime, and local politics. It is certain that violence was a common instrument for these groups and a means for achieving and defending social status for the individuals involved. It is certain, moreover, that the term "mafia" was widely used, albeit in a confusing variety of ways. But there is no historical consensus on the key issue of whether and when Cosa nostra came to constitute an autonomous, "self-conscious" entity based on a pattern common to large parts of western Sicily. Nor does it seem to me that Franchetti can provide the basis for any such consensus in the future.

What I hope my reading of Franchetti's study of public order in Sicily has shown is that interpreting the mafia in terms of a commercial logic is only the beginning of the historical task. What remains is the work of historicizing private protection and plotting its changing relationship with the broader economy, the state, and society. Gambetta's version of the origins of the mafia perhaps does not entirely do justice to the subtlety of his overall understanding in that it risks producing a teleology of the modern mafia by looking back for signs of the once-and-for-all emergence of a particular *supplier*, "for characters who specialize in protection" (77). It is arguably more in tune with Gambetta's theory to try instead to write the history of an evolving protection *market* in which all kinds of shifts in the nature of supply and demand, and their relationship with the social and political context, are possible over time. Historians also need to be able to make allowance for radical alterations in the very structure of the business itself in response to wider economic, social and political change. One thing to which Leopoldo Franchetti can lay claim is to have been the originator of that "commercial" line of analysis, even if it was partly as a result of a certain creative misreading of his work by later scholars. His achievement is indeed remarkable. By locating the social matrices for the mafia's origins in the particular nature of its transition from feudalism to modernity, he was certainly far ahead of his time. Just as striking is the huge labor of systematization of which *Condizioni* is the result. Franchetti's notes from his journey provide few, if any, hints of the highly abstract, theoretical picture of Sicily that was to emerge in the published study.[63] In moving from observation to analysis, Franchetti ingeniously adapted the only sociological language in his repertoire by simply inverting the ideal models implicit in nineteenth-century liberal social analysis. In this way he provided a picture of lawlessness in Sicily that was cogent enough on its own terms to have become a fundamental point of reference for scholars in the field ever since.

Conclusions

Villari and Franchetti both viewed the areas of the South that they studied as in some sense beyond Italy. Yet they also saw the Mezzogiorno as defining the nation's mission, a place where, at the very moment that the weakness of Italian identity was revealed, the potential for its salvation also came to light. Their South, in other words, was caught up in the patriotic game of "us" and "them." The stereotypes of Southern Italy that were produced in the work of the first *meridionalisti* were not unequivocally false. Nor can it be said that these stereotypes merely set up a static, monolithic image of an Other. The stereotypical South is a polyvalent and often contradictory concept that cannot be abstracted from the textual strategies in which it is elaborated. Hence the distinct differences between the type of geographical concept that Villari and Franchetti create. Villari's South is envisioned when he denounces the country's problems to public opinion, or when he exhorts the moral elite to action; it is conjured up when the moralist sets out to know it, or when it is used to measure the gap between words and deeds. Franchetti's Sicily is evoked as the traveler hears with horror of the violence in and around Palermo or contemplates the desolation of the island's interior; it is fabricated as the impartial analyst rescues the traveler from his confusion or as a classical liberal model of society is inverted in the attempt to account for a seemingly anomalous reality. It should be added that there were other, similarly complex and multifaceted Souths created in the 1870s and 1880s: they range from a lyrical, picturesque, tragic version in Renato Fucini's *Napoli a occhio nudo* of 1878, to Pasquale Turiello's racialized South of *Governo e governati in Italia* from 1881.[64]

As I suggested in my introduction, the influence of the early *meridionalisti* really becomes visible only over the longer term, as they come to be seen as the founders of a tradition. It is a tradition that has been subject to both revision and forgetting. In the early 1990s, the idea of the southern question as a national issue was out of favor in Italy. The perceived abject failure of the policy of extraordinary economic intervention pursued since 1950, and the emergence of a vocal minority autonomist movement in the shape of the Northern League, combined to push the idea of the national state's responsibility for the South off the political agenda. Should the South once again be the subject of collective solidarity and state intervention? It is a project whose economic and social merits are better not discussed here.[65] Nonetheless, my investigation into the early *meridionalisti* suggests that there are risks as well as advantages associated with formulating the southern question in national terms. It seems clear from the work of Villari and Franchetti that in some measure we owe stereotypes of a South unvaried in its backwardness to the way the southern question has been framed in the language of nationhood. And as Franchetti's analysis of Sicily shows most clearly, when the *meridionalisti* constructed the stereotype of the South as Other, they were also constructing significant limits to their liberalism. If my reading of Villari and Franchetti has one message to impart to the southern question of today, it is that the cause of scientific analysis and social solidarity has a slippery ally in the "nation."

Chapter 3 ✤

The Power of the Picturesque: Representations of the South in the *Illustrazione Italiana*

The *Illustrazione Italiana* was the leading illustrated magazine of its day; it spearheaded a drive by Fratelli Treves, one of the largest publishing houses in the country, to carve out a market across Italy for its products. In its efforts to follow, interpret, and mold the outlook of its readers, the *Illustrazione Italiana* can give us an insight into how the South was perceived by the bourgeoisie at large in the magazine's golden years between 1880 and 1900. As I will argue, a set of primarily commercial objectives influenced the content and tone of the magazine and made it into a relatively consistent attempt to shape taste in its own interests. What concerns me in this study of the *Illustrazione Italiana* is the magazine's images of bourgeois culture, its efforts to construct a model sensibility. My case is that representations of the South had a central place in those efforts. In describing the workings of what I call the *Illustrazione Italiana*'s discourse of the picturesque I will look at how the magazine constructed Southern Italy in relation to the cultural values it imputed to its readers. As elsewhere, my readings will also have theoretical as well as historical aims: in this case I will be attempting to provide a theoretical description of the imaginary dynamics associated with picturesque stereotypes.

The *Illustrazione Italiana:* commerce, patriotism, aesthetics.

When the *Illustrazione Italiana* was founded in 1873 it was in many ways a pioneer.[1] Other publishers had already tried and failed to launch a similar project, notably Sonzogno with his magazine of the same title, which went under in 1869. Within a few years, the Treves brothers had overcome the technical problems that were the chief obstacle confronted by previous publishers. Heavy investment in machinery enabled the *Illustrazione Italiana* to rival magazines in other European countries for the quality of its images.[2] However, it bears emphasizing that despite Treves's investments, the production of a weekly illustrated magazine of contemporary events was a technically daunting task. The regular use of directly reproduced photographs did not really become feasible until the 1890s. For at least the first twenty years of its existence the *Illustrazione Italiana* relied on engravings on wood plates (often laboriously copied from photographs) by skilled craftsmen such as Aristide Sartorio and Eduardo Ximenes—Treves was keen to regard them as artists in their own right.[3] It seems likely that practical aspects of the magazine's production exerted an influence on its content: a newsworthy event in the outer reaches of the peninsula would mean sending an artist and writer, hindered by their ignorance of the area and by communication problems, to the scene. However, by 1881, illustrated publications had become a key factor in the strong Milanese presence in the national publishing market. By 1883 the sale of Treves magazines was high enough to subsidize the book publishing arm of the company, which itself was the major force in literary publishing in Italy: its list included Verga, De Amicis, and Carducci.[4] The company covered every aspect of publishing, from the editing to the printing and distribution. The Treves plant was very much a factory in the modern sense of the word: highly mechanized and therefore investment-intensive, with a clear division of labor between the ten different stages of the production process.[5] The magazine took several years after its foundation to achieve a consistency of tone and format. Its heyday, and the period on which I concentrate here, was in the 1880s and 1890s before its position as market leader was taken by *Domenica del Corriere,* which first appeared in 1898.

Who were the readers of the *Illustrazione Italiana* and how numerous were they? Unfortunately, the circulation figures that are the obvious source for such information do not exist, nor does any documentation from the publishing house itself.[6] But a relatively well-defined profile of the magazine's readership can be deduced from what we know about publishing in Italy generally and from the content of the *Illustrazione Italiana* itself.

The very low disposable income of the average Italian meant that Italy inevitably lagged behind other European countries in the progress towards a mass reading public, and its publishers continued to prefer to produce upmarket editions for some time after unification. Treves in particular targeted the quality end of the market. The *Illustrazione Italiana* itself was packaged as a luxury item: binders in which to collect and display the magazine were sold. Emilio Treves was considered by a close colleague to have "a sound appreciation of his readership, and not of that vulgar readership whose desires it is profitable to comply with, but of the kind of readership that wants to be led towards higher things, that wants to understand, to participate and to be persuaded in a dignified manner."[7] The advertising in the *Illustrazione Italiana* gives the impression of a readership concentrated, at least initially, in the urban bourgeoisie. In its pages are advertised life insurance, dress materials, cosmetics, novelty gadgets, luxury comestibles, and numerous health fads including "golden anti-hysteria drops," hair restorers, and the services of a famous somnambulist and magnetist. But it is books, and overwhelmingly Treves publications, that are the commodities most often publicized in the magazine. The advertisements clearly also imply that both women and men made up the *Illustrazione Italiana's* readership: Emilio Treves asserted that his periodicals "are very much aimed at families" (quoted in Grillandi 330). What these clues suggest is that the magazine targeted the upper end of the publishing house's middle-class market.[8] While we cannot quantify it exactly, the *Illustrazione Italiana's* undoubted commercial success suggests that it was an important interpreter of the culture of its readership.

The geographical spread of the public addressed by the *Illustrazione Italiana* is also difficult to ascertain. Milan's claim to be Italy's "moral capital" was supported by the strength of its publishing industry.[9] The development of the *Corriere della Sera* and *Il Secolo,* the first newspapers in Italy to operate as something like a fourth estate rather than just as the mouthpieces of particular interest groups, is often cited as evidence of the relative modernity of the Lombard capital's public sphere. But while the core of the *Illustrazione Italiana's* readership, particularly in its first years, must have been Milanese, one does not get the impression that it was speaking to a specific regional public or that it was attempting programmatically to impose the cultural and political agenda of Lombardy on the whole country. Although Emilio Treves subscribed to the myth of the moral capital, and gave Milan that title in some of the pieces he wrote for the *Illustrazione Italiana,* he was too shrewd a publisher to let regionalism hinder his conquest of a national readership (Grillandi 476). Soon after it began, the *Illustrazione Italiana* absorbed a Roman rival, *Illustrazione—Rivista Italiana,* and subsequently carried a picture of the Capitol taken from the Roman magazine on its masthead. The geographical spread of the *Illustrazione Italiana's* public is also suggested by the fact that by 1883 Fratelli Treves had branches in Rome, Bologna, Trieste, and Naples (Grillandi 412). It has also been argued that only increasing penetration of a national market could have supported enterprises the size of Treves (Gigli Marchetti). The distribution problems that contributed to the localized nature of the newspaper market would not have been such a hindrance to a magazine published only weekly, at least as far as reaching the urban centers was concerned.[10] The magazine itself had

a distinctly national profile: its regular contributors, including Emilio
Treves himself, were overwhelmingly not Lombard, for example: Nicola
Lazzaro, born in Naples in 1842; Raffaello Barbiera, born in Venice of a
southern father in 1852; Carlo Sforza, a Tuscan born in Lucca in 1873;
Ugo Pesci, born in Florence in 1842. The *Illustrazione Italiana* certainly has
a more national outlook than its more down-market sister publication, the
Illustrazione Popolare, which had twice the circulation but only cost one
fifth of the price.[11] The magazine's more Milanese focus is evident well into
the 1890s: of the views of land- and cityscapes reproduced in the *Illustrazione Popolare* in 1894, nine were from Milan, one from Sicily and none
from Naples. Further indicators suggest that the *Illustrazione Italiana* developed into a magazine aimed at the bourgeoisie of the whole peninsula:
during the 1880s advertisements for shops in Milan steadily reduced in
number to be replaced by products and services sold nationally including
by mail order. The magazine may have hailed from Milan, but the language
it spoke was national.

One of the *Illustrazione Italiana*'s most interesting aspects from a historical perspective is its diversity of subject matter. It capaciously called itself
the "weekly magazine of contemporary events and people, which deals with
today's history, public and social life, sciences, fine arts, geography and
travel, theatre, music, fashion, etc."[12] Given this range, to read the magazine
in terms of its explicit political stance would clearly be to impoverish it as a
historical document. Nevertheless, there is a significant uniformity of political tone to the *Illustrazione Italiana*'s pronouncements. Under the pseudonym of "Cicco," Emilio Treves himself wrote much of the comment on the
week's cultural, social, and political events.[13] Treves's moderate standpoint
can be read into his writing at certain moments: he was, for example, not
fully behind Crispi, but seems to have relished the Sicilian politician's way
with parliament and respected his patriotism. On colonialism, the *Illustrazione Italiana* shied away from an openly expansionist policy, but the sat-
uration coverage given to North and East Africa in the 1880s and 1890s
strongly suggests a more enthusiastic *africanismo* than might be deduced
from its explicit statements alone. On religion, the magazine occasionally
lamented the lack of a moral influence on the lower orders such as might be
provided by the church.[14] The *Illustrazione Italiana* also displayed a consistent antifeminism.[15] However, the opinions of many of the magazine's contributors differed greatly from those of Treves: Carlo Del Balzo, who wrote
a long series of articles on Naples in the early 1880s, was from the extreme
Left; later on, the irredentist Scipio Sighele became the *Illustrazione Italiana*'s crime correspondent, and pieces by Francesco Saverio Nitti also appeared. What permitted this diversity was the resigned and almost ironic
distance from the day-to-day business of politics established in the pages of

the magazine. Its distaste for politics occasionally becomes open hostility: "[Italy] will withdraw more and more from politics, which bores or disgusts it" (April 23, 1882, 290).[16]

Italy's political life was very [ ] but it rarely found in affairs of gover[ ] ts own brand of celebratory patriotism[ ] with the paraphernalia of government, the ceremonies, personalities, and grand speeches. The *Illustrazione Italiana* clearly considered its preferred subjects to be above politics. It displayed, for example, a limitless appetite for images of the king and queen: state visits were lavishly covered and collectable portraits of the monarchs printed. The army and navy were given increasingly large amounts of space: the magazine reproduced loving illustrations of maneuvers, weapons, and fortifications, and it never failed to remark on the valor of troops engaged in combating civil unrest. Its monarchism and militarism would seem to align the *Illustrazione Italiana,* if only implicitly, with the most conservative forces in Italy. Etchings and diagrams of new tunnels, bridges, and drainage systems signaled the magazine's pride in technological progress and exemplified its preference for engineering solutions to social problems. But the many new patriotic monuments and rites of Umbertian Italy are perhaps the *Illustrazione Italiana*'s favorite of all topics: in 1884 the "national pilgrimage" to the tomb of Victor Emmanuel II took up the front page for six consecutive editions.[17] If the *Illustrazione Italiana* was to sell across a national market, then it had to tap into and cultivate national sentiment. It had to make images of Italy as it competed for readers.

Just as important as the reproduction of public symbols of *italianità* for the *Illustrazione Italiana* was the cultivation of a private patriotic sensibility through the languages of art and literature. Creating a demand for the artistic had an obvious commercial logic for a publisher dealing primarily in literatur[ ] g heavy use of the *Illustrazione Italia[ ]* es for the number of books produced[ ] amental importance of literature for th[ ].

As an incentive to subscribe for 1886 to *Margherita,* "the lady's journal of luxury, fashion and literature," Treves made a free gift of a print by Vincenzo Caprile (this image has been reproduced on the cover of this book).[19] Full-page advertisements in the *Illustrazione Italiana* proclaimed the offer in terms that constituted something like a lesson in taste:

> Paintings have now become a necessary ornament in our salons, and good taste, which is becoming more exquisitely artistic with every day that passes, dictates that a painting should have a genuine value. It is not enough for it to reproduce an elegant and agreeable subject. In the intonation of its colours, in

the movement of its figures, it must give one that pleasing impression that only arises from the works of genuine artists who paint the truth not only with skill, but also with talent. (November 29, 1885, 352)

To have real value, to be part of the ever more artistic progress of taste, the advertisement tells us, a picture must provide the unmistakable (yet inexpressible) frisson of true art. In other words, what the "elegant and cultivated readership" demands of art is that it be recognizably arty (ibid.). The magazine's texts and images insistently proclaim their own status as traditional high culture. While this kitsch aesthetic values sentimental effects, it "tends continuously to suggest the idea that, in enjoying these effects, the reader is honing some privileged aesthetic experience."[20] Yet the taste cultivated by the *Illustrazione Italiana* was more than a status symbol offered as a commercial ploy. The notion of a properly Italian artistic and literary tradition remained a crucial imaginary guarantor of the nation's solidity in the face of political conflict:

> One could not deny it even if one wanted to. Even we are serious people now! Politics has made us lose our grandfathers' traditional good humour: social problems are disturbing our sleep. It seems that every day a new one is invented to make our lives seem more afflicted. . . .
> But at least once a year we rediscover the good old habits in our Italian blood. And foremost amongst these is our love for the theater. (January 6, 1889, 2)

The commercial and ideological interests of the *Illustrazione Italiana* combine in the propagation of a patriotic aesthetic. Art exhibitions, such as those in Naples in 1877 and Rome in 1883, were given relentless coverage. Articles stoutly defended the territory of Art against the encroachment of Science.[21] Literary news habitually took up more space than politics in the pages of the *Illustrazione Italiana*.

Introduction to the picturesque

A taste for things artistic was thus the distinguishing mark that the readers of the *Illustrazione Italiana* used to identify themselves as a patriotic and cultured public. Yet as such, that taste also became one of the key registers through which Italy's uncultured or dangerous elements were understood. It is significant that the picture offered as a free gift in the subscription drive for *Margherita* is an idealized southern peasant woman, the very embodiment of healthy, unpretentious country living: "How agreeable that robust peasant woman is! Joyful, healthy and clean, with splendid, glowing flesh, a pure, sincere smile, and a ready joke" (November 29, 1885, 352). The *Illustrazione Italiana*'s notion of good taste worked simultaneously as a marketing strategy, as the sign of a group identity, and as a language with which to define and examine other social groups who were unable to know art when they saw it. The Italy projected by the Treves magazine is defined by common motifs activated in anniversaries, in the endless unveiling of monuments, in admiration for the monarchy, in the shared appreciation of art and literature. Yet in each of these and other moments of nationalistic meaning, there is the negotiation of the contradiction inherent in post-Risorgimento nationhood between its pretensions to embrace all the people within certain frontiers and the exclusiveness that makes it a useful language in which Italy's upper and middle classes could think social division. The slow and difficult process of negotiating the change from an oligarchic society to a mass society had as its concomitant a constant self-definition on the part of Italy's upper social strata. The *Illustrazione Italiana*'s cult of the artistic should be interpreted as one aspect of the production of a cultural identity through the representation of that which lay beyond the boundaries of the nation as an "elegant and cultivated readership," yet within the confines of the nation-state. The picturesque gains its range of meanings from its key position in those representations.[22]

In 1882 the six hundredth anniversary of the Sicilian Vespers was celebrated. The *Illustrazione Italiana*'s coverage typifies a number of features of its outlook, such as its conversion of regional histories into a calendar of patriotic ceremonies. Nicola Lazzaro's comment on the festival is an example of this strategic appropriation: "We Italians from the continent will join hands with Italians from the island, and our concord, with the unity of the *patria* as our single holy purpose, will serve as a warning to the foreigner, reminding him unambiguously that it is not easy to violate the independence of a people" (February 26, 1882, 150). The events themselves are given much wider coverage a month and a half later in a report by Raffaello Barbiera, "Palermo e il Vespro," which contains all of the themes that characterize the magazine's aesthetic and of nationalism. Barbiera's article contains many references charms of the buildings and countryside of the l ant appeal to the common points of refer in relation to the masses:

incredible feeling of poetry. The octaves of *liberata*, amongst other things, are constantly illustrated the carts that haul mounds of gigantic cabbages or rocks from the mountains crowning the city of Palermo. The beauteous Clorinda, Goffredo, Tancredi and other knights are alive, painted by rough brushes on those vehicles' sides, which serve the same function as illustrated novels:

mobile novels, the delight of the wretched people who still cannot read. (April 16, 1882, 275)

The *Illustrazione Italiana*'s preferred positive stereotype of the lower orders endows them with a crude aesthetic quality of which they themselves are unaware. In this case, their naive artifacts are associated with an earlier moment in the development of the literary tradition by signs that are visible only by those acquainted with Tasso. It is only from the vantage point of high culture that the folkloristic can be appreciated and the final destination of such precocious symptoms of national cultural belonging perceived. They may not know it, but within the masses lie dormant the seeds of a full *italianità* on the *Illustrazione Italiana*'s model. Thus, in the same moment that the magazine produces a knowledge of the popular classes of the South, it renders unthinkable any idea that they might have a right to control their destiny and implicitly arrogates the power to do so to its own readers. Art is the *Illustrazione Italiana*'s favorite code in which to produce safe images of loyalty on the part of the people.

Garibaldi's presence in Palermo is the occasion for a certain populist tone in Barbiera's account: "That unique, unforgettable spectacle, was worth millions of times more than the gala performance of *Aida* stylishly staged at the Politeama where a great many white ties and tail coats were present on two evenings" (ibid., 278). Even when, as here, it is preferred to a stuffy high art, popular culture is valued only insofar as it can be subsumed within the terms of the bourgeois aesthetic, as the raw material of poetry, or here, as the comparison with *Aida* might suggest, as the source of a homely exoticism.[23] Garibaldi's popularity is shown to be a precise analogue of such spontaneous creativity in the political field. He appeals to the crude, ebullient imagination of the people, inspiring a loyalty empty of political content. Of the moment when the parade arrives at the church where the medieval rebellion broke out, Barbiera writes:

And how Michelangelesque was that multitude of common people! Ignoring all attempts to forbid it, they had got past the gates and invaded the alleyways of the cemetery in a confused, panting mass. It was Michelangelesque when, in a flash, the multitude stopped to hear what one citizen was bellowing at them from atop a flight of steps. And it was even more Michelangelesque when, on being asked by him in the name of Garibaldi to clear the area, . . . the crowd waved their arms, hurled their berets in the air, and started yelling "viva Garibaldi!" as they retreated. (ibid., 275)

The name that most often encapsulates this elementary, aesthetic *italianità* for the *Illustrazione Italiana* is the picturesque. The place where the pic-

" . . . the charming and indolent sons of C̲ . . ."

turesqu̲ . . . . ̲ ̲ ̲ ̲ ̲the South seen as a fund of images of peasants and . . . . ̲ ̲ in the things in life that cost nothing: "although poor, ragged an̲d̲ barefoot, they are happy in the sun."[24] Nicola Lazzaro narrates a visit to Capri in July 1882; he is disappointed by the rundown parts of town;

however, on the shore, the full poetry of the place makes a return as we see groups of very dirty children, half covered in rags, squatting on the ground or sitting on benches or rocks in various picturesque poses and enjoying the breeze and the sun. They almost always live on sweet idleness. They are the charming and indolent sons of Capri. (July 16, 1882, 39)

The magazine's contributors were adept at finding the picturesque in even the most obvious poverty. But even when they did so they were doing more than drawing a consolatory veil over an ugly or alien reality. The picturesque, and terms associated with it such as the typical, the characteristic and the folkloristic, form a systematic field of connotation.

Loosely speaking, a picturesque scene, custom, or figure is foreign enough to be exotic, to belong to the poetic margin beyond a humdrum reality, and yet familiar enough to be soothingly Italian. The South and its people exist primarily for the magazine as a set of textual figures inserted into a grid of obsessively reiterated binary oppositions, of which the pair nature-culture is one of the most important. As the favored location in which to hunt the picturesque, the South becomes the privileged arena for the bucolic experience. It is the site of innumerable moments of contemplative reverie recounted in the *Illustrazione Italiana:* "the sweet idleness [*dolce far niente*] of the beautiful southern climate comes out, grabs hold of you and takes away both your energy and your will, leaving only a desire for the pure country air, for sleep and love" (January 21, 1877, 38). The Mezzogiorno is where one goes to cultivate a calm interiority away from the alienating urban hubbub. In the pages of the *Illustrazione Italiana,* a model middle-class sensibility is constantly remade by, on the one hand, a distancing from the natural and uncultivated and, on the other, the ever-surprising discovery of its truest self in that same element. In 1881 Nicola Lazzaro writes of a trip to Bagnoli-Irpino ("the artistic village par excellence") in an article entitled "Una festa campestre" ("A rustic festivity"). His appetite for the picturesque embraces both people and countryside seemingly without distinction: "That mountain scene was populated by thousands of peasants in their picturesque costumes. And the vivid, warm colors of the women's dresses composed a harmonious whole with the various greens of the meadow and the woods." On leaving to return to Naples, Lazzaro bids farewell to his primitive idyll: "Farewell, pure mountain air! Farewell, mild temperature! Farewell, tranquil feelings which raise man up towards vaster and better horizons! Farewell! We are off back to where there is more civilization, but also more corruption" (September 4, 1881, 154).

We can begin to form a clearer theoretical idea of the way the notion of the picturesque works by comparing it to the kind of "median category" alluded to by Edward Said in his discussion of orientalism. According to Said, the strength of such median categories (one might also, it seems to me, call them stereotypes) is their ability to neutralize and harness data that potentially challenge a dogmatic way of seeing (an example might be the spectacle of "i figli di Capri"):

> Something patently foreign and distant acquires, for one reason or another, a status more rather than less familiar. One tends to stop judging things either as completely novel or as completely well-known: a new median category emerges, a category that allows one to see new things, things seen for the first time, as versions of a previously known thing. In essence such a category is not so much a way of receiving new information as it is a method of controlling what seems to be a threat to some established view of things. If the mind must suddenly deal with what it takes to be a radically new form of life . . . the response on the whole is conservative and defensive. . . . The threat is muted, familiar values impose themselves, and in the end the mind reduces the pressure upon it by accommodating things to itself as either "original" or "repetitious." . . . The Orient at large, therefore, vacillates between the West's contempt for what is familiar and its shivers of delight in— or fear of—novelty.[25]

As is often the case, Said's account displays an interesting tension between an approach informed by discourse theory and an empiricism. The belief in a direct experiential encounter with reality here produces an unargued and simplistic psychology: accepting raw information causes a "pressure" that the mind must then reduce through the application of familiar models; or, in the context that interests us here, the troubling sight of poverty in the South produces the need for comforting stereotypes. Conceived in this way, the picturesque would be less a median category than a mediator of experience; its role would be difficult to distinguish from that of language in general as understood by empiricism.[26] The "shivers" provoked by coming face to face with the Orient or the South would have to be attributed to those things that stereotypes could not render "known and therefore less fearsome" (Said, *Orientalism* 60). Understanding stereotypical discourse as a mediator between the subject and a shocking confrontation with the real in this way would be impossible to implement in analysis: it would necessitate having to reconstruct the original psychological moment of the encounter in order to measure to what extent the representations had neutralized that experience.

There is a second logic at work in Said's theory. According to the first, as I have suggested, the purpose of all categories, including orientalist discourse, is to make fearsome sense-information familiar. According to the second, the fearsome and the familiar, the novel and the boring, are themselves categories that have successfully been emptied of emotional content.

On occasion, for example, rather than being the moment of an untreated exposure to the exotic, fear is seen by Said as one of a list of programmed responses indicative of the West's manufacturing of the East as a theater for its own emotions: "sensuality, promise, terror, sublimity, idyllic pleasure, intense energy" (Said, *Orientalism* 118).

Although these implicit theories are not necessarily mutually incompatible on their own terms, they do both imagine a subject too neatly divided between its sense-mechanisms and its meaning-making capacity. The central weakness of Said's theory, I would argue, is that it relates to cognitive rather than noetic processes. The picturesque is not a median category in that it stands between the psyche and the outside world, but in that its function is governed by its relation to sets of antithetically constructed categories that structure the middle-class sensibility—both emotive and intellectual—shaped by the *Illustrazione Italiana*. The picturesque names the South's anomalous position between Italy and the Orient, between the world of civilized progress and the spheres of either rusticity or barbarism. One of its tasks is to regulate and reinforce these polarities, moving the South nearer to "us" when it is pastoral and nearer to "them" when it is uncivilized.

The picturesque encapsulates the whole representative strategy of the *Illustrazione Italiana* toward the South; one senses the term, and notions akin to it, being ready-to-hand in stereotype after stereotype, article after article. But because of the great variety of circumstances in which it was deployed, the discourse of the picturesque presents analytical problems as far as the selection of material is concerned. It cuts across such obvious criteria as author and subject matter, as across the line between fiction and reportage. It can underpin an incidental stereotype as it can the message of a whole article. It is a flexible structure of response rather than a type of political thought or a set of opinions. Variety of analysis is the best response to these problems. The first of the following sections focuses on the magazine's treatment of an earthquake on the island of Ischia. The second examines the links between the picturesque and the *Illustrazione Italiana*'s monarchism. The third, which is also fairly wide in its scope, analyzes an orientalist thematics in the *Illustrazione Italiana* in order to compare the representations of colonial lands and the South. The fourth section examines the magazine's treatment of a particular historical episode, the movement of the Fasci in Sicily. The fifth section looks closely at a particular text, a short story by Contessa Lara. In the fifth section I will also return to the theoretical questions raised by picturesque stereotypes. From these different angles I will attempt to build up an overall impression of the capabilities of the discourse of the picturesque.

Faces of the picturesque

Earthquake on Ischia.

It need hardly be said that the *Illustrazione Italiana* rarely turned its attention to the unnewsworthy social problems of the Mezzogiorno. A set-piece disaster patently provided rather more opportunity for interesting copy. Events such as volcanic eruptions, earthquakes, and epidemics receive relatively dense coverage, giving us an insight into how the magazine responded to genuine suffering on the part of the charming peasants who filled its pages. In March 1881 large parts of Casamicciola on the island of Ischia were destroyed by an earthquake that killed hundreds. Nicola Lazzaro sent in a report for the issue of March 20, 1881. It opens with the first thoughts of those in Naples who heard news of the disaster: "There can be no more doubt. The poetic, delightful, healthy village of Casamicciola in the Ischia area has been destroyed by the earthquake. The ruined houses run into hundreds, so do the dead, and so do the injured."[27] For Lazzaro, as for his readers, it is primarily against the town imagined by the *Illustrazione Italiana*'s discourse of the picturesque that the gravity of the earthquake will be measured.

Lazzaro's article, like many in the magazine, is a narrative organized around the writer's journey to the scene of his report. In the foreground are the journalist's own impressions, his descriptive powers and his command of the resources of a gaudy sapience. Lazzaro sets off by boat to Ischia and takes time to revise some elements of the patriotic culture:

> Ploughing the waves we passed before Capo Miseno and it seemed to me that I saw the shadow of Hercules' trumpeter who was killed there by the Triton who played the sea shell in mythological times. The immortal rebellion of the Sicilian Vespers came to mind as we passed close to Procida and saw the ruined castle that used to belong to John who was the mind and soul of that national epic.

Lazzaro continues, recalling the customs and costumes of the islanders, the various poets and painters who have found inspiration in Ischia's beauties, the different names given to it by ancient Greeks and Romans . . . The preparatory sections of the report remind the reader of what the South is for the *Illustrazione Italiana:* a display case for fragments of folk culture, mythology, landscape, and epic history. On landing, Lazzaro asks:

> Where are the numerous, annoying tour guides who anxiously await to lead the traveller to the volcano's crater? Where are the gentle maidens who dance a sprightly and gay tarantella? Where are the sternly beautiful, bizarrely

dressed women who, with terracotta pots on their heads, cross the curious traveller's path as he follows a maze of paths which are shaded by trees and bordered with myrtle and aloe?

The destruction of Casamicciola is comprehended through the evocation of a lost stock of picturesque scenes. Hardly has he begun his description of the effects of the disaster than Lazzaro pauses to exclaim, referring to a road taken by the journalists touring the area:

> In different times we would soon leave it to turn back to our left and climb to the volcano, following a path that snakes along the mountain's wooded sides and justifies everything nobly rustic described by writers and poets in ancient eclogues. (March 20, 1881, 181)

Lazzaro is willing to be distracted. As if he were indeed "in other times," he carries on evoking the scenic path, the quality of the fruit and wine of the area, the dramatic climb to the volcano. The digression ends with two rhetorical questions: "But what use is it to speak of what we once used to admire? Why tell of the cosmic beauties towards which no one gave a thought on that day?" (ibid.). One could be forgiven for thinking that little else apart from "bellezze cosmiche" had occupied Lazzaro's mind as he viewed Casamicciola. It would seem that Lazzaro's public is incapable of grasping the destruction of Casamicciola without the town's being lavishly reconstructed as a combination of commonplace reference points: mythological, gastronomic, pastoral, artistic, literary, folkloristic, and patriotic-historical. What holds these components of the *Illustrazione Italiana*'s South together is less their reference to a given reality than their availability to the demands of an apparatus of cultural response. They exist only as the furniture of repeated moments of pastoral reverie, of anthropological observation, of descriptive virtuosity, of pathos.

Of those parts of the article not devoted to the picturesque Casamicciola, many are taken up with the activities of "the worthy carabinieri and the equally worthy engineers and infantrymen," or to the pity aroused by the sight of the ruins (ibid., 182). Accompanying the piece are two illustrations of the town before and after the earthquake which show the damage to buildings. The inhabitants are mentioned only once, and they are portrayed as a dumb and pitiable contrast to the singing and dancing local costumes they had been before:

> And behold we came across a stray dog, or a man whose faltering gait and stupefied look seemed to betray the fact that he had lost his reason. They were all like him because misfortune has almost stupefied them: they do not yet understand the full extent of the calamity that has struck them. (ibid., 181)

Such perceptions of the natives reconfirm hackneyed literary expectations: the poor display an uncomprehending simplicity in the face of Nature's hostility.

Remarkably, at least half of Lazzaro's article is devoted to the Ischia made familiar by a touristic aesthetic and described in passages like those quoted above. The central tactic of the piece is not to describe the damage done by the earthquake, but to rework some favorite *Illustrazione Italiana* themes in a tone of mawkish elegy. The magazine is not often quite so monomanic in its dealings with Italy's imaginary outskirts. But Lazzaro's article nonetheless typifies responses to tragedy in the South in its pages. Even in a time of evident crisis and widespread suffering, the *Illustrazione Italiana*'s primary interest is in a dilettante anthropology of the picturesque.

The Monarchy, the people and the picturesque

Between August and October 1884, a cholera epidemic killed thousands in Naples.[28] The poor quarters of the city, where the people's distrust of authority led to frequent attacks on public health officials, "seethe[d] with class hatred" (Snowden 144). Naples became the focus of political and philanthropic concern across the peninsula. King Umberto gained considerable credibility and popularity by staying in the city for some time during the epidemic. Accompanied by leading ministers and officials as well as by the Cardinal Archbishop Sanfelice (a significant symbolic rapprochement between church and state), he visited the Conocchia cholera hospital and even undertook his own tour of the worst slums.[29] The epidemic was lived by the *Illustrazione Italiana* predominantly through Umberto's visit, as a combination of royal event and military exercise:

> The battle of Naples is a great battle fought by pity, generosity and science against misfortune. It is a terrible predicament: and yet Umberto of Savoy hurried to where the danger was and, for the first time in his life as a constitutional King, has given an order, he has imposed his own will on his lieutenants. (September 14, 1884, 162)

In the following week's issue, the magazine cheerily reports the damage to the credibility of republicanism done by the king's actions: "Amidst its anguish Naples found room for enthusiasm, and the people gave him [the King] the title of 'father of the people', a title which will stay with him" (September 21, 1884, 178). The next number of the *Illustrazione Italiana* carries a picture of Umberto on the front cover and a double page spread of "Il Re e il principe Amadeo all'ospedale della Conocchia" ("The King and Prince Amedeo at Conocchia hospital") in which the monarch ministers to

The King and Prince Amedeo at Conocchia Hospital

the Neapolitan *popolino* who strike suitably cholera-stricken poses of supplication and adoration. If, for the readers of the *Illustrazione Italiana*, Umberto is a constitutional monarch, he is imagined in his relations with the masses, whose paradigm in the *Illustrazione Italiana* is the southern masses, as something akin to a benevolent despot, or even a *roi thaumaturge;* he inspires devotion in a semicivilized people more responsive to ritual than to reason, preferring paternalistic authority to a freedom it could as yet only abuse.[30]

Nevertheless, a glance at the *Illustrazione Popolare*'s desultory coverage of the cholera epidemic serves to demonstrate how national were the *Illustrazione Italiana*'s concerns by comparison. The sketch of some poor and sick Neapolitans lying in straw who adorn the front cover of the edition of September 14, 1884 is very different from the more up-market magazine's approach: none of the figures are looking at the viewer; the picture inspires little pathos. The short text accompanying the illustration protests:

> We absolutely did not want to talk about cholera! It seemed to us that more than enough had been said about it in the dailies and in families. We tried to distance the accursed virus's ugly image by inserting cheerful sketches and drawings of happy scenes in the magazine.[31]

Although it quietly approves of the King's visit to Naples, the *Illustrazione Popolare* gives little attention to it and portrays the sovereign only on his return to Milan station.[32] Between these two dates coverage of the cholera is reluctant (much more space is given to the National Exhibition in Turin) and marked with distaste. The magazine juxtaposes two images in a way that can only imply a comment on the "medieval" nature of Neapolitan society: a picture of a religious procession in Naples to ward off the cholera, and a scene from the Florentine plague of 1348 in which the dying are given absolution. The comment on the former picture, from which the element of pathos is again missing, has a tone that is less than sympathetic: "There is nothing which more promotes the spread of the virus than when people who are filthy, and perhaps infected, all crowd together."[33]

The basic ingredients of the *Illustrazione Italiana*'s approach to Italy's marginal cultures remain constant throughout the period in consideration, surviving even the critical years of the 1890s. Domenico Ciàmpoli, the Abruzzese novelist who was one of the most frequent contributors of stories to the magazine, writes a report on a royal visit to Sardinia in 1899 that revolves around the key themes of the monarchy and the artistic or imaginative qualities of the peasantry. Much of the article is taken up with flowery evocations of local costumes. Sardinian women remind Ciàmpoli of a number of phenomena whose only common factor is their strangeness:

> Are they not the daughters and wives of Pharaohs, of phoenixes, of scouts, or of chatelaines risen from the tombs of the year 1,000? Indeed, together and in each group, something about them reminds one of oriental religions, of remote races, of primitive paintings, and they seem like ritual symbols or allusions. (April 30, 1899, 286)

The confidence of the rhetorical question's appeal to the reader, implying that both an immediate impression and a repertoire of points of comparison are shared, combines uneasily with the imprecision of the images conjured up. Ciàmpoli's prose conveys little about the culture he surveys, or indeed of the sentiments aroused in the onlooker; any such specificity is subordinated to the imperative of reminding the reader that he or she is in the presence of something curious, if cute. Predictably, however, the "gaily coloured throng" is redeemed for Italy by both its enthusiasm for Queen Margherita and its status as pictorial raw material[34]:

> The clamour roars irresistibly and heartily when the Sovereigns appear in the stand surrounded by the Court. I saw their faces shine with a new light and it seemed to me that their august features expressed the utmost joy at being loved so much by this people whose adoration and hope embraces God, the King and the Queen together. And whilst the noble lady rejoiced and smiled enchantingly, these peasants, accustomed to their hovels, to the woods, caves, and villages, made such grand and bold gestures of appreciation, wonderment and admiration that they seemed like figures created by Titian in the youthful exuberance of their colour and form. (ibid., 287)

To be picturesque is to be childlike, to have a gauche fondness for the simple pleasures of color and noise; it is to surprise and delight the onlooker with how unknowingly mature one can be; it is to be constantly amazed and constantly trusting; it is to suffer and not understand why; it is to be ruled by the benign power of spectacle.

Italy's Orient

The front cover of the *Illustrazione Italiana* of September 4, 1881 reproduces "The Arab," a painting by Ernest Giroux displayed at an art exhibition in Turin some time before. The subject has his hand on the ornate hilt of a barely concealed dagger. Protruding from under his robe alongside the knife are two equally ornate flintlock pistols. The Arab glares beadily from underneath his headscarf. If there was any doubt about the ethnocentric meaning of the painting, the brief commentary offered by the *Illustrazione Italiana* removes it, and adds a few touches not evident in the picture, including a reference to dirt:

" . . . the impress of concentrated wildness, latent ferocity, haughtiness, filth and ostentation."

this Arab invited one to stop and look, and it was thought-provoking due to
this African type's very pronounced character, bearing the impress of concentrated wildness, latent ferocity, haughtiness, filth and ostentation . . . a type so

far removed from the strangest things that one can come across amongst us. (September 4, 1881, 151)

Just as the picture's title invites the viewer to take its subject as typical of a whole culture, the author of these lines is drawing on a deep well of associations. To "L'Arabo" many more examples of orientalist representation in the *Illustrazione Italiana* could be added, each a different arrangement of the same cluster of stereotypical themes: the harem, the Bedouin camp, the pilgrimage to Mecca; scenes of fanaticism, pomp, and despotism; Islam portrayed as a pseudoreligion licensing debauched desires under the cover of a harsh morality; obsessive rituals observed by a dirty and uncouth people.[35] "L'Arabo" is reproduced in the *Illustrazione Italiana* before the rapid growth of imperialist enthusiasm in Italy in the mid–1880s: indeed the commentary makes a disapproving allusion to French colonialism in North Africa.[36] Rather than a legitimation of Italian designs on African territory, such perceptions, as well as being part of Europe's long fascination with and fear of the Orient, are involved in imaginary self-definition of Europe and Italy: "a type so far removed from the strangest things that one can come across amongst us."

Other writers do not seem to have found the same difficulty in finding comparable types on Italian soil. The Orient is a constant reservoir of comparisons for the South in the *Illustrazione Italiana,* and it is the Orient constructed by texts and images such as "L'Arabo" that determine the meaning of such comparisons rather than, for instance, the historical links between Sicily and Islamic cultures. But the Orient of "L'Arabo" is the most pejorative on a scale of possible similes for the South. The East projected onto the Mezzogiorno in the Treves magazine is more frequently the place where a hackneyed sublimity is discovered by "the curious or sentimental traveller whose mind is prey to imagination."[37] For the Christmas special issue of 1890, the *Illustrazione Italiana* sent one such traveler, Raffaello Barbiera, to Sicily to write about "La Conca d'oro" around Palermo. Most of Barbiera's article admires the different styles of architecture in the area, judging buildings according to which shows more imagination or "most speaks to the heart." The sights of Sicily produce a mixed poetic and patriotic wonderment in the observer. Other parts of Barbiera's piece show a variant of the picturesque. The article is given a context by allusions to a combined cultural and racial history of a city that is "an infinite wealth of memories from different races."

> Later, amongst the prickly pears, a boy who seems like an ancient bronze statue appears. His hair is black and curly, the tint of his face is olive; proud haughtiness and cunning are mixed together in the way he looks at you.

Egyptian types (detail).

For all that Norman blood was mixed with Moorish blood, the latter is still dominant. Here it is not only in the flaming sky that Africa abides; there is even more of it in the race of the Conca d'Oro. (15)

The use of racial terms in the *Illustrazione Italiana* is not unusual, but neither is it the norm. Racist language was very much subsumed within the magazine's own more flexible popular anthropology of the picturesque.[38] The Africa that Barbiera discovers in Sicily is not the Africa of fiendish duplicity, dirt, and fanaticism, but one where "the imagination catches fire and takes flight." He finds in one scene "a whole oriental vision, an enchantment" and listens out for "original expressions, that some poets might envy" and "treasures of picturesque language" from the mouths of fishermen. The Arab blood that flows in Sicilian veins produces not degeneracy but an unrefined creativity: "poetry blossoms generous and abundant in the Sicilian people" (ibid., 14, 18).

The concept of the type, used casually by Barbiera above, is an important point of comparison between the ways in which the *Illustrazione Italiana* sought to know Africa and the Mezzogiorno. An illustration of "Tipi egiziani" ("Egyptian types"), which covered a page and a half of the edition of July 16, 1882, includes the following under the single category of "type": "negress," "Arab type" (with his face shown), "water vendor," "messenger," "camel," "Arab conjurer." Diverse jobs, castes, ethnic groups, and even animals are grouped together as types, as different images of the same generic Arab quality. The society depicted in "Tipi egiziani" has no logic internal to it: the only factor unifying the different phenomena illustrated is the curious gaze of the European onlooker.[39]

Yet the concept of type retains its scientific connotations just enough to provide a cogent-seeming subethnography in the *Illustrazione Italiana*. The growth of colonialism in Italy brought with it a fashion for a vision of the people of the Horn of Africa that seemed less impressionistic and more programmatic than those offered before, a vision befitting the citizens of a country far enough advanced along the path of progress to engage in civilizing those trailing behind it. In April 1889 the *Illustrazione Italiana* printed a full-page diagram of six "Tipi Galla." The images are reproduced from photographs, their subjects portrayed in full face or in profile as if for physiognomical study. The choice of subjects shown, such as "Zingero warrior," "Gimma woman," "young Sidamà," indicates a much greater respect for the racial version of the concept of type.

The South was also subject to this kind of amateur anthropology with pretensions to a certain scientificity. Its pivotal concept, a version of the picturesque, was the characteristic:

. . . a series of sacred performances, that are still acted out in the villages and small towns: the sceptic laughs at them; the lawman looks on them as

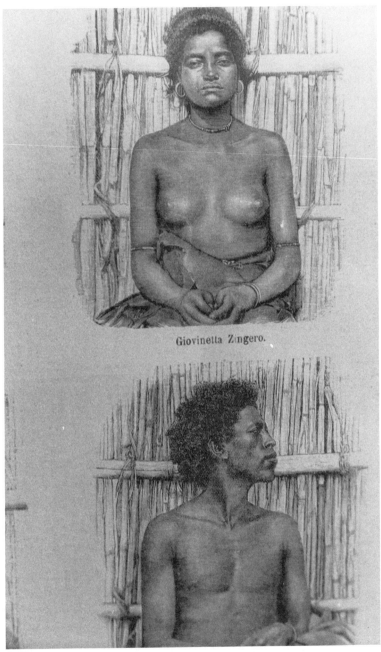

Giovinetta Zingero.

Galla types.

a probable source of disorder; but the scholar collects their characteristic traits.[40]

Characteristic features are collectors' items, curios excavated from superseded popular cultures; from the perspective of progress their function is to intrigue in isolation from the context which produced them. What they are characteristic of, and what types are typical of, is a quaint, generic *sicilianità* or *meridionalità*. Even when racial terms are used in descriptions of Italy's periphery they act merely as one component of an eclectic ethnographic connoisseurship which is fixated on these vague qualities. During the cholera epidemic in Sicily in 1885 the *Illustrazione Italiana* reproduced "Tipi siciliani" by Alfonso Muzii. The magazine describes the picture as follows:

> Our minds still turn to the wretched island of Sicily, to those common people dying amidst superstition, cholera and poverty. Our hearts are consumed by the thought that so many strong, robust lives are succumbing. The Sicilian race is one of the most vigorous there is; the imprint of their faces is virile, their features distinct, the look in their eyes is lively. We have published some Sicilian types, fishermen and peasants drawn from life. At the bottom of the drawing you can see a view of Palermo: the Amiraglio bridge which is now famous in contemporary history because it was over that bridge that Garibaldi first entered the city of the Vespers. The remains of the Temple of Olympian Jupiter in Syracuse stand out at the top, a witness to the noble origins of that unhappy island. Our artist . . . has added to the composition the little hearts, crosses and images that the common people carry round their necks: they live and die with them, never leaving them. (October 11, 1885, 234)

References to Risorgimento history and to a putative classical cultural origin serve to give a second-class *italianità* to the Sicilians depicted, a crude quality more physical than mental. In addition, the three-quarter poses of the subjects who gaze into the distance and the collage form of the composition shift the axis of interpretation of the types shown from the racial-physiognomical (evoked early in the passage) towards the artistic.

Colonialist representations of Africa and ethnocentric perceptions of the Mezzogiorno thus have many aspects in common. The way in which the South's preeminence as a source of exotic images is challenged by colonial Africa in the second half of the 1880s is alone enough to suggest that the two geographical areas served a similar imaginary purpose in the pages of the *Illustrazione Italiana*. When, however, the controversial language of race is used in relation to the South, the effects of that language are generally mitigated by its insertion into the dominant patriotic-artistic discourse to which the magazine endlessly returns. Yet, as we shall see, the Orient of racial degeneracy and incomprehensible ferocity always haunts the picturesque Orient.

"Sicilian types."

The Sicilian Fasci

Fasci was the name given to the workers' and peasants' organizations generally combining the functions of trades unions and mutual aid societies,

which spread throughout Sicily in the early 1890s against the background of an acute economic crisis affecting the island's vital grain, wine, and sulphur production. The novelty and, to the landowners, the particular danger of the Fasci was their mixture of traditional peasant forms of resistance with a relatively modern organization led by educated socialists from the towns.[41] The Fasci would thus seem to provide something of a challenge to the powers of assimilation of the discourse of the picturesque.

Whilst the situation in Sicily was reaching its climax, there was a revolt amongst the marble workers of Northern Tuscany. Carlo Sforza's report on the Lunigiana revolt reads like a phrasebook of the language through which the Italian bourgeoisie sought to understand popular unrest. It refers to anarchists as a "pathological type" and speculates that the "distinctive racial features" of the local people might be behind the disturbances. Those responsible for the "barbaric massacre" are rendered drunk and brutish by the printed word rather than by alcohol. They treat killing soldiers as a sport and behave like "Rabagas's land wardens": "And this barricade is truly and characteristic and picturesque piece of work." The terms of Sforza's report are familiar from their application to disturbances up and down the peninsula, and particularly in the South. Yet Sforza also makes a basic distinction between the Lunigiana uprising and the Fasci: "The Sicilian movement is born from the stomach; here it comes only from the brain" (January 21, 1894, 38). The *Illustrazione Italiana* often feels able to explain and almost to justify the Fasci in similar terms: it is as a bodily revolt, directly springing from poverty, unmediated by dangerous socialist ideas. If plotting is involved, it is not the root cause of the problem but merely a trigger to a fundamentally and almost reassuringly simple reaction on the part of the poor. The Sicilian peasants and sulphur miners somehow cannot help rebelling; they have not yet reached a stage at which they can be considered responsible for their actions. The limited degree of empathy shown towards the Fasci is partially permitted by the *Illustrazione Italiana*'s lack of sympathy for the ruling class of the island. The political page of November 12, 1893 divides the blame for the disturbances between the stubbornness of the landowners and "the Sicilian workers' imagination, that so easily becomes overheated" (November 12, 1893, 320).

There is an unmistakable sympathy for the plight of the peasantry in Sicily, if not for the cause of the Fasci, in "La Sicilia e i Fasci dei lavoratori" by "Renato" (Raffaello Barbiera), the first of three long articles by different journalists that represent the bulk of the *Illustrazione Italiana*'s coverage. Barbiera's article, published in November 1893, dismisses as "timid" fears that the Fasci are a threat to the social order and argues for a clear distinction between criminal brigands and the Fasci who are "the product of poverty" and whose poor minds are clouded by confusion (ibid., 307, 311). Barbiera speaks to a public familiar with the area in question primarily as a source of faintly exotic pastoral imagery. Accompanied by standard picture-postcard images of the Sicilian landscape and people that do not show any of the activities of the popular organizations, the article does not fail to set the movement against the island's picturesque background: "But the poet, the painter and the artist will always admire those people, who are now trembling, uneasy and seething in their suffering. The picturesque, the poetic never leaves them" (311). The natural beauty of Sicily is evoked in what must be the most common of commonplaces relating to the problems of the South: "The island which Nature made into a paradise is about to become hell on earth through the fault of men" (307). Barbiera's reiteration of this formulaic antithesis transposes Sicily's problems onto an abstract plane, inserts them into a conciliatory, unchanging fable of heaven and hell, of the fall from nature. The platitude makes "men" in general responsible: the blame is spread so thinly over all that none are implicated.

Barbiera's article pays a certain amount of attention to the injustices in the island's social structure: it comments that the Fasci were formed "for the protection of the workers against the exploiters" (310). It is an opinion that is possible only because Sicily's "feudal" property relations are seen as safely distinct from every other Italian region. Yet the more factual moments of the report are paired with evocations of the dangers of popular revolt. A paragraph on the large numbers involved in the Fasci concludes in the following way:

> I feel inclined to ask: do those wretched sulphur miners all know what they want? Do they all know what their leaders want? Leaders who are so much better nourished and more respected by the authorities than the unfortunate mob of their followers who are stupefied by suffering, hunger and confused mirages? . . . One of the excellent leaders who thunder loudest against the capitalist bourgeoisie apparently uttered the following wicked words in Palermo. Could they even be true? "Only about a hundred of the Palermo members understand anything. The other eleven thousand are like ras Alula's band: when I need them, with a whistle I summon them to Quattro Canti to scare the bourgeoisie!"
>
> Such are the common people who are agitated, out of control and throwing themselves into civil war; and this is the respect and devotion that the redeemers of the common people have for the common people themselves! (ibid.)

The prose drifts from factual enquiry into a conspiracy theory accompanied by a lurid image of colonial savagery that both borrows and distances itself from the sentiments of the quoted agitator. The patronizing sympathy for the clean and sober Sicilian workers seems to teeter on the brink of a violent disgust. The picturesque island of most articles in the *Illus-trazione Italiana* can easily become the fantastic scene of a bestial violence. Moments of poetic meditation in a romanticized oriental setting constantly risk turning into alarming encounters with a strange enemy. The picturesque has a close affinity with the grotesque. All the writers on the Fasci seem to need at some point to resort to a language of extremity, typically borrowed from the colonial context, with which they rule off a margin of irreducible, incomprehensible Otherness proper to the activities of the islanders.

A similar combination of elements forms the three articles written by Eduardo Ximenes when he was sent in January 1894 to report on the aftermath of the imposition of military rule in Sicily. The journalist relates events, impressions and conversations from his own journey around the trouble spots. Ximenes, who was himself of Sicilian origin, writes with confidence in his knowledge of the island's people. Yet his approach fundamentally echoes the house style. He passes "a succession of paintings and characteristic views" in one village (January 28, 1894, 50). Toward the end of his visit, Ximenes encounters a singing cart-driver who turns out to be a former cavalry soldier and the mouthpiece of the political message of the article: "it needed don Ciccio to calm them down" (Don Ciccio was Francesco Crispi, the prime minister who crushed the Fasci and introduced military rule into Sicily in the first days of 1894) (February 11, 1894, 87). When it is channeled into loyalty, the imaginative quality of the common people of the provinces becomes a reactionary gumption. Yet, according to Ximenes, when it develops in a more dangerous direction, a natural sense of poetry becomes a disturbed "political and moral sense" producing a "kind of savage rebellion" that can have no logic to it (January 28, 1894, 54).

The articles are not without empirical detail: Ximenes carefully lists the financial burdens imposed on the peasants by the land managers. Yet, as in Barbiera's article, such passages coexist with moments of exotic fantasy. Ximenes tells how he photographs a town crier announcing the proclamation to the people:

> You'll see! A real muezzin calling the faithful to prayer from the top of his mosque! Yes, because the Saracen imprint here is as clear and patent as it could be.
>
> In the field where I questioned quite a few peasants, one can only find striking types of an unmistakable African origin. My word what strange intelligence there is in those muddled heads! (ibid., 51)

To a limited extent, it is possible to map Giolittian and Crispian positions onto the articles of Barbiera and Ximenes respectively. But more striking than any such policy differences are the similarities between the ways in which the two journalists use opposing stereotypes of the South in tandem: there is precious little middle ground in either article, and in the *Illustrazione Italiana* generally, between the characteristic and the weird, the faithful and the fanatical, the picturesquely Italian and the shockingly oriental.

A coded warning about "the sincerity and straightforwardness" of the controversial opinions expressed accompanies the first of three installments of "An officer's notes from the state of siege," the last of the major articles on the Fasci in the *Illustrazione Italiana* (April 15, 1894, 238). The fact that the anonymous author is an army officer, and therefore of unquestionable patriotism, allows his contribution to be included without the condescending reserve that normally influences the tone of perceptions of the South in the magazine. "Note di un ufficiale" could arguably be said to typify a certain substratum of received ideas held by the *Illustrazione Italiana*'s public and generally only to be glimpsed beneath an accretion of pretty stereotypes. The articles demonstrate how widespread still was the myth of Southern Italy as the garden of the peninsula: it is argued that Sicily is a "blessed land," a "gold mine" whose resources have been wasted, largely because of certain character faults in the inhabitants which only the moralizing action of strong government can cure (April 22, 1894, 251; May 6, 1894, 280). The officer contends that accidents in the sulphur mines are partly the fault of the "almost fatalistic disposition of the population" and that economic conditions are no worse than elsewhere in Italy, but have been exaggerated by a selective presentation of examples and a general level of filthiness that gives "a look of economic squalor which, in my opinion, is more apparent than real" (April 22, 1894, 251). Indeed the officer's analysis of the condition of the peasantry in Girgenti (Agrigento) is little more than a series of variations on the theme of dirt: "In a manner which is absolutely oriental, packs of wild dogs roam the street and squabble over that filth amongst themselves and with the pigs that are also strays" (April 15, 1894, 238). Comments such as this are more than observations on the state of public hygiene: dirt is the perfect motif to combine a serious-minded concern for hygiene with a powerfully evocative ethnocentric theme. Sicily is dirty for the same reason that it is oriental: it is out of place in the ordered, clean imaginary space of Italian culture that it contrastively defines.[42]

The darker, dirtier, and more menacing colonial world crystallized in "L'Arabo" lurks constantly below the poetic Orient mapped over the South. Whether it intimates a threatening strangeness or denotes objects of revulsion, the more pejorative Orient guards the limits of the discourse of the picturesque: when Sicily or the South fail to fit within those limits, a more violently ethnocentric logic comes into play, placing them at the antipodes of the imaginary world of the Umbertian middle classes.

Murder by stereotype: Contessa Lara's "Un omicida."

The short story "Un omicida" ("A murderer") by Contessa Lara was first published in the *Illustrazione Italiana* in July 1890. The anonymous central character is "a delicate lady from the North of Italy," the wife of a general posted to Naples. She is accustomed to taking trips out into the bay accompanied only by an oarsman, Merulla, a Sicilian conscript who is described as being "a bronze machine, no more and no less":

> He was brown by nature and, as the sun had made him blacker still, he almost had the colouring of a Bedouin. He stayed silent, not daring to sing out of respect for the General's wife.[43]

Merulla is also, we soon learn, a murderer whose behavior since his crime has been so good that the general himself has entrusted him with his rowing duties. "Un omicida" centers on one particular boat trip during which Merulla tells his story to the general's wife. That story takes up the bulk of the text, but it is framed by the expectations and reactions of the general's wife, which, as we shall see, provide the reader with a bad model of how to interpret the oarsman's narrative. The encounter between the general's wife and her boatman, I want to suggest, reveals the dynamics of a type of ethnocentric fantasy that is typical not just of the relationship between the picturesque aesthetic and its objects in the *Illustrazione Italiana,* but also, I would argue, of the relationship between a certain patriotic imaginary and the Mezzogiorno.

Contessa Lara was the Byronic pseudonym of Eva Cattermole Mancini whose fame reached its peak with the appearance of her *Versi* (1883), which was the subject of a typically canny publicity campaign by the publisher Sommaruga.[44] Two dramatic events marked the beginning and end of her writing career: her husband killed her lover in a duel in May 1875; she died at the hands of another of her many lovers in November 1896. Contessa Lara was famous for the way her life seemed to outdo the melodrama, sentimentalism, decadence, and eroticism of her art. She wrote lyric poetry, a novel (*L'innamorata* [1892]), short stories and copious journalism on topics such as fashion.[45] She also edited the society page of *Margherita.*[46]

Critics have been patronizing towards Contessa Lara. Her principal fault seems to have been that she was a "feminine" writer rather than a bad one: Croce referred to her art as being "for the most part made up of the twittering of a little woman who, not without a certain grace, tells of the pains of her heart and her other emotions."[47] My aim here is certainly not use "L'omicida" to argue the case for an aesthetic re-evaluation of Contessa Lara's work. Nor is it to analyze "Un omicida" in the context of her output as a whole.[48] Nevertheless, it is perhaps her almost exclusive interest the "pene di cuore" of the bourgeois woman that makes a text like "Un omicida" into a receptive gauge of the kind of ideological desires and preoccupations which are the object of my study of the *Illustrazione Italiana*. Indeed, the narrative exploration of stereotypes of the South in "Un omicida" can tell us much not only about how the discourse of the picturesque works, but about how ethnic stereotypes in general come to have such a hold on our perceptions.

Stereotypes, as I argued in the introduction to this book, owe their remarkable durability as features of human thought, and their seeming immunity to attempts to disprove them or censure their use, to the function they have in processes of cultural identification and differentiation. The intolerance that stereotypes can articulate aims to reduce the whole range of discursive and imaginative processes implied by cultural belonging and difference to an essentialist binarism, to an assertion of superiority over a reified Other.[49] Homi Bhabha's influential (but, in my view, unnecessarily abstruse) account of the role of stereotypes in colonial discourse proceeds from similar premises:

> The stereotype is not a simplification because it is a false representation of a given reality. It is a simplification because it is an arrested, fixated form of representation that . . . den[ies] the play of difference.[50]

In this case, as with many of the concepts in Bhabha's writing, the precise meaning and provenance of the richly theoretically connotative term "arrested" is far from clear. Are we to assume that the stereotype is a less than fully developed mode of representation, that it is a "limited form of otherness" (77–78)? And does this imply that there is a wholly formed way of representing Otherness against which we might measure the limitations of stereotypes? Or are we to infer that a stereotype in some way halts the machinery of meaning, as the following assertion would suggest? "The stereotype impedes the circulation and articulation of the signifier of 'race' as anything other than its fixity as racism" (75). Bhabha's attempt to account for stereotypical discourse as being fetishistic is also problematic. His argument, in brief, is that the colonialist stereotype at once recognizes difference and disavows it, rather in the way that, according to psychoanalytic theory, the fetish object is used to acknowledge the threat of castration implicit in the knowledge of sexual difference, and yet is also part of an attempt to plug and deny that psychic wound.[51] This is a hypothesis that raises as many questions as it answers. Is it not reductive to try to typify all of the great variety of colonialist discourses with one psychic structure (fetishism) and one ideology (racism)?[52] Could not many other images and types of representation be seen as ambivalent and fetishistic in the same way? What are the problems involved in switching the notion of fetishism from the domain of gender and sexuality to that of "race"?[53] How applicable is the theory to the untold variety of stereotypes that seem to emerge in all facets of social existence?

My own intention is to follow the spirit rather than the letter of Bhabha's theory by taking up his emphasis on the forms of psychic mobility, of imagination, uneasiness, and pleasure, which inhere in the use of "arrested" stereotypical discourse: "the stereotype is a complex, ambivalent, contradictory mode of representation, as anxious as it is assertive" (Bhabha 70). It is these emotions, Bhabha suggests, that must be taken into account if we are to understand how stereotypes inform the discourses through which real agents act out historical events. This insight, I want to suggest, potentially provides a more satisfactory way of explaining the power of the picturesque than does Said's notion of a "median category": it suggests that stereotypes work through the logic of the emotions rather than, as Said seems to argue, by a kind of ritual anesthesia. Contessa Lara's "Un omicida" offers a concise and suggestive example that, when placed in its historical context, can help us to formulate an account of the interplay between what Bhabha calls "fixity" and "fantasy" in stereotypes.

As I hope will become clear as the narrative is explained, the text of "Un omicida" is criss-crossed by cultural strands whose kinship with the *Illustrazione Italiana*'s chief aesthetic and ideological concerns should be apparent. The first is the issue of national identity. As both soldier and Sicilian, Merulla is poised between the figure of the good peasant, redeemed for the nation by the uniform he wears, and that of the dark and silent Bedouin, an image that acts as the symbolic opposite of the loyal soldier. (Like Merulla, of course, Turiddu, the protagonist of Verga's famous tale of a Sicilian crime of honour, *Cavalleria rusticana,* is a *bersagliere.*[54]) Great hopes were placed in the army as an instrument for turning peasants into citizens.[55] Although those hopes often proved to be misplaced, the army, as one of the few organizations with a truly national career structure, did at least have a considerable influence in the Italianization of the officer class. Moreover, as I have already argued, the peasant as storyteller, protopoet, or singer is one of the magazine's favorite encapsulations of a *meridionalità* that is both exotic and familiar, both oriental and Italian. Merulla is a version of that stereotype.

The second strand in the text is that of social and cultural hierarchies. In "Un omicida," attitudes to "popular" culture are shown to be an integral part of the construction of a middle-level culture considered distinct and superior. Merulla and the general's wife belong to different social classes, but the isolation and physical proximity that the boat trips afford them seem to render his subservience contingent, a question of conventional respect. Contessa Lara's text thus foregrounds these social distinctions at a moment when they threaten to break down on the cultural terrain of Merulla's singing and telling his story (the same goes, by implication at least, for the sexual terrain). As we shall see, the general's wife gets rather too close to the low cultural sphere personified by her boatman: correspondingly Merulla is shown, at one level, to be a smarter narrative operator than the "delicata signora."[56]

There is a third thematic strand to the story: "Un omicida" is also about female sexuality imagined as a social danger for which, short of death, marriage provides the only (far from foolproof) remedy. As Anna Nozzoli has argued, the movement between sexual transgression and the reinforcement of maternity as the predominant female role was the central theme of women novelists in this period.[57]

These last two concerns, the erotic and the cultural, are merged when the heroine's appreciation of Merulla's singing is given less than subtle sexual associations:

> with their wide, passionate phrases and with the cadence of the notes which that peasant held for such a long, long time, the songs of his village rang with a penetrating sweetness from his mouth. The lady had listened to them in the cabin where she undressed, and the uncultivated feelings that they contained pleased her much more than the artistically devised romances that she heard in theaters and concerts.

Apart from being potentially adulterous, the desire alluded to here involves the overstepping of imaginary lines of social demarcation between classes, between nation and province, between art and folklore. The songs become the conductor between the antithetically constructed domains of studied bourgeois civility and uncultivated southern spontaneity. As she undresses, the general's wife seems to discard her cultural impedimenta and almost go native in her search for sentimental pleasure.

Viewed in relation to the discourse of the picturesque, the general's wife runs a risk in her eroticized appreciation of Merulla's songs. She crosses the divide between the aestheticizing gaze and its picturesque objects. What power the narrative of "Un omicida" has depends in part upon the *Illustrazione Italiana*'s readers' sensing this danger. When the general tells his wife that Merulla was convicted of murder, her tingling fear of the oarsman is translated into a powerful curiosity, "an observer's rather than a woman's curiosity." If my reading of the story in relation to the house aesthetic of the *Illustrazione Italiana* holds, this reaction involves the woman trying to retreat into the discourse of the picturesque by re-establishing the safe distance between the (genderless) observer and the artifact observed. But the social and sexual tension of the encounter, its sense of menace, is only increased as Merulla begins to answer her request for information about his crime, and we are given a strong hint that he is not as innocent and harmlessly picturesque as the general's wife seems to assume:

> Something like a yellow gleam flashed in the man's eye; there was a nervous movement of his mouth which changed into a smile: but it all happened quicker than a flash. Then he said with his usual indifference, "I killed a woman: my wife."

Merulla's narrative, however, initially seems to be one that might easily have appeared in the *Illustrazione Italiana* in its own right, almost an archetype of the bourgeois narrative of peasant life: simple folk with elemental passions, evoking pathos in their struggle against the forces of a hostile fortune. Merulla portrays himself as hardworking and loyal to family, friends, and country. He seems innocent and happy amid the charms of a homely nature. He stops to weep twice as he speaks of the death of his mother. He is an honest husband and father pushed beyond the limits of tolerance by a fickle wife who is indifferent to the plight of their sick child. Soon after the child's death, Merulla's wife betrays him with a Sicilian friend, Puddu Cassione. By the time Merulla describes discovering them together and murdering her in a fit of righteous rage, the general's wife is inclined to forgive his crime of passion: "'Why give you such a long sentence,' she said, 'when there were so many mitigating circumstances in your favour?'"

In telling his story, Merulla has so far represented himself in terms fully compatible with the discourse of the picturesque. But this comforting role has been set up for a melodramatic reversal. Earlier insinuations, such as his being compared to a Bedouin and the mention of the wolfish "yellow gleam" in his eye, have created a suspenseful prelude. In the last lines of the story it emerges that Merulla has only ten more months to his release.

> "You poor thing! It will not seem real when they let you out!," she said. She was very touched.
>   The former infantryman threw his head back and breathed deeply, as if to fill his lungs with a new, healing air. "You bet!," he said, "I'm going straight off to do Puddu Cassione in."

From underneath the mask of the penitent prisoner emerges the ghastly physiognomy of a murderer who relishes the prospect of violence. The stereotype of the good peasant gives way to that of the bloodthirsty and vengeful Sicilian. A story of crime and redemption is transformed into the case history of an atavistic desire for vendetta. The final twist of Contessa Lara's short story owes its force to the way it reactivates a number of ethnocentric topoi noticeable by their absence in Merulla's story and only tantalizingly evoked in the introductory section of "Un omicida" as a whole. A mechanism of expectation and suspense drives the narrative of "Un omicida" by constructing a series of fearsome commonplaces as the silent and terrible truth behind a suspicious facade.

"Un omicida," as I have just suggested, works on one level as a comment on the *Illustrazione Italiana*'s aesthetic. It undercuts the taste for picturesque clichés, but only by bringing into play a different, more sinister fund of stock representations that constitute the underside of the magazine's perception of the Mezzogiorno. As I have already tried to show, that malign South, where what was exotic has become loathsome, is constantly held in reserve behind the picturesque image. As has often been observed, stereotypes work in such pairs: virgin-whore, and so on; if you aren't one, you must be the other. The narrative constructs this underside as the revealed truth or logical outcome of the positive stereotype that the general's wife so unwisely takes at face value. "Un omicida" thus acts to bolster the normative effect of one particular pair of stereotypes. But how are fantasy and fixity combined in the stereotypes upon which Contessa Lara's story pivots? What forms of pleasure and imaginative projection are present?

The story provides one example of how narrative can elude the patriotic prohibition against regional prejudice. When stereotypes of the South were used, they had to get past, and thereby gain strength from, this taboo. For the reader of "Un omicida," the story procures and legitimates the pleasure of dodging a patriotic interdiction by allowing him or her to bring to bear an ensemble of derogatory associations (the murderous Sicilian stereotype) that the text never makes explicit. At the same time, the negative images conjured up by Merulla's final revelation reinforce certain imaginings of the national space as an area safe from or threatened by the dangers of the South. The story is also suffused with the fear of extending the nation too far, of Italy's being rendered alien as it is adapted in Other minds and mouths.

The climax to "Un omicida" draws on both surprise and familiarity: the "shock" at the end of the tale has been carefully foreshadowed, and consists in the revelation of an all too well-known figure of the Sicilian. In order to appreciate the surprise, the reader has to identify with the responses of the "delicata signora." To sense the familiarity of the murderous figure the boatman is revealed to be, the reader has to tap into received ethnocentric wisdom. Furthermore, in its relation to the complex of patriotism and ethnocentrism in perceptions of the South, that stereotype acts as a wink to the initiated and provokes the pleasure of complicity. Rather than an "objective" shock, it presents itself as a suspended reaffirmation of what the middle classes all "knew" about Sicilians but did not often get the chance to say.

"Un omicida" also builds its ethnic stereotypes into a melodramatic narrative of transgression and punishment. The general's wife's self-indulgence can be enjoyed vicariously because it is protectively surrounded by the suspense and pathos aroused by her credulity, and because it culminates in her punishment. Her surprise at the revelation of Merulla's intention to kill Puddu Cassione constitutes something like a death by association. Thus the conclusion to Contessa Lara's story depends on the pleasure to be derived from dishing out a salutary shock to the general's wife as castigation for her violation of social and cultural boundaries. But enjoying the heroine's punishment and relishing the revelation at the end of the story also involve us in identifying with Merulla's own position as mischievous storyteller. (The general describes him as "an excellent chap . . . and a clever devil.") And, of course, getting too close to Merulla in this way is closely analogous to the misdemeanor for which the general's wife must be punished. The stereotypes at the end of "Un omicida" are conjured up through a kind of prurience that involves the reader in crossing the same prohibitive divide between cultivated, Italian, bourgeois Self and dangerous southern, peasant Other that the text endeavors to establish.

To return to Bhabha's concerns with fixity and fantasy, it seems clear that the stereotype as used in "Un omicida" is far from being only an "arrested" mode of representation. The story certainly tries to trade off and reinforce a hackneyed image of the Sicilian. But it can do so only in a flurry of imaginative activity. Part of the strength of stereotypical images is their obviousness, the way they rely on the rhetoric of the immediately visible: familiar characterological conclusions seem to follow "naturally" from recognizable physiognomic traits, such as Merulla's dark skin. However, stereotypes cannot work if they are boring: they must be charged with mystery, pleasure, and danger. The transition between appearance and ethnocentric meaning must be delayed and inserted into fantasy scenarios of suspense and transgression as they are in "Un omicida." The stereotype evoked by Merulla's announcement of his intention to murder Puddu Cassione offers itself as something like the last word on Sicilians. But while the stereotype finishes off "Un omicida," the effect of this narrative climax on the dynamics of ethnocentric imagination and representation is, as we have seen, far from terminal. We might conclude that stereotypes play a part in what are only *fantasies* of the arresting of representation, fantasies of having the final say. The paradox of these fantasies is that they exist to deny the role of representation and self-projection in the image of the Other.

Stereotypes of the Other are constructed in fields of repulsion and attraction in which the Self is caught. Because its narrative movement is based on the interplay between good and bad images, between fantasy and disavowal, between instances of identification and alterity, Contessa Lara's text reveals particularly clearly both how the positive stereotype always casts a negative shadow, and how the relationship between them is always the sign of a multi-faceted psychic investment that it is the stereotype's job to enable and disavow.

"Un omicida" also allows me to draw together some of my most important points about the discourse of the picturesque in the *Illustrazione Italiana*. This was a discourse that, for all its crassness, was also rewarding enough, in terms both of profit for its publishers and pleasure for its readers, to remain consistent in the face of the changing circumstances of the years from 1880 to 1900. Moments that potentially challenge the discourse of the picturesque, like the protests of the Fasci, or the emergence of Merulla as an unrepentant murderer, only bring out its resourcefulness. The deployment of the group of negative stereotypes that can be seen condensed in the image of "L'Arabo" is not a symptom of a breakdown in the discourse, and certainly not of an objective reality "breaking though" layers of illusion: that such stereotypes had already been incorporated into the narrative mechanism of a story like "L'omicida" shows that they are in fact faces of the picturesque that give it a greater adaptability and a normative force.

The *Illustrazione Italiana* had a double anxiety. It wanted to turn all it encountered into a testament to the unity of the nation. Yet it had also perpetually to assert the superiority of the national culture whose virtues it proclaimed over the darkly different cultures of the masses and the provinces. That anxiety, which produced a particular version of the picturesque, may well be typical of the culture of the bourgeoisie at the national level. The importance of the picturesque to the magazine, and therefore to its commercial success, would suggest that it chimed with perceptions of the South in other domains of bourgeois culture. The *Illustrazione Italiana*'s anxiety is evidence for the weakness of a social group at a loss both for practical strategies of dominance and for sophisticated everyday terms with which to make confident sense of the other Italy. One of the best resourced and most widely read publications in the country could only come up with an astonishingly repetitive vision of the Mezzogiorno. The insistence of the magazine's fascination with monarchic themes and the various components of its own aesthetic demonstrates the very limited number of cultural common denominators of the diverse social and geographical fractions of that class itself. The common ground constituted by king and kitsch was all that identified the nationwide "elegant and cultivated" public to which the *Illustrazione Italiana* sought to sell itself. But once again, it seems to me that it is too simple to conclude from this that the Italian bourgeoisie was "lacking" in national identity: what we have seen in the pages of the *Illustrazione Italiana* is that national identity busily at work in the construction of itself through images of the South.

Chapter 4 ✸

Francesco Crispi's *sicilianità*

Introduction

Francesco Crispi was the first southerner to become prime minister of Italy. He presided over two successive governments between August 1887 and February 1891, and then over two more between December 1893 and March 1896, when the disastrous defeat of Italian forces by an Ethiopian army at Adowa forced his resignation. Crispi has been described as the first literary hero of Italian politics, although his influence as a personality extended far beyond the literary sphere.[1] He is regarded by some as a "charismatic" figure who marked a new phase in the development of relations between the political domain and Italian society. His public image, it is suggested, was a sign that Italy was no longer the oligarchic society of the 1860s and 1870s: the masses now had to be addressed, in however demagogic a way.[2] Crispi saw the statesman's role as being pedagogical as well as governmental. He revitalized old Risorgimento values and created a populist, monarchistic patriotism by portraying himself as the last of the generation of titans who had forged the nation (he had been Garibaldi's agent before and during the Sicilian expedition of 1860). Crispi's ideology has been the subject of suggestive readings by Silvio Lanaro and Umberto Levra.[3] He publicly reconstructed a "national-popular" version of Risorgimento history from which, for example, the figure of Cavour had all but disappeared, overshadowed by the monarchy and the people, whose avatars were Victor Emmanuel and Garibaldi respectively.

Whether Crispi was a charismatic figure in the Weberian sense is still an open historical question, and one on which I can only remain agnostic here: to confirm or refute such a thesis, one would have to study in much greater depth the channels through which his influence was transmitted and the profile of the groups he addressed.

Given the importance of the historical issues surrounding Crispi's public image, it is surprising that no one has yet analyzed a seemingly obvious aspect of it: his "southernness." One reason for this omission, I would suggest, is the biographical and even psychobiographical premises of some studies. Indeed, by assuming that Crispi's southernness is a biographical datum unmediated by cultural representations and identifications, such studies often merely reproduce the stereotypes of Crispi's time and ours.[4] A second reason has been the Sicilian statesman's own insistence that he was he was an *Italian* who only happened to have been born on the island.[5] A passionate patriotism was Crispi's topos, and it left little room for the development, in public, of the "southern" side of his character.[6] Nevertheless, the loose bundle of stereotypes that constituted his public *sicilianità* did strongly influence the way his speeches were received, particularly between 1887 and 1896. Crispi promoted a cult of the *patria,* but that cult was given specific inflections by the fact that its figurehead was a Sicilian. In this chapter, I seek to understand what Crispi's *sicilianità* or *meridionalità* meant to his contemporaries (as we shall see, this vagueness appears in the historical sources). Perceptions of Crispi as southerner need to be placed in their political and social context, and to be seen in their relationship to widespread conceptions of the nation and the South in political discourse in the 1880s and 1890s. Those perceptions, it seems to me, echoed wider concerns among the middle classes about the relation between the "nation" and the institutions that were supposed to represent it. Crispi's southernness is a subtle cultural phenomenon which, at times, is almost completely veiled by the strong patriotic interdiction against regional prejudice. Nevertheless, it powerfully shaped Crispi's influence on the elites and middle classes at least, and demonstrated how profoundly rooted in the collective imagination the multiform idea of the Mezzogiorno had become.

Representations of Crispi's southernness were pervasive and complex, as is apparent from the following three introductory examples from 1876, 1887, and 1905. Sometimes explicitly, sometimes more subtly or covertly, Crispi was consistently seen as stereotypically southern. Both allies and enemies, northerners and southerners, composed their idea of him as a Sicilian from different connotations of the same repertoire of stereotypes.[7]

In November 1876, Crispi gave a brief speech to accept his first official post as speaker of the chamber of deputies. His election to such a prestigious position was a symbolically charged moment. It followed the electoral confirmation of the "parliamentary revolution" of March of that year that had brought the Left to government, heralding the passing of the power of the largely Northern Italian moderates who had managed the establishment of the Italian state. Crispi was considered the antithesis of the moderates, culturally and politically. His roots were in the republican, populist strand of

Risorgimento thought rather than in its liberal paternalist variety. He was a
former patriotic conspirator who had no compun   wrapping himself in the flag. Although a republican before uni   had undergone
a famous conversion to the cause of the monarc   est guarantor of
the country's fragile unity. Yet, despite his con   Crispi's monarchism always remained suspect to the court.[8] W   normally be seen
as conventional avowals of impartiality and devo   established order
in such a speech of acceptance would be hear   ticular attention
from Crispi. Interestingly, it is on such an i   occasion that he
chooses to discuss his *sicilianità* or *meridionali*   es no distinction
between the two).

> It is true that my tormented but untamed love for my country's freedom and
> unity once drove me with passion into supreme and audacious deeds to win
> that great boon. It is true that, in political struggle, my mind's ardent con-
> viction provoked my words into bursting forth with no other restraint than
> that offered by my unlimited faith in all that I considered true and just. It is
> true that my hasty southern temperament itself impelled me along paths that
> were full of danger. Honourable colleagues, you should know that I am fa-
> miliar with this combination of elements which go to make up my person,
> and that here, on this Seat, I will commit all my strength to governing them.
> (*Applause*)
>   Within the bosom of Mount Etna, the ancient fiery matter often holds it-
> self back, whilst the snow lies tranquil and constant on the summit. In just
> the same way I have set the firm command of my unwavering will beside the
> ardour of my mind and the excitability of my fiber. And I will employ all of
> that will in maintaining the strictest possible impartiality (*Excellent!* [*from the
> left*]) when I preside over and guide your discussions.[9]

Crispi's theme is that demanded by the occasion: the subordination of
particular interests to the general interest that the job of speaker presupposes. The autobiographical note is typically Crispian. The speech was de-
livered to a political arena in which regional tensions had been on the
increase: the 1874 elections had been fought amidst accusations and coun-
teraccusations of "regionalism."[10] The various components of the Left,
which tended to have their power bases in the South and Sicily, needed to
appropriate patriotic political discourses, to redefine the political nation
and the place of the South in it. Yet Crispi's representation of his southern
identity remains strikingly entrapped in stereotypical terms: the volcanic
temperament; the passionate rhetoric; the lack of restraint; the need for
strong discipline. It is southern traits that he feels have to be reined in as
unsuitable for a position of national responsibility. These are stereotypes
that owe something to the moderates' own view of the South, shaped by the

process of unification and the struggle against brigandage: the South and its people are seen as somehow constitutionally unsuited to the framework of the liberal polity.[11] At one level, Crispi makes of his own psychological history a parable of Italianization in which his mind transcends his body as the common interest of the *patria* transcends the impetuosity of the South. But of course, the speech is far from self-abnegating. At another level, Crispi's language suggests that being southern means having the selfless, nationalistic dynamism without which public duty becomes ossified and bureaucratic. Crispi's *sicilianità* is imagined as the unbridled passion that drives his patriotism: it is a bodily quality that is unapologetically excessive to reasoned political discourse, yet without it the epic story of the nation's foundation could not have happened. Crispi gives southern stereotypes a proudly positive slant: to be southern is to be *extremely* Italian, to be at the limits of *italianità*.

Crispi was already an old man who had reached an almost mythical status when he first became prime minister in 1887.[12] It had become apparent under Depretis that the government's practice had failed to keep pace with changes in the country at large: legislative work was painfully slow, foreign policy was felt to be timid, and large ministerial majorities came and went with great rapidity. Crispi had staked his reputation in the mid–1880s on wanting the reestablishment of a clear delineation between government and opposition and generally on greater "energy" in state activities. While his backing had its core in an alliance of protectionist interests in steel and particularly shipping, he managed to win unusually broad support in the chamber. With his repeated stress on the unity of both the nation and its politicians, Crispi seemed to many to be the man capable of grabbing parliament by the scruff, revitalizing the institutions, and tackling the social question without making too many concessions to subversive forces. He embarked upon wide-ranging administrative and legal reforms, often characterized as "Jacobin."[13]

Not long after becoming *presidente del consiglio* in October 1887, Crispi gave a policy speech in Turin. It had been planned as a patriotic rite in which the old conspirator and *garibaldino* would stage a symbolic return to the home of the Right as the new prime minister, a context that would inevitably set his southernness amongst the undertones of the occasion.[14] However, throughout his parliamentary career, despite his habitual autobiographical digressions, Crispi's references to his southernness were generally brief and always wedded to an invocation of the nation as a whole. The most that might be said about the typical reference to his *sicilianità* in the Turin speech ("as an Italian born in Sicily")[15] is that it implicitly situates the speaker in a miniature narrative of Italianization in which the regional identity is subsumed within the national. But Crispi spoke to a culture saturated in images of the South, which nonetheless, displayed a high degree of public, patriotic sensitivity to questions of "regional prejudice."[16] Writing in the *Corriere della Sera* after several days of debate on the Turin speech, "Alfred" comments on Crispi's temperament:

> It is a truly Sicilian temperament, but of the taciturn kind. Northern Italian readers will not understand such a distinction without some comment. It ought to be made clear that two races predominate in Sicily: the Romano-Greek (the old race of conquered people) and the Arabo-Norman (the new race of conquerors). The Sicilian who belongs to the former race rather resembles the almost Tartarian type from France's Midi . . . By contrast, the Sicilian of the latter race is reserved, circumspect, shrewd, and loyal; he can forget neither a favour nor an offence until both have been suitably repaid; he changes only with reluctance; he is always armed with an inflexible logic, a limitless self-confidence, and the utmost disdain for cowardice, meanness or pointless busybodying; he is capable of anything as long as he reaches the goal that seems right to him; he is a good friend, but a fearsome enemy; loyal and implacable, he is quicker to act than to speak. . . . This is the race to which Crispi belongs (and to which, by the way, all those Sicilians who achieve anything also belong).[17]

There should hardly be the need to bring into relief the stereotypes used here and their compatibility with those used by Crispi in 1876: the "Arabo-Norman" Sicilian is situated between vendetta and loyalty; between danger and reassurance; between Africa and Europe.

By the time he died in 1901, Crispi was on his way to being incorporated into an authoritarian nationalist mythology that Fascist historiography would inherit.[18] In 1905, Treves published Senator Giorgio Arcoleo's *Francesco Crispi,* based on a commemorative speech. Arcoleo was a Sicilian, a pupil of De Sanctis, a journalist, an essayist, a lawyer, an academic, a politician, and an authoritative constitutionalist. He had served in government under Crispi's rival Di Rudinì in the mid–1890s. Despite not having spared Crispi his famous ironic wit in the chamber, Arcoleo was regarded by many as having inherited the leader's mantle: Carducci said of him "Crispi is quite patently alive again."[19] But if there is a degree of self-projection in Arcoleo's portrait, Crispi is also described in a language, including the terms of racial anthropology and collective psychology, that strongly resembles the confluence of themes that structured perceptions of his *sicilianità* at the height of his power. Arguing that Crispi "cannot be explained without Sicily," Arcoleo portrays the island as a place "where, like the soil, the race displays contrasts: it has Nordic and oriental elements; here it is Greece, there it is Africa; here it is a Nation, there it is a tribe." Arcoleo's meditations on the relationship between *sicilianità* and Italian patriotism are particularly illuminating. They are the culmination of a number of essays on the "semi-barbaric," "infantile" Sicilian character that Arcoleo had produced since the late 1870s:

> The Sicilian element is amongst the most vital and profound of the components which make up Nation's psychic character. A frontier against the Far East and Africa since very ancient times, it became the vanguard of Italianness against internal and foreign domination.[20]

Crispi's function in the national culture is the same as that of the island from which he hails:

> As a Sicilian, Crispi leaves something which is not restricted to the region, but flows back into national life: he leaves two fertile seeds, two knots which tie Sicily to Italy: the notion of the country's unity, and the heroic feeling for the *patria*. Both are genuine motive forces of greatness and civilization.[21]

Sicily and Crispi occupy a border zone where the imagined modern nation fades into an Africa or an Orient. Yet it is also where the nation hopes to find its origins, the most powerful, primeval qualities of *italianità*. These qualities, through that fundamental nationalist homology between the individual and the collective being, are seen to take root in the most intimate substance of the country. Inasmuch as he is seen as a Sicilian, Crispi is imagined as a frontiersman.

To understand Crispi's importance, and the meanings of these kinds of representations of his *sicilianità* for middle-class culture, we need to grasp just how profound was the sense of a political, social, and economic emergency that prevailed, most notably in the months leading up to Crispi's return to government in December 1893. The years 1893 to 1894 saw the economy at the bottom of a long depressive cycle. Throughout the 1880s, governments had failed either to control public spending, increase revenue, or tackle the thorny issue of Italy's inadequate banking system. In 1887 to 1888, agriculture was already several years into a crisis provoked in large measure by the arrival in Europe of cheap American grain, when a period of acute industrial and economic problems began with the collapse of a speculation-driven construction boom and then a trade war with France. In the summer and autumn of 1893, the situation became alarming. The weakness of the lira precipitated a massive exportation of metal currency: silver and even bronze coins became so scarce that banks, mutual aid societies, and shopkeepers' associations in the North had to issue their own tokens. Demonstrations provoked by a massacre of migrant Italian workers at Aigues-Mortes in France displayed distinctly insurrectionary characteristics in Rome and Naples in particular. In Sicily, the confrontation between the landowners and the *Fasci,* or workers' organizations, was becoming increasingly violent. A run on the country's two major credit institutions, Credito Mobiliare and the Banca Generale, forced them to declare a moratorium on payments. The scandal of the Banca Romana, which had been printing millions of lire in excess of its legal limit, had first been revealed to the public at the end of 1892, but continued revelations implicated prominent members of the political class who had being paying for their election expenses with loans from the bank.

It was in such circumstances that, after nearly three years absence, Crispi returned to office as the "savior" of the institutions. He introduced a state of siege and 30,000 troops into Sicily in January 1894 and banned the Socialist party in October of the same year. Crispi had hoped to use the climate of alarm and repression to pass sweeping agrarian reforms that aimed at nothing less than completing Sicily's transition from feudalism. But these radical measures were effectively scuppered by conservative interests. Crispi's finance and treasury minister, Sidney Sonnino, did succeed in stabilizing the fiscal situation and setting up a modern banking system that would be one of the bases for Italy's rapid industrialization in the first decade of the twentieth century. In the year from mid–1894 to mid–1895, Crispi kept parliament and the senate closed for all but eleven days.[22] Arturo Carlo Jemolo has remarked that "Crispi always acted violently towards the two Chambers, and at times he did not even make the effort to disguise or mitigate this violence of his."[23] These tendencies contributed to increasing the centrifugal tendencies in Lombardy, Italy's most economically powerful and socially "advanced" region.[24] Thwarted in his social reforms at home, Crispi embraced a bellicose and expensive colonial policy that culminated in the defeat at Adowa.

The South in the imaginary
geographies of political discourse

Stereotypes of the South, by virtue of their slipperiness and the dynamics of taboo and transgression that often surround their use, do not have the analyzable consistency of political programs or determinate interests. However, whether they underlie the model of collective psychology that informs a political analysis, or provide an imaginative encapsulation of more elaborate ideas, or merely give a polemical edge to an argument, such stereotypes do have their influence. In this section, as a preparation for a reading of perceptions of Crispi as a Sicilian, I will outline the way in which images of the South, parliament, and the nation were interwoven. Even in Crispi's 1876 inauguration speech, at a moment of triumph for the Left during which the nation could at last be given southern inflections, the place of the southern "character" in relation to the nation was formulated in ethnocentric terms. *Meridionalità* is seen as antithetical to norms of institutional behavior, and yet that same assumption about the collective psyche seems to cast doubt upon liberal models of nationhood, to demand a redefinition of Italy. The multiple crises of the late 1880s and early 1890s called into question some of the most reliable commonplaces of nationalist discourse, and with them the stereotypes of the South with which they were pleached. It is this mixture of discourse about the nation and about the South that explains the potent combination of attraction and repulsion which Crispi's *meridionalità* exerted over his contemporaries.

A culture of "antiparliamentarism" was shared by varied political persuasions, from inside and outside the governmental institutions: the chamber of deputies was for many a spectacle of inefficiency, jobbery, and corruption. The diary of Alessandro Guiccioli, who was to become prefect of Rome under Crispi, is unequivocal in its condemnation: "I leave in disgust at the intellectual and moral inferiority of the assembly. This is no longer a Chamber: it is a rubbish dump."[25] The strength of feeling against parliament when Crispi was in power can be estimated from the success enjoyed by Scipio Sighele's *Contro il parlamentarismo* (*Against Parliamentarism*) of 1895. Sighele, a pioneer of "crowd theory" who was closely associated with the Lombrosian school of criminal anthropology, maintained that parliamentarism was best understood in the terms of crowd psychology, as a pathological form of group delinquency closely related to the syndrome that produced the mafia and the camorra.[26] What is more, "the contradictory and cruel" mentality of the chamber was also comparable to feminine psychology: "In short, psychologically the Chamber is a woman, and often even a hysterical woman" (Sighele 258–259). The political programs that incorporated a critique of the parliamentary system were many and varied. But it is striking that frustration with the limitations of government was frequently expressed in a language whose most loaded metaphors were images of Otherness. The putative center of Italy's political life was often portrayed as being taken over by forces associated with its unsavory margins: in the case of Sighele, those forces were women, crowds, and the camorra.

A readily available option for articulating antiparliamentary feeling was treating the apparent decline in the institutions as a southernization of Rome. In his analysis of the social and political situation in late 1893, the historian and moralist Pasquale Villari feels the need to respond to an argument, commonly used at the time, which he paraphrases as follows: "The trouble comes from the Mezzogiorno, which was corrupted by Bourbon despotism. We insisted on unifying the country too early, and the decay in those provinces was soon transmitted to the whole of Italy."[27] This is a point of view which is reflected in Achille Bizzoni's *roman à clef* about the Crispi era, *L'Onorevole,* one of a whole genre of antiparliamentary novels.[28] Bizzoni, a prominent radical politician and journalist, imagines the very heart of the political milieu as contaminated by people, values, and habits associated more commonly with the oriental, the provincial, the dirty, the southern. In Bizzoni's "Rome village," the public realm of politics and the private one of cooking and eating are grotesquely confused in the tavern and the street: "How do you expect . . . the dignity of the legislator to be respected in the Roman taverns, amidst the stink of garlic and frying in rancid oil, or by the ragged customers and street-corner courtesans?"[29] Lastri, an old deputy who is wise to the ways of the capital, describes parliament as a "malaria hospital" (Bizzoni, 272). The narrator voice also makes use of the metaphor of disease to describe the Ministry of the Interior: "Palazzo Braschi is the great lazzaretto of the plague-stricken politicians who are now infecting the whole of Italy" (229). Bizzoni portrays the "southernization" of political Rome, which becomes a city of rustic vulgarity and small-mindedness, of quasi-Neapolitan squalor, dirt and disease: *L'Onorevole's* satirical impact owes a great deal to the way in which it moves the boundary of Italy's imaginary South upwards to include its political center.

There can be few characters in Italian literature who are portrayed with the same painstaking disgust as Baron Carmine Di Santa Giulia in Antonio Fogazzaro's *Daniele Cortis,* published in 1885. Di Santa Giulia, a senator, is loud, ignorant, slovenly, sarcastic, vindictive, corrupt, ungrateful, and grasping. Rarely does he speak; rather he bellows, roars, grunts, mutters, swears, and snarls. What is more, the reader is unambiguously made aware as early as the first pages of the novel that the Baron is a Sicilian. *Daniele Cortis* is Fogazzaro's second novel and his most explicitly political one. Its passages of antiparliamentary polemic are put into the mouth of the book's eponymous hero. But Fogazzaro's beliefs are far removed from Bizzoni's secular radicalism: in the course of a plot set in the months leading up to the law of 1882, which widened the suffrage for the first time, Cortis advocates a reinvigoration of the role of the monarchy and a rapprochement with the church to provide both preventive social reforms and a conservative moral guidance for the populace.[30] Both major plots in *Daniele Cortis,* romantic and political, move between the firs, gardens, and gentle rain of the Veneto and a hectic, shambolic Rome. These geographical oppositions are also encapsulated in the contrast between Cortis and Di Santa Giulia. The two men are implicitly counterposed throughout the novel. Cortis, with his "leonine vigour," is patriotic, honorable, erudite, idealistic, sensitive, strong, and as contemptuous of the public as of his own physical needs.[31] The Baron, on the other hand, is at home in the capital: through his rank and links with the Left, he represents the corrupt establishment. The Baron's "savage nature, mixed with strength and corruption" (Fogazzaro 268) and his "corrupt blood"

(269) become legible in his face: "The senator had grown thinner and more yellow, and his physiognomy showed something darker and more sinister" (226). Di Santa Giulia, in short, is the stereotype of a boorish, delinquent southerner. Yet, since patriotism frowns on too direct a discrimination against fellow Italians, it is the senator himself who most obviously brings up the question of regional identities and prejudices:

> He dragged an armchair to the side of the bed and, yawning, stretched himself out in it with his legs wide apart.
> "I've been good," he said. "I haven't half been good!"
> "And just because I've got this voice," he added, "because I've got the face of an ugly devil from Cefalù, because I've got the fire of the island in me, you lot from the North you take me for a devil, a Dionysius, or something!" (168)

The novel is thus given an ethnocentric tone that is nevertheless always formally consonant with patriotism. While Cortis dedicates his life to Italy and proposes a reconciliation of the ideals of the nation with the moral force of the church, his values emerge in implicit contrast to Di Santa Giulia, who embodies the uncouth parochialism, corruption, and meanness of spirit of a stereotypical South that has come to dominate parliament.

However, the meanings of the imaginary South were highly ambivalent. The land of brigandage, corruption, and malaria could also be seen as a source of elemental but undisciplined nationalistic dynamism that offered a positive contrast to the ankylotic state of the country's institutions. The Neapolitan conservative Pasquale Turiello argued that southerners were potentially the most Italian of all the country's citizens, the most fervent in their support of patriotic monarchical values: all that they lacked was strong government and a regime of moral and physical training.[32] For Turiello, working from the basis of a racial theory, parliament pandered to the typically southern anarchic instincts without the missing ingredients of military-style discipline and selfless, aggressive nationalism. Turiello's *meridionalismo* valorized Southern Italy in very similar terms to some of those conventionally used to explain its problems: in this case the supposedly artistic, undisciplined, impractical, overemotional temperament of its people.

Through the figure of Claudio Cantelmo, the Gabriele D'Annunzio of *Le vergini delle rocce* (1895) produces a more strident and unqualified antiparliamentarism that involves a comparable valorization of the "South." Cantelmo seeks for "ancient barbaric forces" and "the barbaric intoxication of distant ancestors" as an antidote to a massified, debased Rome.[33] D'Annunzio's notion of nobility makes sense as a polemical celebration of an inventory of Others crucial to the self-understanding of Liberal Italy's cultural and political elites. Where the aristocracy are considered a retrograde hang-over from feudalism, D'Annunzio makes of them a repository of racial virtues. Where atavism is anathema to the cult of progress, D'Annunzio embraces it as a source of energy. Cantelmo again flirts with forces demo-nized by Risorgimento ideals when he returns to stay with an old southern aristocratic family and his politics evolve in a dialogue with the father, who dreams of the return of the Bourbon monarchy. D'Annunzio's aesthetic and political mythology inverts hierarchical oppositions such as culture-nature, civility-barbarism, modernity-backwardness, all of which are part of that aggregate of symbolic operations through which the imaginary South was constructed.

The imaginary South offered other possible responses to the perceived crisis in Italy's representative institutions. It could be argued, for example, that liberal policies had in fact been based on a mistaken application of Northern European principles when Italy as a whole was actually a southern nation. Pasquale Villari forwarded this idea in his response to those who maintained that Italy's institutional problems had their origin in the South: "Since we have had neither a grounding in liberty over a long period, nor a severe, rigid religious and moral upbringing, we now find that we have all of the natural, undisciplined attributes of our southern character" (Villari, "Dove andiamo?" 9). For Scipio Sighele, Italy was a Latin or southern na-tion that lived according to the dictates of irrational forces, swinging be-tween chaos and subservience to authoritarian rule. The covertly submissive aspects of the unruly southern character were always likely to come to the fore, bringing about a collapse in democracy:

> Latin countries, even those with a constitutional regime, are often under the concealed dictatorship of one man. The people, who in many respects are still barbaric, feel the need to be guided, directed, commanded by someone . . . Thus, sometimes, one individual rises above the Stygian trench of parliamen-tary mediocrity, an individual . . . who has the qualities of strength, pride and audacity that most appeal to the plebs. Sooner or later he will find himself at the head of the government. He is carried there and kept in his position, per-haps not always by the people's favour, but certainly always by that obscure instinct for servility that is the fundamental psychological trait of Latin and southern peoples. (Sighele 16)

One does not have to read too much into Sighele's text to realize that the man he was talking about, or at the very least the man who had given rise to these speculations, was Francesco Crispi. As we shall see, Crispi provides the occasion for a convergence of the varied themes of the stereotypical South that permeated political discourse in the 1880s and 1890s.

"Siculan fiber, Italian soul"[34]

The most concentrated source of material on Crispi is the large number of pamphlets, poems, biographies, and monographs specifically dealing with his life history and politics. It is in this body of material, written by figures from renowned politicians to otherwise unknown admirers, that I seek to analyze the way in which notions of national and regional character, mythical representations of the "people," and a feeling of political crisis are knotted together in perceptions of Crispi's stereotypical *meridionalità*.

"Statesman" is one of the terms to emerge in almost every account of Crispi's career, and it connotes more than his belief in a strong state or his place in a tradition of southern political thought: "he was *born* a statesman."[35] For many he was the only statesman in the country: the implication being that he was above day-to-day politics, endowed with a direct link to the interests of the nation. Yet it is often Sicilian qualities which are seen to give him such a status. For Guido Pieragnoli, in a study published in 1887, even associations with Africa and a fevered imagination are positive effects of Crispi's Sicilian background:

> the air of his native land, and the burning midday heat of the African sea contributed to waking ever more irrepressibly in his blood and imagination that ardour and those fevers which would then propel him in his adventurous life. They tempered his character into an inflexible resolve which inevitably made Crispi into one of the most eminent Statesmen of his time.[36]

In the eyes of the middle classes of the time, "Sicilian statesman" was something of a contradiction in terms. Writers on Crispi almost invariably home in on the same paradox: he embodies qualities considered unorthodox or unofficial— indeed, he is on the brink of being something other than Italian—and yet he occupies a place in Italy's imaginary center. For Carolina Rosani in her laudatory *A.S.E. Francesco Crispi—Presidente del Consiglio*, "he is the most serious man of government that the nation has today." The common comparison of Crispi to Saladin is made, and his statesmanlike qualities are traced directly back to his racial origins:

> There is a set of traits in the southerner from Sicily: he is serious, calm, tenacious and taciturn; he never jokes or compromises with either his rights or his duties; he abhors posturing; he is proud, frank, and aware of his own strength in defiance of fortune's every trick; he is passionate but serious, impetuous but persistent, compassionate and yet contemptuous. Francesco Crispi is the noblest, strongest and most sincere representative of this race.[37]

The figure of Cesare Bronte in D'Annunzio's political drama *Gloria* of 1899 is a portrayal of Crispi. In virtually his final lines of the play, the aging "colossus" imagines himself as one of D'Annunzio's rough-hewn peasants: "I am a peasant, a real son of the soil, stocky and stiff-necked. . . . I have guided the plough. Going to meet my destiny, I had callused hands, a face browned by the sun, teeth polished by black bread."[38]

Italian public culture placed a fence of patriotic taboos around any display of regional bias. Few commentators on Crispi felt able to give free rein to regionalist sentiments that risked offending these patriotic sensibilities.[39] More often than not, polemics against Crispi skirt the boundaries of the unacceptable with coded remarks left to the reader to extrapolate by tracing a line of ethnocentric associations. That prejudiced reactions to Crispi were habitual at a level just below the public arena is apparent from the *Illustrazione Italiana's* comments on the marriage of the prime minister's daughter:

> What does it matter to this man, with his Napoleonic style, if for the thousandth time his adversaries drag out the Maltese-Siculan legend about his three wives (with the inevitable accompaniment of *maccheroni alla siciliana*) in an attempt to spoil his pleasure as he sees the daughter he adores garlanded in orange blossom?[40]

But it is noticeable that almost all of the positive characteristics attributed to Crispi are versions of more derogatory ethnic stereotypes: eulogy and execration are composed from different connotations of the same language, although Crispi's supporters can refer far more freely to "his well-known characteristic of being a Sicilian in the full sense of the term."[41] If Crispi's critics see him as overimaginative and unrealistic, for his supporters he is a visionary able to bend the world to his will: he has an "an exceptionally vigorous energy of fiber, so that his actions correspond to his mind's conceptions."[42] If, for some, he has an "excessive, unreasonable pride," for others he has a Sicilian ardor or an Arab independence of mind.[43] Alfredo Oriani's "Francesco Crispi," published in September 1901, is largely a history of Italy since unification through Crispi's eyes. Crispi's *sicilianità* is an important aspect of Oriani's myth-making:

> A Sicilian, his eyes and words were shot through with the flash of the island sun, a burning sun which sears all the fleshy plants on the ground and sets fire to the soul, illuminating its blindest recesses. Like almost all of his fellow islanders he was impetuous, with a sharp mind and a tenacious will. He was lucid in his ambition, guileless and voracious in his love, sincere and stubborn in his hatred.[44]

Representations of Crispi similar to those analyzed here were widespread in the court. For Alessandro Guiccioli, whose career became closely

"Faith is a fine thing . . . but it must not become fanaticism . . ."

linked to Crispi's from the late 1880s, ethnic stereotypes created a mystique around him: "unlike Zanardelli, Crispi does not conduct his business in the town square, but uses discretion and mystery like old conspirators and Sicilians."[45] Yet Guiccioli also saw in Crispi a man who "personified the most elevated principles."[46] At a court ball early in 1893, a young member of parliament maligns Crispi and casts doubt on his commitment to a united Italy with Rome as its capital, claiming that Crispi had said "when we [the Italians] leave Rome." Domenico Farini, the speaker of the senate, is quick to disagree and remind him, "that nobody has the right to cast doubt upon the existence of the *Patria;* and that in any case when we leave we will go to a civilized region, Crispi to an uncivilized one" (Farini 198). Crispi's very proximity to barbarism makes him the best defender of civilization.

Cartoons of Crispi seem to follow the same rules.[47] While there was great sensitivity about regionalism, the field of southern topoi provided plenty of options, not always of any great subtlety, for dodging that patriotic interdiction, such as the not-infrequent depiction of him as a bandit.[48] In 1887, "Teja" of *Il Pasquino* depicts Crispi as an Arab leader in a cartoon based on the ceremony of the "Dóseh" or "trampling," which is described as performed by the "Sheykh of the Saadeeyeh darweeshes" in Edward Lane's *An Account of the Manners and Customs of the Modern Egyptians.*[49] Crispi, bearing what seems like a sacred scroll marked "Turin speech," rides his horse over the prostrate bodies of his admirers.[50] An illustration from *Il Fischietto* in January of 1890 even more explicitly trades off imaginary links between Africa and Sicily in its representation of Crispi receiving a visit from a Moroccan delegation. Crispi shows his guests around a personal museum of trophies. We see him "fare le corna" (extending his index and little fingers as a gesture to ward off the evil eye) as he displays his typically southern coral amulet which he calls "the secret of *my* omnipotence, *my* talisman against *my* enemies."[51] Crispi thinks in the same "primitive" terms as his guests. In his *meridionalità,* clearly evoked here through references to southern "superstition," "don Ciccio" seemed to have something of the oriental despot or the African chief; there is something alien or primitive about his power.

Each conception of Crispi's authority corresponds to one of a series of representations of the Italian people which informed hopes and fears about nation building. He can be both "a lover of the people" and "a loather of the plebs" (Arcoleo, *Francesco Crispi,* 11). Guido Pieragnoli argues that the proper role of government, "which incarnates . . . the feeling of the nation," is to temper the "outbursts of enthusiasm which easily occur in a young people which is keen to hurl itself fearlessly into life's great turmoil." It is a task that Crispi is ideally suited to carry out:

"The Moroccans visit Crispi."

For the sake of Italy's very existence, Francesco Crispi consecrated his possessions, the best years of his life, and the boiling enthusiasm he was prone to as
a young man and a Sicilian. As Prime Minister of the government of that
country, he is truly one of those men who, like few others, can contribute to
making Italians. (Pieragnoli, *Francesco Crispi* 6)

Guglielmo Ferrero's *Il fenomeno Crispi e la crisi italiana* (*The Crispi Phenomenon and the Italian Crisis*) of 1894 is a contrasting example. Ferrero,
from Naples, was a socialist and close colleague of Lombroso. In his polemical study, typically "southern" aspects of Crispi's personality are much in evidence, although they are not specifically labeled as such: for example, his
psychology is more suited to the Middle Ages, when individual destinies
were determined by the "intensity of the imagination" rather than by "realism."[52] In an attempt to explain how Crispi can run Italy like a South American republic, Ferrero explains that the prime minister "is not an Italian
type." Especially in his strength of will, Crispi is unlike the average Italian,
whose ideal is described as a "social Buddhism."[53] For Ferrero, the two questions of Crispi's un-Italian character and his charisma are thus related: that
he should exemplify certain abnormal character traits is both a criticism of
him and an explanation of his power over the people, whose political psychology is understood through another set of negative qualities often associated with the Mezzogiorno, such as passivity in relation to authority,
imagination, indolence. Crispi, the antithesis of enlightened, rational government, is seen to rule over a nation that is the antithesis of a responsible,
hardworking populace.

The "people" imagined in relation to Crispi is a very flexible notion: it
can be used to erase divisions between the masses and the upper strata, yet
in doing so it betrays the ideological anxieties of those strata. For "Giorgio
Siculo," the country needs a strong leader like Crispi because "our political culture is not very substantial; in too many respects it is still unformed
or needs to be reformed. We move very easily from one excess to another."[54] Crispi is widely perceived to have a mysterious power over, and
affinity with, an alternately unruly and servile nation. In 1901, Carlo Del
Balzo, a literary journalist, produced *Le ostriche* (*The Oysters*), a transparent novelization of the political events of the mid–1890s. Del Balzo's Paolo
Barnaba (Crispi) is a scheming manipulator of the impressionable masses.
Here he plans to use the wedding of his daughter to distract public attention from his machinations: "Showy theatricality has always entranced
common folk, and especially Latin peoples who love rich things and who
indulge without repentance in the sin of admiring beautiful forms." Yet
Crispi/Barnaba is also associated with more exotic forms of power through
the orientalist imagery with which the text is replete. After closing parlia-

ment to protect himself from corruption investigations, Barnaba "saw himself as the sultan throwing the handkerchief down amongst the odalisques."[55]

In 1895 Leone Fortis, a journalist whose magazine columns of political and social comment became something of an institution, wrote a monograph on Crispi as part of a series popularizing the lives of heroes of the Risorgimento. For Fortis, Crispi's relations with public opinion are characterized by "ups and downs which are like the constant arguing and making up between lovers." He was particularly acclaimed following the defeat at Dogali, which caused an outbreak of "our excessive and neurotic Italian impressionability."[56] Crispi's attraction for the people is bodily, jealous, irrational: his charisma seems to prevail upon a feminized nation. Hypnosis is a frequent metaphor for Crispi's charisma. Its status, somewhere between fairground attraction, charlatan science aimed at duping women, and pioneering experimental encounter with the paranormal, effectively represents the same ambiguities of Crispi's public image.[57]

Scarcely any of the writers on Crispi can resist comparing him to one particular metonym of the South. Emilio Di Natale's pompous lionization of "Italy's Giant" in *A Francesco Crispi—Canto politico* is typical:

> Ben chi comprese 'l tuo pensier ch' ha lampi
> E rombi e scosse di vulcano, quando
> Roggia erompe la lava e i campi invade;
> E chi sovra 'l tuo capo, ove scintilla
> Il fosforo latente, il roseo raggio
> Vide brillar de la corrusca stella
> D'Italia e piover luce gloriosa
> Su tutta la penisola, concordi
> Inni sciolsero a Te, Gigante, in mezzo
> A' colossi che in mano avean le sorti
> D'Europa . . .

Your thought is clear to anyone who has seen volcanic flashes and rumblings and shakings, when the lava bursts from its channel and invades the fields. Or to anyone who, where the concealed phosphorescence sparkles above your head, has seen the rosy ray of Italy's glittering star as it shines and rains glorious light over the whole peninsula. Oh Giant, they raised a united hymn to you, amidst the colossuses who had the destiny of Europe in their hands.[58]

The commonplace significance of comparing Crispi to a volcano lies as much in its meanings for national mythology as for its associations with the South. For example, Renato Fucini's journey to Vesuvius in 1877, described in *Napoli a occhio nudo,* is a kind of patriotic pilgrimage.[59] For Fucini, as for

Di Natale, the volcano fuses patriotic culture with the primordial power of
nature. More sober commentators than Di Natale are also captivated by the
volcano simile, which attempts to capture an ambivalence in Crispi's public
persona: it is both picturesque and powerful; a symbol of Italy and a synec-
doche of the un-Italian South; an uncontrollable force of nature and a vital
energy at the heart of the national culture.[60] Leone Fortis reproduces the full
ideological resonance of the volcano image. Crispi has a superstitious southern faith in himself, and, predictably enough, a "volcano bubbling away inside."[61] But the parallel is also used of the state of the nation in late 1893
and the public's call for Crispi to return to government:

> In December last year, when Giolitti fell, Italy was, as Dante put it, a "ship
> without a helmsman in a great storm." The storm was an appalling economic
> and financial crisis, whose huge waves smashed against our institutions. Italy
> was dismayed by the powerful roar of an underground volcano which might
> burst forth anywhere. It was blinded by the livid flashes which furrowed the
> horizon, ripping through the blackish clouds gathered there. It was then that
> the name of Crispi burst forth from the Nation's heart. . . . and this shout was
> so strong that it even smothered the noise of the storm, and the flow of pub-
> lic faith was such that it swept away all resistance. (Fortis 5–6)

These few phrases encapsulate many of the paradoxical myths that circulate
around the figure of Crispi. Three seemingly diverse phenomena are
grouped together as *volcanic:* the troubles facing the state; the public acclaim
for Crispi; and the savior of the nation, the "ardent Siculan" himself. Crispi,
the savior of the institutions, is perceived as having a preternatural affinity
with vital and dangerous forces in the nation outside those institutions.

Conclusion

There are many other aspects to Crispi's public image: his impetuousness,
"energy" and faith in his own power; the not always unfounded accusations
of demagoguery; his conspiracy theories; his admiration of Bismarck; the
assassination attempts and the accusations of bigamy and corruption
against him. Many of these themes are woven with representations of Crispi
as southerner. Then, of course, there is the enormous importance of his past
as a *garibaldino,* republican, and conspirator. *Sicilianità* is, moreover, just a
small part of the culture of *crispismo.*[62] It meshes with a whole phenomenon of political culture in which it is difficult to separate image and reality,
style and content: where stereotypical representations of his *meridionalità*
overlay the real influence of Crispi's early political development and his networks of support and influence in the South; where rhetorical invocations

of the people and the nation mix with moments of genuine political contact with the masses; where Crispi's self-projection and public perceptions of him are entwined with the definite personal stamp on his policies and the way he offered a very distinctive interpretation of the social and political conjuncture. Crispian patriotism has many dimensions. Crispi moved nation building to the center of political discourse in what Lanaro has called a "pedagogical authentication of the political."[63] He interpreted social problems in the language of the Risorgimento, as a matter of defending the unity of Italy. Anarchism, socialism, and foreign conspiracy were all but conflated as threats to the national order in his world-view. Self-citation and autobiography helped to place Crispi in a lineage of great patriots. He called upon the bourgeoisie to renew their patriotic mission and be protagonists of the social question as they were of the birth of the nation.[64] The nation's internal problems were to be resolved on the grand stage of colonial conquest. But for all the complexity and coherence of *crispismo* as an ideology and as a social and political project, the *sicilianità* of Crispi's public persona should remind us of the strong element of paradox that Crispi represented for the patriotic culture of his age.[65] An important part of Crispi's fascination as a persona for his contemporaries is the contrast between an *italianità* that went as far as to claim to incarnate the nation, and a *meridionalità* that was stereotypically considered Other to the nation.

It is fairly easy to see why a southern "frontiersman" image might capture the public imagination in the Crispian decade. The state seemed under threat from the outside: Catholics and socialists were becoming increasingly important as social forces; popular action was beginning to exert a determining influence on strategic choices in the political sphere (Manacorda, *Crisi economica e lotta politica*, 47–49). The myth of Dogali, the protests over the Aigues Mortes massacre, and the Sicilian *Fasci* themselves show the mixture of politicization and nationalization involved in these early contacts between the masses and the public sphere.[66] Complex lines of division ran through the elites: North and South; industry and agriculture; reform and conservation. The role of the state itself was being rethought though the issues of protectionism, antiparliamentarism, and the decentralization or reinforcement of the executive. Yet, while "transformism" and "parliamentarism" had become terms of abuse, parliament retained undeniable functions as a mediator of interests and a lightning conductor for the institutions. In 1893 and 1894 the situation was so dramatic as to have "psychological" and "moral" aspects.[67] Faced by "strange, fantastic conflicts" on the nation's frontiers, and by lurid crime, violent popular disorder, financial chaos, and Byzantine corruption at its center, the middle classes certainly found in Crispi an author of political strategies.[68] But they also found in his image in general, and in his *meridionalità* in particular, a condensed and displaced way of thinking these circumstances. Crispi was both beyond the pale marked out by motifs normally associated with the nation and, as a statesman and great patriot, seen as occupying a privileged place inside it. He was perceived to be both *of* the other Italy and a rampart *against* it, as he was a politician considered to be above or against politics. These two-sided understandings have their counterpart in conceptions of the masses as by turns a loyal or even zealous people and a disorderly mob; as potential Northern European citizens or as incurable Latin minions. Equally am-bivalent are the images used to describe the parliament over which Crispi rules: it is at once the center of the nation and a corrupting force from its underside. Aspects of Crispi's *sicilianità* also provided an image of his re-sponse to the situation. It seemed to encapsulate the way he combined a le-galistic view of the social action of the state with a violent intolerance of anything that he considered a formalistic obstacle to his initiatives. After 1887, it could symbolize the "Jacobin" combination of reform with a strengthening of the defenses of the system against popular organization and the "dangerous" classes. After December 1893, it provided an image of both repression and popular appeal.[69] In a sense, then, the oxymorons to which many historians have resorted in describing Crispi ("authoritarian democrat," "revolutionary statesman") are foreshadowed in the culture of his time by the oxymoronic stereotype of a "Sicilian Italian."

Conclusion ❧

fter 1860, the concept of the South was (re-)invented and a massive
accretion of real and symbolic problems rapidly began to shape that
concept as a national concern. It would be convenient, for the sake
of obeisance to historiographical convention, if I could claim that the beginning of the twentieth century marked a transformation in the way the
South was represented, thereby justifying my chosen temporal break. I cannot make that claim, and those conventions have to be broken for the same
reason that, in my introduction, I suggested that my four essays had no pretensions to being an exhaustive treatment of the theme. Because the bank of
hackneyed representations of the Mezzogiorno lends itself to such varied
uses, and because context is so important in determining the significance of
stereotypical images, there was no unitary discourse, no "regime of truth" determining what could and could not be said about the South and that could
have undergone any such epochal shift. I owe the periodization of this book
not to reasons internal to stereotypical discourse on the Mezzogiorno, but to
the broader transformations in Italian society associated with the early twentieth century: the season of rapid industrialization in the Northwest; the
great wave of emigration from the southern countryside; the growth of more
modern forms of mass party; the first developments in consumerism and the
mass media; the greater openness of the institutions that culminated in
Italy's first elections with universal male suffrage in 1913; the First World
War.[1] The Southern question also took new forms in the Giolittian era. In
different ways, the state's special laws and Francesco Saverio Nitti's proposals for government intervention aimed at promoting industrialization both
signaled that the South's "backwardness" had become an explicit object of
public debate and policymaking. With Luigi Sturzo, a Catholic discourse on
the South also developed.

The South certainly continued to be perceived in a stereotypical fashion
in the early twentieth century. The earthquake that devastated Messina and
Reggio Calabria in December 1908 made the South the subject of what is
probably Italy's first great cross-class movement of national solidarity. Yet at
the same time, the disaster reinforced the image of a tragic South, an eternal

reminder of the fragility of human progress. Umberto Zanotti-Bianco began a lifetime of campaigning for the southern peasantry following a visit to the devastated villages of Calabria in the aftermath of the earthquake. But the South, which he perceived as a domain of timeless desolation, poetry, and moral simplicity, also offered a penitential resolution to his own spiritual-patriotic crisis.[2] For nationalist mythology, southern emigration came to be seen as the ebbing away of the nation's life blood, its very numerical substance. Luigi Pirandello's 1913 novel of the "bankruptcy of patriotism," *I vecchi e i giovani,* embodies Sicily in the memorable character of Mauro Mortara: a former *garibaldino* who is closer to nature than to human civilization, yet evinces an uncomplicated human sympathy, Mortara is also "the purest incarnation of the island's ancient soul," and the personification of an aboriginal, uncorrupted *italianità.*[3] Before and during the First World War, militaristic ideologies produced the myth of the patriotic redemption of the "primitive" Sardinians in uniform.[4] In 1919, the Futurist painter, poet and war veteran Ardengo Soffici found in Naples, "an oriental marvel," a place where the narrator, "the ultimate *lazzarone,*" could discover a primitive harmony and sensuality away from the conflict.[5] Clearly these and other representations of the Mezzogiorno from the early twentieth century echo the ones I have analyzed here. But the new century offered a broadly different set of contexts in which the patrimony of stereotypes of the South could be reworked. These contexts would require the same kind of detailed, localized analyses as I have endeavored to undertake in this book.

Still today, Italian culture is dense with stereotypes of the South and with the anxieties about national identity that those images often signal. Fascination, disgust, exoticism, and fondness are still on the palette of responses to the South's difference. Stereotypical images of the South continue to be fenced around with interdictions that signal the limits of appropriate public behavior. Today, as in Umbertian Italy, ethnocentric remarks about the South can be made with a kind of transgressive relish; it is something one does more readily in private rather than in public. Yet the notion of a corrupt or maladministered South, alien to norms of modernity, is also still used to shame the nation into remedial action. "We are not in Europe," the inhabitants of a crime-ridden suburb of Palermo exclaim to the TV cameras.

Stereotypes of Southern Italy have perhaps never been as important in Italian political life as they became in the late 1980s and 1990s with the rise of an autonomist movement in the North. The roots of the growth of the Northern League lie in the crisis of a traditional Catholic subculture; in the social upheaval brought by the breakneck economic acceleration and subsequent crisis in areas of "diffuse industrialization"; in the inefficiency of Italy's administrative and political system.[6] But the success of this populist regionalism is also due to the way it has managed to get people to think these political and social problems in territorial terms (Diamanti, *La Lega* 3–16). The League has attempted to construct a home territory, whose imprecise and mobile boundaries (Lombardy, the North, Padania) are held in place by the imaginary circle of hostile forces seen to lie beyond them. The League has seen itself as merely a legitimate defensive response to forces such as immigration and the central state, which are constructed as antithetical to supposedly locally rooted values. Among these Others, the South has been a constant presence, although its relative importance to *Lega* ideology, as is inevitable with so volatile a phenomenon as intolerance, has fluctuated. Even the crude instrument of opinion polls has shown sufficiently clearly that, even when such ethnocentrism is absent from official *Lega* discourse, it is present among supporters and those supporters see the party as in some way giving political expression to that ethnocentrism.

The South provides a powerfully charged emblem of threats and problems, which, in seeming to come from outside the League's territory, actually serve to define a territory of the imagination.[7] Rising crime, social decay, and drugs can be thought of as entirely the product of the mafia. The fear of "invasion" informs campaigns against the confinement in the North of organized crime suspects; it also finds expression in hostility towards immigration (whether from the South, or, more often, from outside Western Europe). The wastefulness of the Italian state can be selectively blamed on the presence of southern workers in state jobs, and on a dependency culture and clientelism in the South, all of which are seen to contrast with the image of a widespread self-reliance in the North. Vague aspirations to a European identity can be seen as a move away from "Africa": as Umberto Bossi argued, when commenting on his party's success in the 1992 general election, "The North has chosen federalism and Europe, the South has chosen Africa and Fascism."[8] Indeed, the kind of images of the South evoked by *Lega* supporters seem to have changed little from the stereotypes abroad in Liberal Italy. One example is the "Arabic" nature of South. Whether in this century or the last, when aspects of Southern Italy are described as Arabic or oriental, it is to the Orient seen as a "living tableau of queerness" that they are compared, as in the following extract from the letters page of *Lombardia Autonomista* in July 1988[9]:

> I find it humiliating that we have been invaded and colonized. . . . It is unnatural that "administrators" from regions which, geographically and ethnically speaking, can be considered North-African or Arab, should "govern" us and lord it over us in our home, with the arrogance that we all know.[10]

So the *Lega*'s habit of thinking political problems in geographical and ethnic stereotypes is not new. However, there is no direct thread of influence to be followed from Niceforo to Bossi. They clearly belong to very different political conjunctures and do not form part of anything like a linear tradition of intolerance towards the South. The League has certainly made use of a powerful patrimony of stereotypes, but it has endowed it with very different meanings. The complex of nineteenth-century ethnocentrism I have analyzed is generally incorporative or centralizing when translated into a politics; it is related to the process of national state-formation and to the identity of the patriotic classes. By contrast, the ethnocentrism of the Northern League is tied into a centrifugal regionalism; it is a function of the invention of a regional political identity. Where the texts I have studied are part of a set of attitudes on the part of the classes represented in the institutions towards their supposed social inferiors, the populism of the League poses as a puncturing from below of the hypocrisies of the political class. The League as a "political entrepreneur" is faced with a task, that of constructing a territorial consensus, which is analogous, at the level of symbols, to the nation building of Italy's first rulers.[11] The often ridiculous Padanian national rituals created by the League show how self-conscious that nation-building project has become. But our amusement at Bossi's antics should not blind us to the historical irony that similar ethnocentric representations of the South have been involved in two comparable but diametrically opposed social and political projects separated by a century of Italian history.[12]

This book is not, therefore, a prehistory of the Northern League. Stereotyping of the Mezzogiorno in the postunification period cannot be explained as regionalism or located only in the North. Nor can it be restricted to racism or even to obviously pejorative conceptions of the South. It is just one aspect of the way in which for the upper and middle classes the South was both a problem to be addressed and a symbolic resource to be exploited. The perceived disorder of the South helped organize concomitant ideas of the nation.

Stereotypes of the South in Umbertian Italy are hooked into well-known mechanisms of identity and alterity, of taboo and transgression. However, the history of stereotypes of the Mezzogiorno cannot be boiled down to a psychological or anthropological truism. Stereotypes are vague and flexible enough to be adapted to very different circumstances. My individual essays analyze moments of particular intensity in the traffic in stereotypes of the South between the different contexts of bourgeois culture. To take one example: the notion of "impressionability" reappears in very many of the texts I have analyzed as a way of marking out southerners as different. But it is given different meanings and put to different uses: it legitimates public atrocities in the antibrigand campaign; in the political thought of Pasquale Turiello, it is seen as the instinctual basis for a new, aggressively monarchistic patriotism with southern inflections; it manifests itself in the charmingly gaudy colors of peasant costumes for the *Illustrazione Italiana;* it suggests a reason for Crispi's grip on the popular imagination in the late 1880s and early 1890s. Yet the vagueness and versatility of stereotypes also make them a very sensitive analytical instrument, a revealing moment in the process of constructing social identities.

On one interpretation, the contribution that my analyses of ethnocentrism towards the South make to the history of nation building is minimal: the subject at hand has been how the Italianized classes viewed the country beyond, and not how the use of the language of nationhood was made more widespread. Yet in another interpretation, the essays constitute examples of how the Italian nation was constantly rebuilt in discourse. No project to Italianize sections of the population, such as was involved in legitimating the war against brigandage or incorporated into the presentation of the *Illustrazione Italiana,* can escape the ambiguous, shifty, and divisive nature of nationalist discourse. Even for the most patriotic of citizens, for a Franchetti or a Villari, thinking in the language of nationhood means using it to discriminate and integrate, and to hypostatize the elusive concept of "Italy." A history of nation building, as well as describing the social changes that encourage the spread of nationalism, must address the crucial question of how patriotism is then acted out, of how the available nationalist jargons are appropriated and activated. That question is just as dense and problematic whether one's object of study is would-be nation builders, as it is here, or their target audience; it is a question that can be tackled only by studies prepared to engage with the close and texture of national belonging. If historians are to use the concept of national identity productively, and not merely to describe the same old historical phenomena in crudely dualistic terms like identity-diversity, integration-disparateness, that concept must be analyzed at the textual level on which its strongest and most intricate effects are registered.

Alberto Banti has recently argued that patriotic discourse was central to the social identity of Liberal Italy's diverse bourgeoisie.[13] This study of the relationship between patriotic discourse and images of the Mezzogiorno adds a little more weight to that argument. In the drive to articulate bourgeois identity, and to know and manage the popular classes in Liberal Italy, discourses of statistics, criminality, hygiene, sexuality, and demography were deployed, as well as the discourses of geography and ethnicity examined here. The terminology of nationhood acted as a kind of switchboard between these different discourses and conditioned their access to the public sphere. But perhaps my research also adds a qualification to Banti's case, to the extent that he still stresses the unifying rather than differentiating role of the idea of nation. My own studies show some of the ways in which the concept of nation lends itself to reinscribing, managing, and also disavowing class divisions. For example, images of the South as Other to the nation allowed the problem of representing class relationships to be transposed onto a geographical axis. The southern peasantry, perhaps because more than any other group, they were unable to represent themselves in Italy's cultural centers, became a pliable synecdochic representation of the masses of the peninsula, available to the discourse of the picturesque as to the sober moralist discourse of the first *meridionalisti.* Crispi's charismatic *sicilianità,* as a function of a relationship of fear and desire toward the masses on the part of the bourgeoisie, seems in part to have owed its force to the way that the imaginary South provided a condensed emblem of the problematic of Italianizing the lower orders in general. Each of these moments involves defining ideas of the Italian nation. Each also suggests that we should be posing different questions about national identities. In seeking to understand the national identity of a class like Liberal Italy's bourgeoisie, the historian's instinctive questions have tended to be "what united and divided them?" or, very simply, "what were they like?" Yet we should also learn to ask how they invented a sense of themselves through what they feared and what they desired, what they found fascinating, alien, or exotic. An important part of the answer to these questions about national identity in the Liberal period, and throughout Italy's postunification history is "the South," that space "beyond" Italy, which is also taken to betoken the whole country's failure to live up to the standards putatively set by nationhood, Europe, or modernity.

Notes

Introduction

1. A. Niceforo, *L'Italia barbara contemporanea (Studi ed appunti)* (Sandron, Milan-Palermo, 1898), p. 247.
2. The sentence is quoted in G. Bocca, *L'inferno. Profondo sud, male oscuro* (Milan, Mondadori, 1992), p. 28.
3. The texts I have chiefly in mind in writing this introduction are: M. L. Salvadori, "L'interpretazione razzistica della inferiorità meridionale," in *Il mito del buongoverno. La questione meridionale da Cavour a Gramsci* (Turin, Einaudi, 1963), pp. 184–205; M. W. Battacchi, *Meridionali e settentrionali nella struttura del pregiudizio etnico in Italia,* second edition (Bologna, Il Mulino, 1972); A. Gramsci, *Il Risorgimento* (Rome, Riuniti, 1975); G. Galasso, "Lo stereotipo del napoletano e le sue variazioni regionali," in *L'altra Europa. Per un'antropologia storica del Mezzogiorno d'Italia* (Milan, Mondadori, 1982), pp. 143–190; V. Teti, *La razza maledetta. Origini del pregiudizio antimeridionale* (Rome, Manifestolibri, 1993). More detailed references to these works are made at appropriate points below.
4. Perhaps because of this, the concept of regionalism has a muddled history in the peninsula. For some interesting reflections on the idea of the region in Italian history, see: L. Gambi, "Le 'regioni' italiane come problema storico," *Quaderni Storici,* 34, 1977, 275–298; "Il concetto storico spaziale di regione: una identificazione controversa," debate between various authors including Immanuel Wallerstein, *Passato e Presente,* 9, 1985, 13–37. On regionalism after unification see D. Mack Smith, "Regionalism," in E. R. Tannenbaum and E. P. Noether (eds.), *Modern Italy. A Topical History Since 1861* (New York, New York University Press, 1974), pp. 125–146. The essay is, however, clouded by an implied definition of regionalism that fluctuates between "regional sentiment" and decentralizing and federalist political programs based on the recognition of regional diversity. For various authoritative contributions on regionalism see C. Levy (ed.), *Italian Regionalism. History, Identity and Politics* (Oxford, Berg, 1996). For some stimulating observations on regionalism in literature in the Liberal period,

see A. Asor Rosa, *Scrittori e popolo. Il populismo nella letteratura italiana contemporanea,* second edition (Turin, Einaudi, 1988), pp. 56–57.

5. Salvadori, p. 186. Salvadori follows Gramsci, according to whom the racial thesis provoked "a North-South polemic on races and the superiority and inferiority of the North and the South" (Gramsci, *Il Risorgimento,* p. 9).

6. The fact of Niceforo's being from the South is very rarely highlighted: Daniel Pick, in his otherwise cogent study, would even seem to imply that Niceforo was a Northern Italian. See D. Pick, *Faces of Degeneration: A European Disorder, c. 1848–c. 1918* (Cambridge, Cambridge University Press, 1989), p. 114. Giuseppe Sergi, from whom Niceforo borrowed theories of southern inferiority based on craniometric data, was himself from Messina.

7. F. Fonzi, *Crispi e lo "stato di Milano"* (Milan, Giuffré, 1965), p. xix.

8. See Mack Smith, "Regionalism."

9. See, for example, the recent account in G. Gribaudi, "Images of the South: the Mezzogiorno as seen by insiders and outsiders," in R. Lumley and J. Morris (eds.), *The New History of the Italian South. The Mezzogiorno Revisited* (Exeter, Exeter University Press, 1997), pp. 83–113, especially pp. 95–98.

10. The debate on the racial interpretation of the southern question is contained in A. Renda (ed.), *La questione meridionale* (Milan-Palermo, Sandron, 1900).

11. The work of "criminal anthropologist" Cesare Lombroso—a major influence on Niceforo—has been read by Daniel Pick as part of a comparable nation-building "project of social differentiation, obsessed by the distinct visual image of the criminal," D. Pick, *Faces of Degeneration,* p. 150.

12. In the *Quaderni,* Antonio Gramsci offers a brief but influential interpretation of the "race" debate of the 1890s. For Gramsci, those who attributed an innate inferiority to southerners were providing a pseudoexplanation that covered up their ignorance of the real conditions of the South and of the role played by the unified state in perpetuating those conditions. Gramsci's argument is that the poverty of the South was inexplicable for the northern masses, who could not see its objective, "external" causes. The only explanation remaining for them was one based on natural, "internal" causes: "men's organic inability, their barbarism, their biological inferiority," Gramsci, *Il Risorgimento,* pp. 98–99. However, if one ascribes prejudices to ignorance, one tends to be prevented from explaining their effects. As an absence of knowledge, ignorance cannot be an effective presence in our thought. A lack of awareness of the real causes of a phenomenon may well be considered to open up a space for other attempted explanations. But there cannot be the relation of determination between that lack of awareness and the characteristics of those explanations implied by Gramsci's juxtaposition of "external" and "internal" causes.

13. See Salvadori, *Il mito del buongoverno,* and Teti, *La razza maledetta.* On the ethical and political dangers of the rhetoric of the "last word" in racism, see J. Derrida, "Racism's Last Word," in H. L. Gates Jr. (ed.), *"Race," Writing, and Difference* (Chicago, Chicago University Press, 1986), pp. 329–338.

14. See A. Montagu, *Man's Most Dangerous Myth: The Fallacy of Race* (Cleveland, Meridian, 1964), p. 76: "the so-called 'races' are populations that merely represent different kinds of temporary mixtures of genetic materials common to all mankind."

15. H. L. Gates Jr., "Introduction: Writing 'Race' and the Difference It Makes," in H. L. Gates Jr. (ed.), *"Race," Writing, and Difference* (Chicago, Chicago University Press, 1986), pp. 1–20 (p. 5).

16. R. Miles, *Racism* London, Routledge, 1989, p. 48. The book also contains a useful discussion of problems in definitions of racism (pp. 41–68).

17. Battacchi, *Meridionali e settentrionali* (first published in 1959 as a response to the problems associated with the migration from the South to the industrial triangle) is the only monograph of which I am aware that is entirely devoted to the issue of North-South prejudices. Interesting and problematic though the book may be on its own terms (such as in its assertion that ethnic prejudice is typical of some "infantile" and "primitive" forms of thought [p. 64]), it interprets the problem of ethnocentrism entirely in psychological, rather than historical or social, terms. Its psychological model is derived from a questionable developmental interpretation of Freud and sees stereotyping as the opposite of scientific knowledge rather than as part of "normal" social relations.

18. On stereotypes, see also S. L. Gilman, *Difference and Pathology. Stereotypes of Sexuality, Race, and Madness* (Ithaca, Cornell University Press, 1985), although Gilman's account is weakened by being inserted into a developmental account of the individual psyche. Richard Jenkins, *Social Identity* (London, Routledge, 1996) usefully situates the study of stereotypes within an identity framework (pp. 122–123 and 159–170). For a further theoretical discussion of stereotyping, see chapter 3 below.

19. Teti, *La razza maledetta* seeks to find the "origins" of anti-southern prejudice in racial thinking.

20. See L. Cafagna, "Italy 1830–1914," in C. Cipolla (ed.), *The Fontana Economic History of Europe*, Vol. IV, *The Emergence of Industrial Societies*, Part One (London, Collins/Fontana, 1973), pp. 279–328 (p. 285): "Propaganda and action for the railways was the most important watchword of the movement for the modernisation of Italy on the model of the north-west European countries." See also T. Kemp, *Industrialisation in Nineteenth-Century Europe* (London, Longman, 1969): Kemp writes of the "captivating effect" of the railways "on the minds of public men, entrepreneurs, bankers and middle-class investors" (p. 168). One example of the train used as a mobile platform of civilization from which to view the national outlands is the series of articles by N. Trevellini published in the *Illustrazione Italiana* from June 7, 1874 and called "Lungo le ferrovie meridionali": "even here progress has opened its breach by using that formidable cannon, the locomotive!" (August 2, 1874, p. 84).

21. Again it is Salvadori in *Il mito del buongoverno* who produces a reductive reading of Niceforo along these lines.

22. For a stimulating history of the South, see P. Bevilacqua, *Breve storia dell'Italia meridionale dall'Ottocento a oggi* (Rome, Donzelli, 1993).

23. On approaches to the problem of regional diversity before and after unification, see G. Talamo, "Diversità e squilibri regionali nella cultura politica del Risorgimento," in *De Sanctis politico e altri saggi* (Rome, Editrice De Santis, 1969), pp. 115–156.

24. The archetypal statement of this view is Cavour's death-bed speech as reported by Ernesto Artom via his uncle Isacco. See his "Il Conte di Cavour e la questione napoletana" in B. Caizzi (ed.), *Antologia della questione meridionale* (Milan, Edizioni di Comunità, 1955), pp. 251–263.

25. Paolo Alatri quoted in M. Petrusewicz, *Come il meridione divenne una Questione. Rappresentazioni del Sud prima e dopo il Quarantotto* (Catanzaro, Rubbettino, 1998), p. 158.

26. See also chapter 2, "Representing and Ruling the South in the Piedmontese Political Correspondence of 1860–61," N. Moe, *Representing the South in Post-Unification Italy, c. 1860–1880* (Johns Hopkins University Doctoral Thesis, 1994), pp. 101–173.

27. Bevilacqua quotes the statistics from the early years after Unification for the number of cotton spindles working in the South (70,000) and in Piedmont, Liguria, and Lombardy (320,000) compared to the 30 million working in Britain, Bevilacqua, *Breve storia dell'Italia meridionale*, p. 29.

28. For more on the South at unification, see chapter 1 below.

29. See G. Manacorda, "Crispi e la legge agraria per la Sicilia," in *Il movimento reale e la coscienza inquieta. L'Italia liberale e il socialismo e altri scritti tra storia e memoria* (Milan, FrancoAngeli, 1992), pp. 15–84.

30. M. Barbagli, *Disoccupazione intellettuale e sistema scolastico in Italia (1859–1973)* (Bologna, Il Mulino, 1974), pp. 140ff is useful on the North-South dualism in education. Barbagli identifies "an inverse relation between the economy and education" in the South for pupils aged 15 to 21 (p. 143).

31. On malaria and the South, see F. M. Snowden, "'Fields of Death': Malaria in Italy, 1861–1962," *Modern Italy,* 4 (1) 1999, 25–57.

32. J. A. Davis, "Changing Perspectives on Italy's 'Southern Problem,'" in Levy, *Italian Regionalism,* pp. 53–68 (p. 62). For another recent summary of these debates, see A. M. Banti, *Storia della borghesia italiana. L'età liberale* (Rome, Donzelli, 1996), pp. 93–96.

33. For recent reformulations of this point, see S. Lanaro, "Le élites settentrionali e la storia italiana," *Meridiana,* 16, 1993, 19–39, and Gribaudi, "Images of the South," pp. 90–92.

34. The comparison I have in mind is with C. Vann Woodward's study of representations of the southern states of the United States in *American Counterpoint. Slavery and Racism in the North-South Dialogue* (Boston and Toronto, Little, Brown and Co.), 1964.

35. I owe these points to M. Meriggi, *Breve storia dell'Italia settentrionale dall'Ottocento a oggi* (Rome, Donzelli, 1996), pp. 3–37.

36. For introductions in English to the new work on the South, see Adrian Lyttelton's "A new past for the Mezzogiorno," *TLS,* 4618, October 4, 1991, 14–15, and J. Morris, "Challenging *meridionalismo:* Constructing a New History for Southern Italy," in Lumley and Morris (eds.), *The New History of the Italian South,* pp. 1–19. For introductory surveys, see also: P. Craveri, "Un nuovo meridionalismo," *La Rivista dei Libri,* 1, 1993, 11–13; and R. Romanelli, "Esiste il Mezzogiorno?" *La Rivista dei Libri,* 5, 1993, 26–28.

37. M. Petrusewicz, *Latifondo. Economia morale e vita materiale in una periferia dell'Ottocento* (Venice, Marsilio, 1989); and "The demise of *latifondismo,*" in Lumley and Morris (eds.), *The New History of the Italian South,* pp. 20–41.

38. For more on the origins of the southern question, see chapter 2 below.

39. C. Donzelli, "Mezzogiorno tra 'questione' e purgatorio. Opinione comune, immagine scientifica, strategie di ricerca," *Meridiana,* 9, 1990, 13–53 (p. 19, p. 35).

40. E. W. Said, *Orientalism* (Harmondsworth, Penguin, 1978), p. 20. The interpolations are mine: Said is obviously referring to the Orient. The ethnocentric discourse of Orientalism, as understood by Said, bears some similarities to the representations of the Mezzogiorno studied here. I would, however, take my distance from Said on a number of theoretical grounds, chiefly relating to the way in which he fails to analyze the difficult construction of the position of the western observer, or of ideas of the West, in the process of representing the Orient. The best critiques of Said are: J. Clifford, "On Orientalism," in *The Predicament of Culture. Twentieth Century Ethnography, Literature, and Art* (Cambridge, Mass., Harvard University Press, 1988), pp. 255–276; H. Bhabha, "The other question: Stereotype, discrimination and the discourse of colonialism," *The Location of Culture* (London, Routledge, 1994), pp. 66–84; and R. Young, *White Mythologies. Writing History and the West* (London, Routledge, 1990), pp. 119–140. Said's understanding of the mediating function of orientalist categories is discussed below in chapter 3. For a recent interpretation of representations of the Mezzogiorno based on an uncritical transposition of Said's thesis into the Italian context, see J. Schneider, "Introduction: the dynamics of neo-orientalism in Italy (1848–1995)," in J. Schneider (ed.), *Italy's "Southern Question": Orientalism in One Country* (Oxford and New York, Berg, 1998), pp. 1–23. For further discussion of this book, see my "Many Souths: Many Stereotypes," *Modern Italy* 4 (1) 1999, 79–86.

41. R. Romanelli, *L'Italia liberale (1860–1900)* (Bologna, Il Mulino, 1979), contains a useful statistical appendix.

42. On popular education in Italy see D. Bertoni Jovine, *Storia dell'educazione popolare in Italia* (Bari, Laterza, 1965), especially pp. 148–167. On the limits of policy and practice after unification with regard to literacy, see also G. Vigo, "Gli italiani alla conquista dell'alfabeto," in S. Soldani and G. Turi (eds.), *Fare gli italiani. Scuola e cultura nell'Italia contemporanea. 1. La nascita dello Stato nazionale* (Bologna, Il Mulino, 1993), pp. 37–66.

43. G. Candeloro, *Storia dell'Italia moderna,* Vol. V, *La costruzione dello stato unitario 1860–1871* (Milan, Feltrinelli, 1978), p. 27.

44. B. Tobia, *Una patria per gli italiani. Spazi, itinerari, monumenti nell'Italia unita (1870–1900)* (Rome and Bari, Laterza, 1991), esp. pp. 114–129.

45. A. Giddens, *The Nation-State and Violence,* Vol. II of *A Contemporary Critique of Historical Materialism* (Cambridge, Polity, 1985), p. 219.

46. See, for example, S. Woolf, *A History of Italy 1700–1860. The social constraints of political change* (London, Methuen, 1979), p. 331. The best short analysis of the Risorgimento is L. Riall, *The Italian Risorgimento: State, society and national unification* (Routledge, London, 1994).

47. For the key role of questions of law and order in these relations see J. A. Davis, *Conflict and Control: Law and Order in Nineteenth-Century Italy* (London, Macmillan, 1988), pp. 262–289. See also L. Riall, "Elite resistance to state formation: the case of Italy," in M. Fulbrook (ed.), *National Histories and European History* (London, UCL Press, 1993), pp. 46–68.

48. For some recent work in this area see, for example, the chapter "Le strutture elementari della clientela" in Emilio Franzina's *La transizione dolce. Storie del Veneto tra '800 e '900* (Verona, Cierre, 1991), pp. 105–170, and L. Musella, *Individui, amici, clienti. Relazioni personali e circuiti politici in Italia meridionale tra Otto e Novecento* (Bologna, Il Mulino, 1994). See also Banti, *Storia della borghesia italiana,* esp. pp. 23–49 and 181–212.

49. See G. Galasso, "Le forme del potere, classi e gerarchie sociali," in *Storia d'Italia,* Vol. I, *I caratteri originali* (Turin, Einaudi, 1972), pp. 401–599 (pp. 549–52), especially on the prefects' role in this process.

50. M. Meriggi, "The Italian 'Borghesia,'" in J. Kocka and A. Mitchell (eds.), *Bourgeois Society in Nineteenth-Century Europe* (Oxford, Berg, 1993), pp. 423–438.

51. The figures are from Barbagli, *Disoccupazione intellettuale,* p. 65. On lawyers in Liberal Italy see H. Siegrist, "Gli avvocati nell'Italia del XIX secolo. Provenienza e matrimoni, titolo e prestigio," *Meridiana,* 14, 1992, 145–181.

52. Recent work on the Italian bourgeoisie includes the following texts. A. Lyttelton, "The middle classes in Liberal Italy," in J. A. Davis and P. Ginsborg (eds.), *Society and Politics in the Age of the Risorgimento. Essays in honour of Denis Mack Smith* (Cambridge, Cambridge University Press, 1991), pp. 217–250 is an interesting sketch of the middle classes of Liberal Italy that, in focusing on professional rather than capitalist groups, is substantially compatible with Meriggi's analysis. For stimulating assessments of some recent work on the Italian bourgeoisie, see R. Romanelli, "Borghesi d'Italia," *La Rivista dei Libri,* 1, 1993, 29–32, and A. Lyttelton *et al.,* "Élites, famiglie, strategie imprenditoriali: Macry e Banti sull'Ottocento italiano," *Meridiana,* 6, 1989, 231–259.

53. For all the differences between them, E. J. Hobsbawm, *Nations and Nationalism since 1780: Programme, Myth, Reality* (Cambridge, Cambridge University Press, 1990) and E. Gellner, *Nations and Nationalism* (Oxford, Blackwell, 1983) have had a considerable influence, in the UK as in Italy, in spreading this model of the nation.

54. For an introduction to a theory of nations as "social fictions" see my "Imagined Italies," in D. Forgacs and R. Lumley (eds.), *Italian Cultural Studies. An Introduction* (Oxford, Oxford University Press, 1996), pp. 19–33. Benedict Anderson's thesis is set out in *Imagined Communities. Reflections on the Origin and Spread of Nationalism,* revised edition (London, Verso, 1991). A perceptive recent assessment of Anderson's book is Alberto M. Banti's review, "Comunità immaginarie," *Storica,* 6, 1996, 189–194.
55. W. B. Gallie, "Essentially contested concepts," *Proceedings of the Aristotelian Society,* vol. LVI, 1955–1956, 167–199.
56. Samuel Johnson quoted in *Boswell's Life of Johnson,* edited by G. Birkbeck Hill, Vol. II, *Life (1765–1776)* (Oxford, Clarendon, 1887), p. 348.
57. See my *"La macchina da scrivere:* the Victor Emmanuel Monument in Rome and Italian nationalism," *The Italianist,* 14, 1994, 261–285, (esp. pp. 266–273).
58. John A. Davis has made the point that the distinction between "legal Italy" and "real Italy," when coined by Stefano Jacini, "was not a statement of fact . . . but an ideological manifesto" that sought to promote a conservative valorization of "older and more personal bonds of deference and social obligation" seen to have been trampled on by a distant state (Davis, *Conflict and Control,* pp. 262–263). The metaphor belonged to the relations between the state and the local elites rather than the state and the masses, as it has often been taken to do. Davis argues that histories that have taken Jacini at his word have often assumed too simple a divide between the public and the private domains, or imagined a "traditional" real Italy undisturbed by socioeconomic transformations and confronted by a hungrily centralizing governmental apparatus. It is worth making clear, therefore, that the distinction between real and legal Italies is employed here in the (strictly speaking) improper sense, as a useful way of describing the state's incapacity to win hegemonic adherence amongst the laboring population (see, for example, Galasso, "Le forme del potere," p. 552).
59. G. Bollati, "L'italiano," in R. Romano and C. Vivanti (eds.), *Storia d'Italia, I caratteri originali,* vol. II, 951–1022, (Turin, Einaudi, 1972), p. 958.
60. A version of this point is also made by Bollati on the basis of a reading of Lévi-Strauss, although he oversimplifies the dynamic of alterity by assuming that it involves only the "devaluing or negation" of the identity of the other (p. 955).
61. See Dickie, "Imagined Italies."
62. On stereotypes in the historical process of forming national identity in France, see E. Weber, "Of stereotypes and of the French," *Journal of Contemporary History,* 25 (2–3) 1990, 169–203 (pp. 180–181).
63. Emilio De Marchi, *Demetrio Pianelli* (Milan, Mondadori, 1979), p. 336.
64. For a history of stereotypes of Naples and the South organized on linear narrative lines see Galasso, "Lo stereotipo del napoletano." It seems to me that one of the weaknesses of such an approach is that the relationship stereotypes presuppose with earlier stereotypes does not take the form of a unidirectional

tradition or movement of influence from past to present. The sense that stereotypes have all been said before (while always demanding to be said again, to be given new inflections) is an aspect of the play of novelty and familiarity, of difference and similarity that is part of their effect. For further theoretical reflections on stereotyping, see chapter 3 below.

65. See some of the texts anthologized in and quoted in the introduction to A. Mozzillo, *Viaggiatori stranieri nel Sud* (Edizioni di comunità, Milan, 1964). See also: C. De Seta, "L'Italia nello specchio del Grand Tour," in C. De Seta (ed.), *Storia d'Italia, Annali 5*, "Il paesaggio" (Turin, Einaudi, 1982), pp. 125–263; N. Moe, "Imagining the South," chapter 1 of *Representing the South in Post-Unification Italy, c. 1860–1880* (Johns Hopkins University Doctoral Thesis, 1994), pp. 1–100; J. Pemble, *The Mediterranean Passion. Victorians and Edwardians in the South* (Oxford, Oxford University Press, 1988); and Gribaudi, "Images of the South."

66. A. Recupero, "La Sicilia all'opposizione (1848–74)," in M. Aymard and G. Giarrizzo (eds.), *Storia d'Italia. Le regioni dall'Unità a oggi. La Sicilia* (Turin, Einaudi, 1987), pp. 39–85.

67. Petrusewicz, *Come il meridione divenne una Questione.*

68. Meriggi, *Breve storia dell'Italia settentrionale,* pp. 39–43.

69. C. Duggan, *Fascism and the Mafia* (New Haven, Yale University Press, 1989) includes a history of the instrumentalization of the idea of the mafia by the postunification state (pp. 15–91).

70. For a fine introductory survey of stereotypes of the South since unification, see Gribaudi, "Images of the South." The article is nonetheless limited predominantly to revealing misrepresentations in political and social scientific discourse. Giuseppe Giarrizzo produces an extraordinarily erudite and suggestive reading of certain myths of Sicily as a historical and cultural anomaly in his introduction to M. Aymard and G. Giarrizzo (eds.), *Storia d'Italia. Le regioni dall'Unità a oggi. La Sicilia* (Turin, Einaudi, 1987), pp. xix-lvii.

Chapter 1

1. The figure is from Franco Molfese, "La repressione del brigantaggio postunitario nel mezzogiorno continentale (1860–70)," in *Archivio Storico per le Province Napoletane,* CI (1983), 33–64 (p. 52). Giorgio Rochat and Giulio Massobrio estimate the proportion at two-thirds, *Breve storia dell'esercito italiano dal 1861 al 1943* (Turin, Einaudi, 1978), p. 49.

2. The most plausible typology and chronology of banditry at this time is in Franco Molfese, "Il brigantaggio nel Mezzogiorno dopo l'Unità d'Italia," in *Archivio Storico per la Calabria e la Lucania,* XLII (1975), 99–136.

3. J. A. Davis, *Conflict and Control: Law and Order in Nineteenth-Century Italy* (London, Macmillan, 1988), p. 175.

4. F. Molfese, *Storia del brigantaggio dopo l'Unità* (Milan, Feltrinelli, 1964), p. 342.

5. E. Hobsbawm, *Bandits* (London, Pelican, 1972), pp. 68 and 63. Sergio Romagnoli sees the brigandage of 1860–1870 in a similar way: "that form of

social delirium which brigandage was, in so many respects: a delirium that alienated the people from historical reality. Although it aimed to subvert existing power relations, in the instant it was translated into action it destroyed any chance that it might become an instrument of decision-making power and participation in progress because of its uncontrolled, irrational violence" ("Il brigante nel romanzo storico italiano," in *Archivio Storico per la Calabria e la Lucania*, XLII [1975], 176–212 [p. 212]).

6. G. Candeloro, *Storia dell'Italia moderna. Vol. 5. La costruzione dello stato unitario, 1860–71* (Milan, Feltrinelli, 1968), p. 168.

7. See for example the article by Niccolò De Ruggieri on a study of the bandit Ninco Nanco (N. De Ruggieri, "Indagine antropologica sulla personalità del brigante Giuseppe Nicola Summa, detto Ninco-Nanco," in *Archivio storico per la Calabria e la Lucania*, XLII [1975, 231–233]. Lombroso worked as a doctor in Calabria during the war.

8. Both quotations are from G. Doria, *Per la storia del brigantaggio nelle province meridionali* (Naples, extract from *Archivio Storico per le Province Napoletane*, 1931), p. 5.

9. A. Guarnieri, *Otto anni di storia militare in Italia* (Florence, Galletti, 1868), p. 462.

10. On the history of the terms "bandit" and "brigand," see Davis, *Conflict and Control*, pp. 73–75.

11. See Davis, *Conflict and Control*, pp. 66–90. For more specific studies, see for example: P. Ginsborg, "After the Revolution: Bandits on the plains of the Po 1848–54" (pp. 128–151), and G. Fiume, "Bandits, violence and the organization of power in Sicily in the early nineteenth century" (pp. 70–91), both in J. A Davis and P. Ginsborg (eds.), *Society and Politics in the Age of the Risorgimento. Essays in honour of Denis Mack Smith* (Cambridge, Cambridge University Press, 1991); P. Brunello, *Ribelli, questuanti e banditi. Proteste contadine in Veneto e Friuli 1814–1866* (Venice, Marsilio, 1981); S. C. Hughes, *Crime, Disorder and the Risorgimento. The Politics of Policing in Bologna* (Cambridge, Cambridge University Press, 1994).

12. On brigandage in the preunification South, see Davis, *Conflict and Control, loc. cit.*, and the following essays, all contained in Angelo Massafra (ed.), *Il Mezzogiorno preunitario. Economia, società e istituzioni* (Bari, Dedalo, 1988): M. Themelly, "Trasgressione, criminalità, comportamenti collettivi nelle province meridionali" (pp. 1039–1054); A. Albanese, "Crimini e criminalità in Terra di Bari nell'età della Restaurazione (1818–1835). Le comitive armate" (pp. 1055–1068); M. Platania, "Instabilità sociale e delinquenza" (pp. 1069–1085); R. Marino, "Nuova borghesia e amministrazione locale nelle cronache giudiziarie del principato Citra" (pp. 1087–1101); M. Autuori, "Storia sociale della banda Capozzoli (1817–1827): lotte municipali e brigantaggio" (pp. 1127–1141); M. P. Vozzi, "La comitiva armata dei fratelli Capozzoli e la rivoluzione cilentana del 1828. Lotta politica e brigantaggio" (pp. 1143–1157).

13. See, for example, the assessment of the state of the South contained in the report by Diomede Pantaleoni to Minister of the Interior Bettino Ricasoli in

October 1861, which is reproduced in P. Alatri, "Le condizioni dell'Italia meridionale in un rapporto di Diomede Pantaleoni a Marco Minghetti (1861)," *Movimento Operaio,* 5–6 (1953), 750–92.

14. On the relations between clergy and state in the South, see B. Pellegrino, *Vescovi "borbonici" e stato "liberale" (1860–61)* (Rome and Bari, Laterza, 1992).

15. A. Scirocco, *Governo e paese nel Mezzogiorno nella crisi dell'unificazione (1860–61)* (Milan, Giuffrè, 1963), and *Il mezzogiorno nell'Italia unita (1861–5)* (Naples, Società Editrice Napoletana, 1979).

16. G. Massari, "Relazione della commissione d'inchiesta del deputato Massari letta alla camera nella tornata segreta del 3 maggio 1863," in T. Pedìo, *Inchiesta sul brigantaggio* (Manduria, Lacaita, 1983), pp. 105–229 (p. 208).

17. A. Bianco di Saint Jorioz, *Il brigantaggio alla frontiera pontificia, 1860–63* (Milan, Daelli, 1864), p. 36. Ironically Alessandro was the son of Carlo, the man who proposed the use of guerrilla tactics in patriotic warfare during the Risorginento.

18. Aurelio Saffi from "La commissione parlamentare d'inchiesta nelle province meridionali attraverso le lettere di Aurelio Saffi" in Pedìo, *Inchiesta sul brigantaggio,* pp. 57–90 (p. 61).

19. From a letter reproduced in M. Scherillo "Gaetano Negri alla caccia dei briganti" in Gaetano Negri, *Opere di Gaetano Negri I—Nel presente e nel passato* (Milan, Hoepli, 1905), pp. 3–65 (p. 30).

20. Bianco di Saint Jorioz, *Il brigantaggio,* pp. 9, 67, 43. Major General Lopez declared that "the mysteries of brigandage will never be known!" (quoted in P. Costantini, *Silvio Spaventa e la repressione del brigantaggio* (Pescara, Attraverso l'Abruzzo, 1960), p. 24). Aurelio Saffi, then a member of parliament for a Basilicata constituency and chosen to represent the Left on the Commission of Inquiry, writes to his Mazzinian wife from Avellino in January 1863: "brigandage is like a shadow that fades away as soon as one gets near it" (in Pedìo, *Inchiesta sul brigantaggio,* p. 70). On Saffi's politics and the background to his being chosen for the Commission, see A. Scirocco, "Aurelio Saffi nella vita parlamentare," *Il Risorgimento,* 1 (1991), 5–33.

21. For example, in Massari's report to parliament: "In the eyes of the common people who are so full of imagination and so angered by the deprivation they suffer, the brigand seems very different to what he really is; for them he becomes transformed and becomes a fantastic being, the symbol of their checked aspirations, the avenger of the wrongs they have endured. . . . the vile reality is replaced by an imaginary fiction with opposite characteristics" (Pedìo, *Inchiesta sul brigantaggio,* p. 123).

22. The photos from the antibrigand campaign have been widely reproduced: see, for example, photos 80, 81, and 84–88 in C. Bertelli and G. Bollati, *Storia d'Italia, Annali* 2, "L'immagine fotografica," Vol. 1 (Turin, Einaudi, 1979). The quotation is from M. Milani, *La repressione dell'ultimo brigantaggio nelle Calabrie, 1868–9* (Pavia, Biblioteca pavese di storia patria, 1952), p. 39.

23. On the affiliations between the political class and the military cadre see Rochat and Massobrio, *Breve storia dell'esercito italiano,* pp. 40–41. Maurice Pearton describes the military ethos of the time: "war was considered a duel on behalf of the state or the nation by those who considered themselves governed by its codes. It was the antithesis of peace but, like peace, operated in a framework of moral codes; it was not outside the moral order or a negation of it" (*The Knowledgeable State: Diplomacy, War and Technology since 1830* (London, Burnett, 1982), p. 28). On the sociology of nineteenth-century warfare, see also M. D. Feld, *The Structure of Violence: Armed Forces as Social Systems* (Beverly Hills/London, Sage, 1977). On the "professionalization" of the military before and after unification, see Giorgio Rochat, "La professione militare in Italia dall'Ottocento alla seconda guerra mondiale," in *L'esercito italiano in pace e in guerra. Studi di storia militare* (Milan, RARA, 1991), pp. 29–40.

24. For an account of the reforms implemented by La Marmora in 1854 and of the construction of the Italian army by Fanti, see: P. Pieri, *Storia militare del Risorgimento* (Turin, Einaudi, 1962) and *Le forze armate nell'età della destra* (Milan, Giuffrè, 1962); J. Whittam, *The Politics of the Italian Army 1861–1918* (London, Croom Helm, 1977); Rochat and Massobrio, *Breve storia dell'esercito italiano;* and J. Gooch, *Army, State and Society in Italy, 1870–1915* (Basingstoke, Macmillan, 1989). According to Rochat and Massobrio, two out of three of the officers of the Italian army in 1860 were from the Piedmontese army or had been trained in Piedmont (Rochat and Massobrio *Breve storia dell'esercito italiano,* p. 26).

25. Rochat and Massobrio mention that beyond the political motives for hostility toward the *esercito meridionale* there was also a strong corporate jealousy on the part of the army (*Breve storia,* p. 29). Roberto Battaglia summarizes the competing military ideologies of moderates and democrats with concision: "The entire organization given to the army by the moderate leadership was substantially inspired by the desire that the 'nation should be born from the army'; whilst for the democrats the point of departure was exactly the opposite, and consisted in ensuring that the 'army be born from the nation,' according to Cattaneo's formula: 'every man a militiaman, no man a soldier'" (R. Battaglia, *Risorgimento e Resistenza* (Rome, Editori Riuniti, 1964), p. 42). For Garibaldi an army other than one composed of volunteers drawing its strength from "all of the Nation's living forces" is "contrary to Italy's interests . . . it is not Italian, it is not worthy of the Nation" (quoted in Pieri, *Storia militare del Risorgimento,* p. 739).

26. See Battaglia, *Risorgimento e Resistenza,* p. 33. One of the most important and lasting features of Fanti's reforms was the switching of officers and men from different areas in order to minimize regionalism and prevent potentially dangerous links with the local population. Rochat and Massobrio argue that the integration of the army at officer level was a much greater success than amongst the ranks, where failure to respond to the call-up was initially at very high levels (*Breve storia dell'esercito italiano,* p. 45).

27. Both quotes are from Molfese, *Storia del brigantaggio,* p. 190.

28. General Cialdini quoted in Count A. Maffei, *Brigand Life in Italy: A History of Bourbonist Reaction* (London, Hurst and Blackett, 1865), Vol. II, pp. 289–290.

29. Bianco di Saint Jorioz, *Il brigantaggio*, p. 27. See also ibid., p. 27.: "There was only one moralizing agent in these provinces . . . and it was the Army." Guarnieri refers to the army as "a select part of the new generation" (*Otto anni di storia militare*, p. ix). Colonel Mazé de la Roche, in command of the Campobasso area in 1861, lists his powers: "In this district I am mayor, judge, commander of the carabinieri . . . and I exercise an almost sovereign authority over some fifteen communities," quoted in C. Buffa di Perrero, *Biografia del Conte Gustavo Mazé de la Roche* (Turin, Bocca, 1888), p. 80.

30. A young officer, Enea Pasolini, complains to his old teacher, listing the functions he performs, including "even executioner (horresco referens)" (see the letters reproduced in chapter 23 ("Enea in Calabria") of P. Pasolini dall'Onda, *Giuseppe Pasolini 1815–1876—Memorie raccolte da suo figlio*, Vol. II (Turin, Bocca, 1915), pp. 229–273 (p. 251). Enea died in 1868 of an illness contracted in Calabria. For Guarnieri the campaign was a series of "sterile struggles" (*Otto anni di storia militare*, p. 462); and in Massari's report to the parliamentary commission the war is described as "inglorious and sad" and "obscure and distressing" (Pedìo, *Inchiesta sul brigantaggio*, pp. 180 and 183).

31. C. Cesari, *Il brigantaggio e l'opera dell'esercito italiano dal 1860 al 1870* (Rome, Ausonia, 1920), p. 83. According to Cesari, the government, more than generous in the honors given to the combatants of the wars of unification, "did not judge it appropriate to be similarly generous in handing out rewards for a war which was a harsh necessity but was unfortunately at the same time an internal wound for the Nation" (ibid., p. 167). The long-term effects of the campaign on the ability of the army to fight are impossible to gauge accurately. Molfese refers to the relative solidity of the new army ("Il brigantaggio nel Mezzogiorno," p. 136), while Battaglia asserts that the disorientating experience of the war in the South contributed in large measure to the defeat at Custoza (*Risorgimento e Resistenza*, p. 55).

32. Scherillo, "Gaetano Negri alla caccia dei briganti," p. 34. Negri sums up the effects of the campaign on morale: "Imagine the immense virgin forests, where the army cannot enter without running the risk of getting lost and can only be certain of not getting any good results . . . because the brigand knows every lane, every opening, every hiding place. In the mean time we are condemned to lead the most miserable life imaginable . . . it is real hell! But the worst thing is the continual uncertainty we live in. In the early days of my exile, an existence of this kind had its pleasurable side for me, and the novelty of it was fun; but now I'm completely blasé and brigand emotions have lost all their attraction" (ibid., p. 52).

33. In C. Cavour, *Carteggi: la liberazione del Mezzogiorno e la formazione del Regno d'Italia*, Vol. III (October–November 1860) (Bologna, Zanichelli, 1952), letter from Farini dated October 27, 1860, p. 208.

34. N. Bixio, *Epistolario*, Vol. II (1861–1865) (Rome, Vittoriano, 1942), letter dated February 18, 1863, p. 143.

35. "Sul brigantaggio—note di un uffiziale italiano," in *Rivista Contemporanea*, May 1862, 185–201. General La Marmora was chosen to lead the fight against brigandage because of his experiences in Algeria; see Battaglia, *Risorgimento e Resistenza*, p. 45.

36. Pasolini dall'Onda, *Giuseppe Pasolini*, p. 241. The letter quoted is to his brother, and dated June 24, 1868.

37. Bianco di Saint Jorioz, p. 391. Certain practical dimensions of the war would tend to make the radical imaginative juxtaposition of the army and its enemy very problematic. The foot soldiers and their antagonists would have been from the same peasant background. Ex-subjects of Francis II employed in the Savoyard army would be as likely to have common cultural ground with their opponents as with their fellow soldiers, who, for instance, included a large number of Hungarians (see R. Riviello, *Cronaca potentina dal 1799 al 1882* (Potenza, Santanello, 1888), p. 348). G. Zanzi mentions that the troops under him spoke a Neapolitan dialect (*Memorie di Zanzi Guglielmo Maggior Generale della Riserva sulla repressione del brigantaggio negli Abruzzi e Terra di Lavoro* (Milan, Cogliati, 1913), p. 66). There were many incidences of deserters from the Italian army joining the bandits. On the other hand, General Pallavicini offered one prisoner his freedom on condition that he teach the army brigand tactics and act as a guide (see A. De Jaco (ed.), *Il brigantaggio meridionale: cronaca inedita dell'unità d'Italia* (Rome, Editori Riuniti, 1969), p. 33). Molfese reports that troops, in their search for intelligence on brigand movements and support, would get drawn into local intrigues and corruption (Molfese, *Storia del brigantaggio*, p. 188), while Zanzi is proud of the fact that the soldiers under his command have managed to "domesticate" some of the local "brigantesse" (he uses the term synonymously with "peasant women") by taking them as lovers (Zanzi, *Memorie di Zanzi Guglielmo*, pp. 52–53). It is well known that the army had to resort to such unconventional practices as disguise, treachery, and concealment in the peculiar circumstances of the war, for example, by dressing up as brigands to expose *manutengoli*. It has even been argued that the officers, partly through necessity and partly through affectation, began to "go native" in their dress, adding local garments to their uniforms (V. Gibellini, "Esercito italiano (1861–70): la lotta al brigantaggio," in *Rivista Militare*, 105, 2 (1982), 123–126. Gibellini offers little evidence in support of his case, which must be treated with circumspection.

38. Aurelio Saffi in Pedìo, *Inchiesta sul brigantaggio*, p. 88.

39. G. Govone, "Memoria sulle cause del brigantaggio," in U. Govone, *Il generale Giuseppe Govone. Frammenti di memorie* (Turin, Casanova, 1902), pp. 393–408 (p. 393).

40. A. Dumas (père), *Cento anni di brigantaggio nelle province meridionali d'Italia*, translated by E. Torelli (Naples, De Marco, 1863), p. 8.

41. G. Bourelly, *Brigantaggio nelle zone militari di Melfi e Lacedonia dal 1860 al 1865* (Naples, Mea, 1865), pp. 52, 69.

42. L. Gargiulo, *Relazione sulla vera sorgente del brigantaggio* (Naples, De Angelis, 1863), p. 24. The army seemed itself to be prepared to try out unconventional methods of producing a satisfactory knowledge of brigandage: Gaetano Negri describes the arrest of a priest "with a very brigand-like physiognomy" (Scherillo, "Gaetano Negri alla caccia dei briganti," p. 30).

43. The most comprehensive analysis of the legal aspects of the antibrigand war is in R. Martucci, *Emergenza e tutela dell'ordine pubblico nell'Italia liberale* (Bologna, Il Mulino, 1980). For a cogent short account of the state's response to the situation in the South, see also Davis, *Conflict and Control,* pp. 168–182.

44. Nicola De Luca quoted in Scirocco, *Il mezzogiorno nell'Italia unita,* p. 94.

45. Quoted in ibid., p. 128.

46. Massari in Pedìo, *Inchiesta sul brigantaggio,* pp. 223, 203.

47. *Inferno* XX, 12. The translations are from *The Divine Comedy,* translated and with a commentary by C. S. Singleton (Princeton, Princeton University Press, 1977).

48. *Inf.* XX, 27–30.

49. In Pedìo, *Inchiesta sul brigantaggio,* p. 224.

50. "Sul brigantaggio—note di un uffiziale italiano," p. 193.

51. In a written order of February 3, 1861, quoted in G. Buttà, *Un viaggio da Boccadifalco a Gaeta. Memorie della rivoluzione del 1860 al 1861* (Naples, Benso, 1966 [1875]), p. 427. The rest of Pinelli's order is interesting for the language used to describe banditry, which Pinelli blames on priestly plotting: "A pack of that race of thieves is still lurking in the mountains, flush them out; be as inexorable as destiny. Against such enemies pity is a crime; they are the hired cut-throats of the Vicar not of Christ, but of Satan. We will annihilate, we will crush the priestly vampire which has for centuries been sucking the blood of our mother with his foul lips. With iron and fire we will purify the areas infested with his unclean slaver, and liberty will arise fresher and healthier from the ashes."

52. From Maffei, *Brigand Life in Italy,* Vol. I, p. 223.

53. The two letters quoted are Ricasoli to La Marmora, October 24, 1861 and La Marmora to Ricasoli, February 2, 1862, in A. La Marmora, *Carteggi* (Turin, Chiantore, 1928), pp. 115 and 141.

54. Massari in Pedìo, *Inchiesta sul brigantaggio,* p. 225.

55. F. Carcani, *Sul brigantaggio—osservazioni* (Trani, Cannone, 1863), p. 34.

56. A letter from the Advocate General to the War Minister dated December 16, 1864 (ACS 193/(misc. correspondence)) discusses the issue of what counts as an armed band under the law: "to pretend that carrying a rasor, a knife, a carving-fork . . . do not make the band an armed one as defined by the law is one of those objections which one would hardly tolerate from the lips of a defence lawyer whose every other means of defence had failed." It need hardly be stated that in an overwhelmingly agrarian society, to label "an in-

finity of sharp, pointed and blunt instruments" (ibid.) as weapons associated with banditry gives enormous scope to the repressive forces.

57. *Atti Parlamentari,* Sessione del 1863, Discussioni, August 1, 1863, p. 1795. See also Martucci, *Emergenza e tutela dell'ordine,* p. 126.

58. Letter dated November 23, 1863 to military tribunal in Chieti (ACS 127/1424).

59. ACS 127/1425 (Chieti). The looseness of the term also allowed the law to work retrospectively: "the crime of brigandage is a continuous crime with a comprehensive character, so the Military Tribunals must necessarily deal with all of the crimes which can be imputed to the accused, even those committed before the law, as long as after the law the accused continued to remain in a state of brigandage" (ACS 2/11 (Aquila) Circular from Advocate General, November 29, 1863).

60. There is, for example, the case of Sabato Cibelli, described as "a desperately poor man," given twenty years hard labor by the Salerno military tribunal for doing some shopping for the brigands (ACS 192/2310). The list of items is interesting, and perhaps suspiciously picturesque: "seven hats, six pipes, four silk handkerchiefs, a packet of coloured sweets, a bottle of rosolio, six shirt-fronts, a razor, a pair of scissors and two jars of brilliantine."

61. See Molfese, *Storia del brigantaggio,* pp. 288–289. P. Alvazzi del Frate, "Giustizia militare e brigantaggio. Il tribunale di guerra di Gaeta (1863–5)," in *Rassegna Storica del Risorgimento,* IV (1985), 447–464, contains some interesting conclusions about the workings of the Pica law in the Gaeta area.

62. General Pallavicini, in a set of instructions to his forces in Calabria (which caused no small embarrassment to the government on their becoming public) makes explicit the army's tactics: "Crime, which in this province has no other aim than robbery, is a war waged on the rich by the poor; from this special characteristic of the current bandits, it is clear which class should preferably be suspected of helping the brigands . . . the whole rigour of military authority should thus fall chiefly on the relatives of brigands," quoted in Martucci, *Emergenza e tutela dell'ordine,* p. 196. A routine letter of November 6, 1865 from the commander of the military zone to the military advocate of the Avellino area mentions the arrest of brigands' relatives (ACS 38/514 [Avellino]).

63. ACS 37/510 (Avellino) contains a letter on the arrest of *manutengoli* dated August 30, 1864 from the area delegate responsible for Baiano to the lawyer of the military tribunal of Avellino outlining the difficulty of finding brigands and *manutengoli* and concluding: "From that I was permitted to pick out with complete peace of mind the people who are most indicted by public opinion." A great many of the verdicts published by the military tribunals in the South mention that the reputation of the accused was taken into account before the punishment was prescribed. As an example of the suspicions and intrigues which the military tribunals had to unravel, ACS 38/514 (Avellino) contains a letter from some locals denouncing canon D. Mariano Valente for *manutengolismo.* An explanatory note from an official in Cervinara mentions

that the letter is signed by fictitious witnesses and was probably written in revenge for denunciations made by Valente, whose brother had been killed by brigands.

64. General Cialdini was a firing-squad enthusiast: "Publish the fact that I will shoot all the armed country people I catch, and that I will only have mercy on regular soldiers. I have already started today." (Cialdini (October 21, 1860) quoted in Molfese, *Storia del brigantaggio,* p. 55. Concerned about European public opinion politicians and commanders at various times tried to moderate the use of shooting, decreeing that only band leaders should be executed. Officers on the ground simply responded by claiming that all the brigands they captured were leaders and shooting them anyway (E. Della Rocca, *The Autobiography of a Veteran* (London, Unwin, 1899), p. 206).

65. Article 593 (pp. 398–400) of *Regolamento di disciplina militare per le truppe di cavalleria ed artiglieria* (Turin, Fodratti, 1840), p. 399. The regulations were in force from August 1840—those applying to the Piedmontese forces were extended to cover the new Italian army.

66. M. Foucault, *Surveiller et punir. Naissance de la prison* (Paris, Gallimard, 1975), p. 17.

67. The officer was Borjès. There are many accounts of his execution including that in M. Monnier, *Notizie storiche sul brigantaggio nelle provincie napoletane dai tempi di Frà Diavolo sino ai giorni nostri* (Florence, Barbèra, 1862), p. 162. The principal aim of Monnier's text is to show that the problems in the South were largely due to a papal and legitimist conspiracy. There is also a French version of his book: M. Monnier, *Histoire du brigandage dans l'Italie méridionale* (Paris, Lévy, 1862). It was also translated into English as Vol. I of Maffei, *Brigand Life in Italy.*

68. From *Il Bruzio* of January 4, 1865. The article is by Vincenzo Padula (V. Padula, *Il brigantaggio in Calabria (1864–5)* (Rome, Carlo M. Padula, 1981), p. 100).

69. Massari felt obliged to argue along similar lines to refute the familiar notion that brigands "died well": "It is not true that all of them go to meet their deaths with courage; this has been true in some cases, but it is not the general rule; unless one is intent on confusing stupidity with stoicism, or the strong man's disdain for life with the coldness that brutishness brings," Pedìo, *Inchiesta sul brigantaggio,* p. 184.

70. The inconsistency with which the penalty of shooting in the back is cited in the records of the military tribunals might attest to its being only a semiofficial measure. Some accounts of shootings before the introduction of the Pica law mention that the victims were shot from behind, others not. After the law, as appears from a rough estimate based on a cross-section of the papers of the military tribunals, over half of the sentences specifically mention shooting in the back. It may well be that the method did not need to be specified, that different regions had different practices, or that the method of shooting was left to the discretion of the commander of the firing-party. In the documents for the Ariano tribunal (ACS 193/2317) shooting in the

back is made explicit, whereas in Avellino (39/[1863–4]) it is rarely mentioned. In some cases where simple peasant brigands are shot alongside ex-soldiers of the Bourbon army, the latter are given the penalty of "death by means of shooting in the back following reduction to the ranks" (ACS 71/sentenze 1863–4 [I] [Caserta] quoted from the case of Pasquale Silvestro) while the former are simply shot. In Avellino (ACS 39/[1865]) they get the same treatment.

71. *Codice penale militare per gli stati di S.M. il Re di Sardegna* (Turin, Fodratti, 1859), article 8, p. 12.

72. *Regolamento di disciplina militare,* article 594, pp. 400–402.

73. It was decreed in the Pica law that judgements should be read out loud and copies posted in prominent places in the town and by the house of the culprit. On the practice of displaying mutilated corpses, De Jaco reproduces the following from one officer: "Many brigands were unknown in the villages where they were put to death. At first we took them, judged them, shot them and buried them. Everything ended there, not just for them, but also for others. Who knew them? Who got to hear of their wicked actions? or about their sad and deserved end? . . . Nobody . . . The earth covered everything up. But when the bodies of the executed were visible in the churchyards or piazzas, whether they were from the area or not, and when they were exposed to the sun and rain, things suddenly changed. The punishment served as a salutary example to the bad, and gave faith and courage to the good who then became tractable and even effusive." (De Jaco, *Il brigantaggio meridionale,* p. 53).

74. Letter dated May 1, 1864 (ACS 193/[misc. correspondence]).

75. ACS 193/(misc. correspondence), letter dated May 28, 1865. The quotations that follow are from ibid.

76. Ibid., letter dated June 18, 1865.

77. A. Blok, "The Peasant and the Brigand: Social Banditry Reconsidered," in *Comparative Studies in Society and History,* 14, 4 (1972), 494–503 (p. 502).

78. Ibid., p. 501.

79. E. Hobsbawm, "Social Bandits: Reply," in *Comparative Studies in Society and History,* 14, 4, (1972), 503–505. Having stated that "the myth cannot be entirely divorced from the reality of banditry," Hobsbawm briefly argues that the "social bandit" is chiefly the product of peasant expectations which are very difficult to realize given that the brigand is often forced to seek protection from the powerful. These ideas are left undeveloped as Hobsbawm tackles the question "Does he [the social bandit] exist at all?" (ibid., p. 504).

80. Massari's report to parliament categorically asserts, "they drink blood, they eat human flesh" (Pedìo, *Inchiesta sul brigantaggio,* p. 185).

81. Riviello, p. 357. The diary of a Swiss, I. Friedli, captured by a brigand band in the 1860s often describes how its members' favorite entertainment was telling stories, particularly about brigands: "We could only listen stupefied at how . . . one after they other, they told a sort of fairy story in one way or another. And what surprised me was that they did it with a talent, a skill of which I would

never have thought these extremely rough and uncultivated men capable" (A. Caiazza, *La banda Manzo* [Naples, Tempi Moderni, 1984], pp. 118–119). Before they become brigands, peasants are tellers of brigand stories.
82. C. Lévi-Strauss, *Le totémisme aujourd'hui* (Paris, Presses Universitaires, 1962), p. 132.

Chapter 2

1. See A. Asor Rosa, *La cultura* in *Storia d'Italia*, Vol. IV, *Dall'Unità a oggi*, 2 (Turin, Einaudi, 1975), p. 911.
2. P. Villari, "La camorra" (pp. 1–16) in "Le lettere meridionali" (pp. 1–74), *Le lettere meridionali ed altri scritti sulla questione sociale in Italia*, second edition (Turin, Bocca, 1885).
3. "La mafia," pp. 17–34 in ibid.
4. "Il brigantaggio," pp. 35–55 in ibid.
5. "I rimedii," pp. 56–70 in ibid., p. 67.
6. See, for example, C. Donzelli, "Mezzogiorno tra 'questione' e purgatorio. Opinione comune, immagine scientifica, strategie di ricerca," *Meridiana*, 9 (1990), 13–53.
7. Asor Rosa, *La cultura*, p. 920. For a comparable judgment from the conservative side, see E. Tagliacozzo, *Voci di realismo politico dopo il 1870* (Bari, Laterza, 1937). See also N. Zito, "Le inchieste del 1875–76 in Sicilia. Appunti per un'analisi comparata," in *Nuovi Quaderni del Meridione*, 51–2 (July-December 1975), 263–293 (p. 269) on their "lack of bias."
8. P. Villari, *Le prime lettere meridionali* (Rome, La Voce, 1920).
9. On Villari's early life and work, see M. L. Cicalese, *Note per un profilo di Pasquale Villari* (Rome, Istituto storico italiano per l'età moderna e contemporanea, 1979), pp. 9–53.
10. M. L. Salvadori, "Villari," in *Il mito del buongoverno. La questione meridionale da Cavour a Gramsci* (Turin, Einaudi, 1963), pp. 34–61 (p. 34). See also Asor Rosa, *La cultura*, p. 914.
11. See the extensive appraisal of Villari's changing reception by Mauro Moretti in "Preliminari ad uno studio su Pasquale Villari," *Giornale Critico della Filosofia Italiana*, V serie, LIX (LXI), fascicolo 1–4 (1980), 190–232, and "La storiografia italiana e la cultura del secondo ottocento. Preliminari ad uno studio su Pasquale Villari," *Giornale Critico della Filosofia Italiana*, V serie, LX, fascicolo 3 (1981), 300–372.
12. The best account of Villari's work on *la morale* and national character is in R. Romani, *L'economia politica del Risorgimento italiano* (Turin, Bollati Boringhieri, 1994), pp. 228–235.
13. "La filosofia positiva ed il metodo storico," in P. Villari, *Arte, storia e filosofia. Saggi critici* (Florence, Sansoni, 1884), pp. 437–489.
14. Maria Luisa Cicalese makes some interesting observations on Villari's ambiguities about the distinction between individual psychology and social life in *Note per un profilo di Pasquale Villari*, pp. 76–7.

15. "Tommaso Errico Buckle e la sua *Storia della civiltà*," *Nuova Antologia*, July 1, 1883, subsequently published in Villari, *Arte, storia e filosofia*, pp. 221–271.

16. On Villari's relationship to Mill in general, see N. Urbinati, *Le civili libertà. Positivismo e liberalismo nell'Italia unita* (Venice, Marsilio, 1990). Villari's idea of the moral and his project to understand and reform the national character bears the impress of Mill's notion of an ethology, or science of character, as projected in chapter V, book VI of *A System of Logic Ratiocinative and Inductive. Being a Connected View of the Principles of Evidence and the Methods of Scientific Investigation, Collected Works of John Stuart Mill*, vol. VIII, edited by J. M. Robson (Toronto, University of Toronto Press, 1974), pp. 861–874. On Mill's ethology see J. Carlisle, *John Stuart Mill and the Writing of Character* (Athens-London, University of Georgia Press, 1991), esp. pp. 127–167.

17. "Di chi è la colpa?" is in Villari, *Le lettere meridionali*, pp. 255–305. For a fuller account of the war, see G. Candeloro, *Storia dell'Italia moderna*, V, *La costruzione dello stato unitario, 1860–1871* (Milan, Feltrinelli, 1968), pp. 287–307. Cattaneo is quoted in ibid., p. 305.

18. "La scuola e la questione sociale in Italia," in Villari, *Le lettere meridionali*, pp. 147–204.

19. "Di chi è la colpa?," p. 299. In his review of Turiello's *Governo e governati in Italia* ("L'Italia giudicata da un meridionale," first published in *Nuova Antologia* December 1, 1883 and reproduced in Villari, *Le lettere meridionali*, pp. 101–143) Villari criticizes Turiello's use of a racially grounded national character to explain the country's problems. However, his objection is not to the category itself; rather, he accuses Turiello of failing to take account of the possibilities and realities of change and improvement in the character. Historical events such as "the history of our revolution" both affect and are affected by the national character (p. 103).

20. "Ciò che gli stranieri non osservano in Italia," Villari, *Le lettere meridionali*, pp. 227–251 (pp. 250–251). The essay dates from June 1877 and was first published in Germany in *Italia*, no. 4.

21. Cicalese says that the army and navy "were always close to Villari's heart" (Cicalese, *Note per un profilo*, 143). On the ideological role of the army in this period, see I. Porciani, *La festa della nazione. Rappresentazione dello Stato e spazi sociali nell'Italia unita* (Bologna, Il Mulino, 1997), pp. 78–88.

22. Speech to House of Deputies on the bill for an agrarian inquiry, April 26, 1876 in Villari, *Le lettere meridionali*, pp. 405–412 (p. 408). In the letter on brigandage published in March 1875 Villari cites the Massari report following the brigandage enquiry as an authoritative voice on the social problems in the South. He makes particular reference to General Govone's views and includes selections from his memoirs in "Le lettere meridionali." After the publication of his letters Villari was sent the memoirs of an officer who fought against the brigands and had come to similar conclusions about the causes of the problem; it is this text that he quoted in parliament.

23. "Regulations have become the bureaucracy's only anchor, its gospel, just as rhetoric is the gospel of pedants. But in the same way that rhetoric never made a writer, no regulations will be enough to form a good administration. The letter of the law has taken the place of its spirit, first because of difficulties in getting at the real purpose of our laws, and second because of the want for the authority needed to take on the responsibility for interpreting them" ("Di chi è la colpa?," pp. 276–277).

24. "Lettera VII," first published on October 20, 1861, Villari, *Le prime lettere meridionali*, pp. 49–65 (p. 62).

25. Cavalieri describes the equipment in his 1925 introduction to the second edition of the inquiry ("Introduzione alla seconda edizione," L. Franchetti and S. Sonnino, *Inchiesta in Sicilia*, Vol. I (Florence, Vallecchi, 1974), pp. vii–xlix (p. xiii)). The travelers also took folding campbeds and four copper basins each in which to bathe their feet as a precaution against insects.

26. R. De Mattei, "L'inchiesta siciliana di Franchetti e Sonnino," *Annali del Mezzogiorno*, Vol. III (1963), 113–147 (p. 113).

27. L. Franchetti, "Le condizioni economiche ed amministrative delle provincie napoletane," in *Mezzogiorno e colonie* (Florence, La Nuova Italia, 1950), pp. 3–152 (p. 52). Franchetti's earlier inquiry in the southern mainland is reputed to have been provoked by an English newspaper article that claimed that foreigners knew the Mezzogiorno better than the Italians did. See M. L. Salvadori, "Sonnino e Franchetti," in *Il mito del buongoverno. La questione meridionale da Cavour a Gramsci* (Turin, Einaudi, 1963), pp. 62–114 (p. 73).

28. S. Sonnino, *I contadini in Sicilia*, Vol. II of Franchetti and Sonnino, *Inchiesta in Sicilia*. On Sonnino's economic and political beliefs, and on the intellectual background to the *Inchiesta* in general, see Z. Ciuffoletti, "Nota storica" in Franchetti and Sonnino, *Inchiesta in Sicilia*, Vol. II, pp. 281–343.

29. L. Franchetti, *Condizioni politiche e amministrative della Sicilia*, Vol. I of Franchetti and Sonnino, *Inchiesta in Sicilia*.

30. On the problems of defining the mafia and delimiting the field of study, see for example chapter 1 of S. Lupo, *Storia della mafia dalle origini ai nostri giorni* (Rome, Donzelli, 1993), pp. 3–18. For a survey of the different schools of thought on the mafia, see R. Spampinato, "Per una storia della mafia. Interpretazioni e questioni controverse," in M. Aymard and G. Giarrizzo (eds.), *Storia d'Italia. Le regioni dall'Unità a oggi. La Sicilia* (Turin, Einaudi, 1987), pp. 881–902. The diversity of the most recent approaches emerges clearly in the debate between Diego Gambetta, Salvatore Lupo, Paolo Pezzino, and Nicola Tranfaglia, "La mafia e la sua storia. Radici locali e dimensione internazionale," *Passato e Presente*, 31 (1994), 19–40.

31. D. Gambetta, *The Sicilian Mafia. The Business of Private Protection* (Cambridge, Mass., Harvard University Press, 1993), p. 2.

32. P. Pezzino, "Nota introduttiva," in L. Franchetti, *Condizioni politiche e amministrative della Sicilia* (Rome, Meridiana, 1992), pp. xii–xx (p. xv).

33. C. Tullio-Altan, *La nostra Italia. Arretratezza socioculturale, clientelismo, trasformismo e ribellismo dall'Unità ad oggi* (Milan, Feltrinelli, 1986), p. 60.

This much criticized study of Italy's "socio-cultural backwardness," of the missing sense of civic responsibility in the national mentality, explicitly takes its ethical and scientific cue from *Condizioni.*

34. Gambetta, *The Sicilian Mafia,* p. 2. Gambetta's book puts forward an elegant argument for the case that *mafiosi* are distinguished from criminal entrepreneurs, extortionists, and hired enforcers by the fact that their central concern is the provision of protection backed by violence, a business that can be interpreted in commercial terms.

35. Lupo does, however, point out that Franchetti is better than his epigones in marking a distinction between the cultural background and the autonomous class of criminals, Lupo, *Storia della mafia,* pp. 31–38. His critique of Franchetti is part of his broader case. He takes an inductive approach, using predominantly judicial sources to tell the story of the mafia as the story of specific historical actors.

36. See, for example, F. Renda, "La 'questione sociale' e i Fasci (1874–94)," in Aymard and Giarrizzo (eds.), *La Sicilia,* pp. 157–188 (pp. 169–171). On the Right and public order in Sicily, see L. Riall, *Sicily and the Unification of Italy: Liberal Policy and Local Power, 1859–1866* (Oxford, Oxford University Press, 1998).

37. See M. I. Finley, D. Mack Smith, and C. Duggan, *A History of Sicily* (London, Chatto and Windus, 1986), p. 189. For the origins of the southern question in the political events of the years from 1874 to 1876, see G. Procacci, *Le elezioni del 1874 e l'opposizione meridionale* (Milan, Feltrinelli, 1956), especially pp. 9–16.

38. *La Perseveranza,* May 31, 1874, quoted in Procacci, *Le elezioni del 1874,* p. 27; D. Pantaleoni, "Le ultime elezioni politiche in Italia," *Nuova Antologia,* 12 (1874), 928–944 (p. 929).

39. On the commonplace image of an inherently "rebellious" Sicily, see A. Recupero, "La Sicilia all'opposizione (1848–74)," in Aymard and Giarrizzo (eds.), *La Sicilia,* pp. 39–85.

40. See, among others, P. Pezzino, "Stato, violenza, società. Nascita e sviluppo del paradigma mafioso," in Aymard and Giarrizzo (eds.), *La Sicilia,* pp. 903–982 (pp. 913–921).

41. On the official inquiry, see the account in G. C. Marino, *L'opposizione mafiosa (1870–1882). Baroni e mafia contro lo stato liberale* (Palermo, Flaccovio, 1964), pp. 137–157.

42. U. Zanotti-Bianco, *Meridione e meridionalisti* (Rome, Collezione Meridionale Editrice, 1964), pp. 254–255. See also the account of Franchetti's death in ibid., pp. 261–263.

43. Quoted in G. Carocci, "La caduta della destra," *Belfagor,* January 31, 1955, 37–69 (p. 56). On the reception of the inquiry, see also Ciuffoletti, "Nota storica," pp. 330–332.

44. Sonnino was in Paris at the time of the Commune. For Sonnino on Tuscan sharecropping see "La mezzeria in Toscana" of 1874 in S. Sonnino, *Scritti e discorsi extraparlamentari,* Vol. I, *1870–1902* (Bari, Laterza, 1972),

pp. 105–149. See also F. Chabod, *Storia della politica estera italiana dal 1870 al 1896*, Vol. I, *Le premesse* (Bari, Laterza, 1951), p. 343–346, on the unimaginative, charity-based conclusions of other debates thrown up by the Commune and the extent of the general ignorance of the problems of the peasantry.

45. A. Jannazzo, "Introduzione" in L. Franchetti, *Politica e mafia in Sicilia. Gli inediti del 1876* (Naples, Bibliopolis, 1995), pp. 9–25 (pp. 18–19).

46. On the *Rassegna Settimanale,* see P. Carlucci, "La 'Rassegna Settimanale' (1878–1882). Il percorso originale di una rivista militante," in Massimo M. Augello *et al.* (eds.), *Le riviste di economia in Italia (1700–1900). Dai giornali scientifico-letterari ai periodici specialistici* (Milan, Franco Angeli, 1996), pp. 443–470.

47. See, for example, Francesco Barbagallo's introduction to Pasquale Villari, *Le lettere meridionali ed altri scritti sulla questione sociale in Italia* (Naples, Guida, 1979), pp. 5–19. See also Ciuffoletti, "Nota storica."

48. There are numerous versions of this "hiatus" reading: for example, M. Corselli, "Un esempio di ideologismo nella questione meridionale: l'inchiesta di Franchetti e Sonnino," *Nuovi Quaderni del Meridione,* 51–2 (July-December 1975), 17–35 (p. 32); also, Simone Gatto, "Attualità di un'inchiesta del 1876 sulla Sicilia," *Belfagor,* March 31, 1950 (229–233).

49. Alberto Asor Rosa refers to Franchetti's "scientific sangfroid," *La cultura,* p. 915.

50. See the section of the book entitled "How, according to the system of government in force in Italy, the dominant class is considered to be the interpreter of the needs of the whole population," pp. 208–10.

51. C. Vivanti, "Lacerazioni e constrasti," in *Storia d'Italia,* Vol. I, *I caratteri originali* (Turin, Einaudi, 1972), pp. 867–948 (p. 936).

52. Manlio Corselli remarks that in Franchetti, "there is no continuity between the various stages of civilization, rather there is a rigid opposition and distinction," "Un esempio di ideologismo nella questione meridionale," p. 27.

53. Corselli is astute on the implications of Franchetti's describing Sicily as feudal: "if Sicily is still a feudal world well into the nineteenth century, then at the opposite pole the Italian nation embodies . . . the constitutional state which has a mission to undertake" ("Un esempio di ideologismo nella questione meridionale," pp. 27–28). It has also been remarked that for Franchetti and Sonnino conditions in Sicily are "quite the reverse of the Italo-Tuscan and European stereotype," P. Mazzamuto, "La Sicilia di Franchetti e Sonnino e i suoi stereotipi socio-letterari," in *Nuovi Quaderni del Meridione,* 51–2 (July-December 1975) 36–67 (pp. 44–45).

54. A similarly normative and teleological vision of history underpins Franchetti's 1872 essay on local government, "Dell'ordinamento interno dei comuni in Italia," in *Mezzogiorno e colonie,* pp. 433–491, for example, in his assertion that England is the only place where the "natural" process in which private interests coalesce to form the basis for local government has actually happened historically (p. 438).

55. There is a contrast here between *Condizioni* and Franchetti's earlier inquiry in the mainland South in 1873 to 1874. Perhaps because of Franchetti's desire to shock his public into discussion and action, *Condizioni economiche e amministrative delle provincie napoletane* is a text in which ethnocentric keywords such as "barbarism," "savagery" and "primitive" proliferate. Of the poor state of agriculture in large areas of Calabria and Basilicata, he writes: "At the sight of that desolation, the outsider is tempted to think that in that village . . . there lives a particular kind of man who, in the midst of cultivated land, has preserved the lack of foresight characteristic of the savages of the American prairies, and who, after he has eaten well or badly, does not feel the desire that is common to all men to improve his own lot" (*Mezzogiorno e colonie*, pp. 59–60). Parts of the South are labeled as both several rungs behind the rest of Italy on the ladder of social evolution and yet also as almost a non-society, ignorant of or lacking in the moral and commercial fabric of civilization. Franchetti takes his cue from reports of the horrors of brigandage: "All of these facts seem contradictory to a man who is used to civilization. And when one contemplates them, they all seem equally to characterize that primitive state of being, a state of barbarism, ignorant of all of the relationships, the laws that hold the social fabric together, from the laws of the family to those of public order" (ibid., pp. 21–22). Both forms of thought tend to bar Franchetti from attributing any logic to important aspects of southern society in general and peasant culture in particular: that peasants prefer their "lurid" small towns and "dirty, unlit, airless" hovels to farmhouses in the fields is attributed to the blind force of custom rather than to the socioeconomic structure of southern agrarian life or even to an assessment of the dangers of malaria and banditry in the countryside. On the determinants of the "agro-town" structure of rural communities in Southern Italy and Sicily in particular, see, for example, A. Blok, *The Mafia of a Sicilian Village, 1860–1960: A Study of Violent Peasant Entrepreneurs* (Cambridge, Polity Press, 1988 [1974]).

56. Paolo Pezzino has pointed to the way Franchetti portrays "an anti-institutional middle class which is exactly the opposite of the middle class which had supported the rise and consolidation of liberal regimes across the whole of Europe," "Nota introduttiva," pp. xvii-xviii. One can only assume that Pezzino thinks that Franchetti is right.

57. Jane and Peter Schneider start from Sicily's position on the periphery of the global market and specify a type of "broker capitalism" (p. 11) predominant on the island. When Sicily was incorporated into the Italian state, it was this economy that shaped the mafia's mediating role. In such circumstances the mafia has an economic function in, for example, preserving technologically outdated and commercially conservative monopolies (p. 180), *Culture and Political Economy in Western Sicily* (London, Academic Press, 1976).

58. S. Lupo, *Il giardino degli aranci. Il mondo degli agrumi nella storia del Mezzogiorno* (Venice, Marsilio, 1990).

59. See Gambetta, *The Sicilian Mafia*.

60. For Gambetta's account of the origins of the mafia, see ibid., pp. 75–99.

61. Salvatore Lupo, *Storia della mafia dalle origini ai giorni nostri,* revised edition (Rome, Donzelli, 1997, pp. 54–63).

62. For Lupo's critique, see ibid., pp. 24–28. He criticizes Gambetta on a number of counts: for estimating the importance of a political dimension to the mafia; for underestimating the role of extortion as opposed to negotiated protection in mafia power; for constructing too neat a separation between the entrepreneur of protection and the protected entrepreneur or trafficker, figures often found combined in the individual *mafioso;* and for the way the patronage typical of *mafiosi* does not fit with the interpretation of the mafia as a business. For a comparative analysis of Lupo and Gambetta, see M. Marmo, "Le ragioni della mafia: due recenti letture di storia politica e sociologia economica," *Quaderni Storici,* 88 (1995), 195–212.

63. See Franchetti, *Politica e mafia in Sicilia,* in which many opinions on criminality and the mafia are reported without comment by the author. If anything emerges from this text, it is the variety of meanings attributed to the term "mafia." In the revised edition of his *Storia della mafia,* Lupo points out that some of the Sicilians interviewed by Franchetti were *mafiosi* whose explanation of the word "mafia" as a special feeling of pride proper to the Sicilian character was actually the mafia's own "official" and deliberately misleading view. Less convincingly, Lupo suggests that Franchetti has adopted this theory from his sources and merely given it a pejorative coloring, pp. 74–78.

64. R. Fucini, *Napoli a occhio nudo* (Turin, Einaudi, 1976); P. Turiello, *Governo e governati in Italia* (Turin, Einaudi, 1980).

65. Piero Bevilacqua has recently argued this case. See P. Bevilacqua, "New and old in the southern question," *Modern Italy,* 1, 2 (1996), 81–92. See also the subsequent debate between Bevilacqua and Anna Cento Bull: A. Cento Bull, "The South, the state and economic development: remarks on Piero Bevilacqua's 'Old and new in the southern question,'" *Modern Italy,* 2, 1/2, (1997), 72–76; P. Bevilacqua, "A reply to Anna Bull," *Modern Italy,* 2, 1/2, (1997), 77–80.

Chapter 3

1. Its original title, *La Nuova Illustrazione Universale,* was changed in October 1875.

2. The technical achievements of the Treves were viewed by Eugenio Torelli-Viollier with a degree of patriotic pride: "they created a school for wood engraving headed by the excellent Foli, an electrolysis workshop, a photoengraving studio, and they managed to give them such a great level of artistic and commercial development that, where once we only ever saw foreign stereotypes in Italian magazines, we now very often have the pleasure of seeing Italian illustrations copied by foreign magazines," "Movimento librario," in *Mediolanum* III (Milan, Vallardi, 1881), pp. 341–361 (pp. 346–347).

3. M. Grillandi, *Emilio Treves* (Turin, UTET, 1977), p. 436.

4. The indicator of the commercial success of magazines compared to literature is from Grillandi, p. 410. Mario Bonetti comments that "The Treves brothers' tills were the coffers which subsidized Italian literature for almost half a century," M. Bonetti, *Storia dell'editoria italiana* (Rome, Gazzetta del Libro, 1960), p. 102.

5. See A. Gigli Marchetti, "Lo stato e i caratteri dell'industria tipografica," in *I tre anelli. Mutualità, resistenza, cooperazione dei tipografi milanesi (1860–1925)* (Milan, Franco Angeli, 1983), pp. 9–33.

6. The Treves archive, which had passed on to Garzanti, was destroyed by Allied bombing during the Second World War. The only (isolated and unsubstantiated) figure I have been able to discover for the magazine's circulation is 15,000, quoted in N. Bernardini (ed.), *Guida della stampa periodica italiana* (Lecce, Tipografia Editrice Salentina, 1890), p. 518.

7. A. Comandini, a close colleague of Treves's, quoted in Grillandi, p. 319.

8. "The Treves supplied the reading matter for the Italian bourgeoisie of the Umbertian era, and they were already feeding the lesser bourgeoisie . . . that was just becoming aware of itself with the spreading range of social classes brought into being by economic progress and industrialization," Bonetti, p. 103.

9. "Milan was once described as Italy's moral capital. The truth of that statement is proved by the extraordinary progress that some book and magazine publishers have had in our city," *Mediolanum* IV, p. 240. On the "myth of the moral capital" see G. Rosa, *Il mito della capitale morale. Letteratura e pubblicistica a Milano fra Otto e Novecento* (Milan, Edizioni di Comunità, 1982). On the limits of middle-level culture in Naples, by comparison, see P. Macry, "La Napoli dei dotti. Lettori, libri e biblioteche di una ex-capitale (1870–1900)," *Meridiana*, 4 (1988), 131–161.

10. See D. Forgacs, *Italian Culture in the Industrial Era 1880–1980. Cultural industries, politics and the public* (Manchester, Manchester University Press, 1990), pp. 33–34.

11. Bernardini, *loc. cit.*

12. From the front page of year 1884.

13. Emilio Treves dominated the *Illustrazione Italiana* during the Umbertian period. Treves was born in Trieste in 1834 into a Piedmontese-Jewish family. The death of his father forced him to abandon a precocious career in theatrical writing to work in publishing and journalism, which he pursued in several different places, including Paris, before settling for good in Milan in 1858. Treves fought under Garibaldi in 1859 but remained throughout his life a man of the moderate Right. Treves's career as a publisher in his own right began with the launch of *Il Museo di Famiglia*, "the magazine which is truly for families and the people," in 1862 (quoted in Grillandi, p. 265). In the expanding publishing market opened up by unification, Treves built up a magazine and book list while continuing his journalistic activity. In 1871 he joined forces with his more commercially minded brother Giuseppe, and

their publishing company rapidly developed into one of the most powerful in the country, with a dominance in the literary market. In 1875 Emilio was elected president of the Associazione libraria italiana, the organization of publishing, printing, and bookselling interests.

14. Two examples are the items on Pope Leo XIII in *Illustrazione Italiana,* September 28, 1884 and January 1, 1888.

15. See for example the satirical illustration "La donna emancipata" on the cover of the issue of March 13, 1881.

16. Where possible, references from the *Illustrazione Italiana* will be given in the text with the date of the issue and page number.

17. For an account of the pilgrimage, see B. Tobia, *Una patria per gli italiani. Spazi, itinerari, monumenti nell'Italia unita (1870–1900)* (Rome-Bari, Laterza, 1991), pp. 130–142.

18. See *Mediolanum* IV, p. 241. Of the 972 different titles printed, 235 were counted as "novels, short stories, travel literature," making up by far the biggest category. But this number did not include the 79 "comedies, dramas, tragedies" and the 42 "poems." The second biggest category, that of "scientific and philosophical books," included 111 titles.

19. On *Margherita* in particular, and on nineteenth-century women's fashion magazines in Italy in general, see S. Franchini, "Moda e catechismo civile nei giornali delle signore italiane," in S. Soldani and G. Turi (eds.), *Fare gli italiani. Scuola e cultura nell'Italia contemporanea,* vol. 1, *La nascita dello Stato nazionale* (Bologna, Il Mulino, 1993), pp. 341–383 (pp. 378–380).

20. U. Eco, "La struttura del cattivo gusto," in *Apocalittici e integrati* (Milan, Bompiani, 1964), pp. 65–129 (p. 71).

21. See, for example, "Conversazioni letterarie," January 22, 1882, p. 70, and March 11, 1883, p. 148.

22. What follows is an analysis of the specific variety of connotations given to the picturesque in the *Illustrazione Italiana.* The term obviously has an important role in other contexts, notably in eighteenth-century British landscape aesthetics, although, as is well known, it showed itself to be a particularly vague concept even then. See S. Copley and P. Garside, "Introduction" in S. Copley and P. Garside (eds.) *The Politics of the Picturesque. Literature, landscape and aesthetics since 1770* (Cambridge, Cambridge University Press, 1994), pp. 1–12.

23. On Verdi's *Aida* and its place in European representations of the colonial world, see E. Said, *Culture and Imperialism* (London, Vintage, 1994), pp. 133–159.

24. February 17, 1884, p. 107. The author is commenting on a drawing by Fausto Zonaro set in Naples, "The song of the day."

25. E. W. Said, *Orientalism* (Harmondsworth, Penguin, 1978), pp. 58–59.

26. In the middle of the quoted passage ("In essence such a category . . . some established view of things") Said attempts to assert a distinction between the role of orientalist discourse and the cognitive function of language in general ("a way of receiving new information"). In order to make that distinction, however, he has to imply an impoverished definition of orientalism

(compared to the central theoretical tenets of his text) as a hidebound view of the world, an "established view of things."

27. *Illustrazione Italiana*, March 20, 1881, p. 180. The next two quotations are from the same reference. It is possible that Lazzaro never went to Casamicciola after the earthquake: the local detail he gives could be read as protesting too much. Whether or not he actually went to the island does not change what I have to say below.

28. For a compelling account of the epidemic, see F. M Snowden, *Naples in the Time of Cholera, 1884–1911* (Cambridge, Cambridge University Press, 1995), pp. 59–178. Estimates of the total number of deaths varied from the 7,143 recorded at the municipal cemetery to the 18,000–20,000 considered a more honest figure by the *Times* (ibid., pp. 104–105).

29. On Umberto's visit, see Snowden, pp. 163–169.

30. Tobia argues that the monarchy was influenced by its perceived role in the South. His hypothesis is based on an interesting reading of statues on the facade of the Royal Palace in Naples (*Una patria per gli italiani*, pp. 165–167).

31. *Illustrazione Popolare*, September 14, 1884 "The cholera in Naples—a poor quarter." The illustration is on p. 577, the text on p. 578.

32. Ibid., October 12, 1884, "King Umberto's return from Naples—The King's arrival at Milan Central Station," p. 649.

33. Ibid., October 5, 1884, p. 626. The two illustrations are on pp. 628–629: "Present times: Public prayers to stop the cholera in Naples"; "Old times: Public absolution for those dying of the plague in Florence—year 1348."

34. On the cult of Queen Margherita see G. Bollati, "Il modo di vedere italiano (note su fotografia e storia)," in *L'italiano. Il carattere nazionale come storia e come invenzione* (Turin, Einaudi, 1983), pp. 124–178 (pp. 153–156).

35. For another example see "Il ramadan," *Illustrazione Italiana*, August 29, 1880, p. 139.

36. As late as November 9, 1884 in the *Illustrazione Italiana*, Treves could write "Italy does not have, nor can it have, great colonial adventures" (p. 291). The free gift for subscribers to the magazine for 1888 was a map of the theater of war in Ethiopia.

37. "S. Giovanni degli Eremiti a Palermo," July 11, 1880, p. 31. Although the examples examined in this chapter are all of comparisons between Sicily and the Orient or Africa, Naples is also the subject of such comparisons. One of a regular series of letters from Naples in the *Illustrazione Italiana* of October 1, 1876 describes how convincingly a group of people were dressed as Arabs for a festival: "and if there wasn't much Arab in them, there was a lot of Neapolitan: because it almost amounts to the same thing" (p. 286).

38. Lombrosian theories were similarly appropriated. In November 1882 Lombroso contributed a piece on "Crime in the popular mentality" that argued that certain popular proverbs displayed a primitive awareness of some of criminal anthropology's findings (ibid., November 5, 1882, p. 299). The attribution of a timeless, homely wisdom to the peasantry very much fitted in with the *Illustrazione Italiana*'s favored themes.

39. The same points can be made about the *Illustrazione Italiana's* commentary on the etching "La carovana" printed in March 1883: "Marinelli's painting is a merry composition. Characteristic types abound in it: Turks, Egyptians, Circassians, Bedouins, Persians, Moors, Negroes, Nubians, old men with their great white beards yellowing around their mouths, camels and camel-drivers, bundles, fluttering rags, people on foot and on horseback. The whole thing is a feast of varied colours, of clashes and harmonies of shade, and its rich composition portrays an oriental caravan in the most picturesque way" (ibid., March 11, 1883, p. 154). From using type to imply racial group at the beginning of the list, the article moves to pointing out any features of the illustration that are picturesque, a term that here serves as a commonplace identifier of the exotic. The figures gathered in the etching are once again bound together not by any feature common to them but by a taste for their colorful effect when juxtaposed.

40. November 4, 1883, p. 299, "Scorse letterarie" on Francesco Torraca's *Studi di storia letteraria napoletana*.

41. See F. Renda, *I Fasci siciliani (1892–94)* (Turin, Einaudi, 1977).

42. See M. Douglas, *Purity and Danger* (London, ARK, 1984).

43. All quotations from the story are taken from *Illustrazione Italiana*, July 13, 1890, p. 26; July 20, 1890, pp. 38–39. The version published in *Storie d'amore e di dolore* (Milan, Chiesa & Guindani, 1893), pp. 251–282 has some slight changes.

44. Much speculation was generated about the identity behind the pseudonym. Eventually Sommaruga's own *Cronaca Bizantina* was "forced" to publish a portrait of the (very beautiful) Contessa Lara on February 16, 1883 (4, III, vol. I). See G. Squarciapino, *Roma bizantina. Società e letteratura ai tempi di Angelo Sommaruga* (Turin, Einaudi, 1950), pp. 172–180.

45. The novel was recently republished: *L'innamorata* (Rome, Il Sigillo, 1981). Further information on Contessa Lara can be found in: R. Barbiera, *Il salotto della contessa Maffei* (Milan, Garzanti, 1943), pp. 312–315; M. Borgese, *La contessa Lara. Una vita di passione e di poesia nell'ottocento italiano* (Milan, Treves, 1938).

46. See Franchini, p. 379.

47. "La contessa Lara—Annie Vivanti," in *La letteratura della nuova Italia. Saggi critici*, Vol. II (Bari, Laterza, 1914), pp. 315–333 (p. 321). See also the judgment of Sergio Romagnoli, for whom Contessa Lara's realism "only has aspirations to a private meaning, like a diary or a secret confided between women," *Storia della letteratura italiana*, Vol. VIII, *Dall'Ottocento al Novecento* (Milan, Garzanti, 1968), pp. 592–596 (p. 592).

48. Contessa Lara's writing is in fact replete with stereotypes of the South: I will cite only the sonnet "Amore meridionale" ("Southern Love" from *E ancora versi* (Florence, Sersale, 1886), pp. 147–148) because of the final narrative twist that makes it comparable to "Un omicida." The poem tells the story of a southern man whose love is "wild and hot-tempered / sudden, capricious, like his sea." His lover, unaware of the dangers, laughs at this tragic passion:

"But she laughed no more the day when, in a new / torment he drove a blade into her heart / in a last, insane embrace."

49. Many of the ethical and political questions that stereotypes raise derive from the fact that it is not possible to draw a distinction, other than a willed one, between the workings of harmless and harmful stereotypes. As I will argue below, for example, positive and negative stereotypes are in some ways interdependent. The theoretical problems associated with stereotypes are further complicated by the difficulties involved in deciding what is, and what is not, a stereotype. This is not just because one person's cliché will seen by another as the truth. If a differentiating effect is central to stereotypical discourse, how does one distinguish it from the differentiating effects in all kinds of language use? In other words, to talk of stereotypes as a distinct mode of representation, one has, in the last analysis, to stereotype them. The problem is related to the questions of iterability and recognition discussed in J. Derrida, "Signature Event Context," in *Margins of Philosophy* (Brighton, Harvester, 1982), pp. 307–330.

50. H. Bhabha, "The Other question. Stereotype, discrimination and the discourse of colonialism," in *The Location of Culture* (London, Routledge, 1994), pp. 66–84 (p. 75). For a very acute account and critique of Bhabha's work on colonial discourse, see R. Young, "The ambivalence of Bhabha," in *White Mythologies. Writing History and the West* (London, Routledge, 1990), pp. 141–156. I should make it clear that, in using Bhabha's work on colonial stereotypes, I am in no way suggesting that the stereotypes of southern Italy I analyze here have a straightforward colonial situation as their historical background.

51. See S. Freud, "On fetishism" (1927), in *On Sexuality* (Harmondsworth, Penguin, 1977), pp. 345–357.

52. See, for example, the following untenable generalization: "The objective of colonial discourse is to construe the colonized as a population of degenerate types on the basis of racial origin," Bhabha, "The Other question," p. 70.

53. Freud assumes, for example, that all fetishists are male. The question of translating the theory of fetishism to the issue of race is only incompletely addressed in Bhabha, "The Other question," p. 78.

54. The theatrical version of this story is in G. Verga, *Teatro* (Milan, Garzanti, 1987), pp. 207–229.

55. One need only think of the many invocations of the army's "moralizing" role in the work of Pasquale Villari.

56. "Un omicida" may also be read as differentiating a middle-level cultural ethos from a higher one. As the wife of a general, Contessa Lara's central character would have been above the social station of the average reader of the *Illustrazione Italiana*. It is likely that her behavior would, to that readership, have seemed an example of a certain dangerous bohemianism to which the wealthy were considered to be prone.

57. A. Nozzoli, "La letteratura femminile in Italia tra Ottocento e Novecento," in *Tabù e coscienza. La condizione femminile nella letteratura italiana del Novecento* (Florence, La Nuova Italia, 1978), pp. 1–40.

Chapter 4

1. R. Romanelli, *L'Italia liberale (1861–1900)* (Bologna, Il Mulino, 1979), p. 353. See also the classic C. Salinari, *Miti e coscienza del decadentismo italiano (d'Annunzio, Pascoli, Fogazzaro e Pirandello)* (Milan, Feltrinelli, 1960).

2. See S. Lanaro, *L'Italia nuova* (Turin, Einaudi, 1988), pp. 151–156. Lanaro's analysis is suggestive but problematic on a number of counts, including its uncritical adoption of a Weberian model of charisma as set out in M. Weber, *The Theory of Social and Economic Organization* (New York, Free Press of Glencoe, 1964), pp. 358–392. Among other problems, Weber's theory seems to me to be based on a rigid dualism between rational and irrational forms of political discourse.

3. S. Lanaro, *Nazione e lavoro. Saggio sulla cultura borghese in Italia, 1870–1925* (Venice, Marsilio, 1979), pp. 190–217, and "Il Plutarco italiano: l'istruzione del 'popolo' dopo l'Unità," in C. Vivanti (ed.), *Storia d'Italia*, Annali 4, *Intellettuali e potere* (Turin, Einaudi, 1981), pp. 553–587; U. Levra, "Il Risorgimento nazional-popolare di Crispi," in *Fare gli Italiani. Memoria e celebrazione del Risorgimento* (Turin, Comitato di Torino dell'Istituto per la Storia del Risorgimento Italiano, 1992), pp. 299–386.

4. Denis Mack Smith argues that he was a "volcanic revolutionary by temperament" and claims that "like many Sicilians he was proud and oversensitive to criticism," *Italy—A Modern History* (Michigan, University of Michigan Press, 1959), p. 138. Mack Smith cites Guglielmo Ferrero's *Il fenomeno Crispi e la crisi italiana* (Turin, Roux and Frassati 1894) as the source of some of his opinions on Crispi: a clear indicator of the origins of his argument in an insufficiently critical reading of the sources relating to the charisma question. Massimo Grillandi attributes his authoritarianism in part to the same cause: "As a good southerner, Crispi knew how much importance needs to be given, in moments of transition, to the police," *Francesco Crispi* (Turin, UTET, 1969), p. 408. Sergio Romano mentions many of Crispi's "southern" qualities, such as superstition, and identifies in him a personality split between a pugnacious patriotism derived from his southern nature and conditioning, and a political culture that he acquired later in life: "His love for Italy, his nationalism and his touchiness when it came to anything that might offend or diminish the *patria* corresponded to his southern temperament and education . . . By contrast, his liberal and social impulses originated in his legal training and juridical knowledge. . . . Power forced him to choose and reveal his true self," *Crispi—progetto per una dittatura* (Milan, Bompiani, 1973), pp. 167–168.

5. See, for example, "La Sicilia di Crispi" by Gaetano Falzone in *Rassegna Storica Toscana*, XVI, 1 (1970), 25–35, "In the end, Sicily was only a contributory factor in shaping the way in which Crispi was made ready for *italianità* and parliamentary democracy" (p. 35).

6. In the hope of currying favor, Sicilian citizens who wrote to Crispi often appealed to his *sicilianità*, but in this case what was invoked was obviously

common origins on the island rather than the ensemble of commonplaces that is the subject of this chapter. See D. Adorni, "Lettere ai potenti: i siciliani che scrivevano a Crispi e a Rudinì (1887–1898)," *Studi Storici,* 2 (1994), 327–403.

7. As is well known, some northern socialist writers saw Crispi as the product of reactionary, feudal forces originating in the "barbaric" society of the island. The discussion of Crispi in *Critica Sociale* in the spring of 1898 is an interesting example. See pp. xl-xli of Mario Spinella, "Politica e ideologia politica" in M. Spinella *et al.* (eds.), *Critica Sociale,* Vol. I (Milan, Feltrinelli, 1959), pp. ix-lxxix. F. Fonzi, *Crispi e lo "stato di Milano"* (Milan, Giuffré, 1965), particularly chapters VII (pp. 219–256) and X (pp. 335–362), is fundamental for the attitudes of Milanese socialists to Crispi and the South.

8. According to Silvio Lanaro, Crispi's monarchism "was not based on an acquiescence to dynastic feeling; rather it took the form of a saddened conviction that the fragility of unification created the urgent need for a symbol, for the kind of solemn pledge of no return which no system centered on a republican assembly could guarantee," "Il Plutarco italiano," p. 556. Crispi made no reference to the monarchy in the speech he made on taking office: for the immediate context of his election as Speaker of the Chamber, see R. Colapietra (ed.), *Storia del parlamento italiano,* Vol. VIII, *La Sinistra al potere* (Palermo, Flaccovio, 1975), pp. 65–67.

9. F. Crispi, "Crispi Presidente della Camera," in *Discorsi parlamentari di Francesco Crispi,* vol. 2 (Rome, Tipografia della Camera, 1915), pp. 287–288 (p. 287).

10. See G. Procacci, *Le elezioni del 1874 e l'opposizione meridionale* (Milan, Feltrinelli, 1956).

11. Procacci quotes the northern conservative organ, *La Perseveranza:* "they [southerners] are less fit to govern Italy and feel less of a calling to do so because they have a worse understanding than anyone of the Italian conception of politics," May 31, 1874, quoted in ibid., p. 27.

12. See R. Romanelli, "Francesco Crispi e la riforma dello stato nella svolta del 1887," in *Il comando impossibile. Stato e società nell'Italia liberale,* second edition (Bologna, il Mulino, 1995), pp. 279–351 (p. 314).

13. The administrative reforms juggled demands for greater democratization and/or devolution with the overriding urge simply to streamline the centralized structures within which the liberal state had always responded to regional pressures (see Romanelli, "Francesco Crispi e la riforma dello stato"). Elsewhere Romanelli contrasts the "undoubted openings toward a liberal position" of Crispi's legislation in the field of civil and political rights with a tendency to "make the system's social defences more rigid" (*L'Italia liberale,* p. 349).

14. The press of the Left in general and the Crispian press in particular stressed this message: "Let us put to one side the legitimate pride that we islanders must feel more strongly than others, knowing that this man is the son of the glorious land of the Vespers. We are products of his school: for us the region,

and the town bell-tower have never counted for anything," *Giornale di Si-cilia,* October 29, 1887. The contrast of regional provenance, among many other things, between Crispi and his predecessor, Depretis, would also have highlighted his *meridionalità.*

15. F. Crispi, "A Torino," speech given October 25, 1887, in *Scritti e discorsi politici (1849–1890)* (Rome, Unione Cooperativa Editrice, 1890), pp. 695–712 (p. 696).

16. See Procacci. An anecdotal example of this sensitivity comes from 1889, when the parliamentary leader of the radicals, Felice Cavallotti, even fought a duel with a General Corvetto on the merest suspicion that the General had voiced such prejudice. The incident followed the publication of a letter written by the General some eleven years previously in which he reported from his posting in Palermo that "Italy is lucky that it only has one Sicily." The event is discussed in the "La settimana" section of the *Illustrazione Italiana,* March 31, 1889, p. 210. By contrast, see below for the ethnocentrism displayed by one of Cavallotti's lieutenants, Achille Bizzoni.

17. *Corriere della Sera,* October 29–30, 1887.

18. See F. Bonini, "Il mito Crispi nella propaganda fascista," *Rivista di Storia Contemporanea,* 4 (1981), 548–574.

19. Quoted in A. Casulli, *Giorgio Arcoleo,* second edition (Rome, Voghera, 1914), p. 43. Casulli also portrays Arcoleo as having "the indomitable energy of the island temperament" (p. 129) and as being "rich in the most fervid southern vivacity" (p. 130) in the concluding pages of his biography.

20. See also "Canti del popolo in Sicilia," *Opere,* I, *Studii e profili* (Milan, Mondadori, 1929), pp. 121–135, first published by Morano in Naples (1878) as the text of a speech given to De Sanctis's *Circolo filologico* in the city, May 1878. Arcoleo argues that, despite all of the invasions, the Sicilian people has maintained more than any other "its autonomous character, a certain barbaric and savage something, a feeling of its own superiority, a perennial rebelliousness against something indefinite" (p. 123). Sicilian popular song can be regarded as a "a faithful portrait of a semi-barbaric society which is unexplored and unknown" (p. 148). See also "Palermo e la cultura in Sicilia," in *Opere,* I, *Studii e profili* (Milan, Mondadori, 1929), pp. 205–243. The essay is the transcript of a paper given May 15, 1897 in Milan to the *Circolo filologico* that was translated into French and published by Guillaumin, Paris, 1898. In it, Arcoleo offers a racial-characterological history of the island, and concludes with a portrait of its nature today which will be picked up textually in his biography of Crispi: "And, like nature, the race displays contrasts: it has nordic and oriental elements; here it is Greece, there it is Africa; here it is a Nation, there it is a tribe; here it is legend and there history. In the Sicilians' deference for status, their long silences, and their cult of arcane powers one can see the adoring and self-abnegating Semite or Oriental. In their frenzied desire for conquest, their love of adventure, their feeble mettle, and their invasive fanaticism, one can see the Arab, the Orient itself struggling and expanding," p. 207.

21. G. Arcoleo, *Francesco Crispi* (Milan, Treves, 1905), pp. 10, 9, 52, 50. For a comparable interpretation of Crispi's character, See also W. J. Stillman, *Francesco Crispi—Insurgent, Exile, Revolutionist and Statesman* (London, Grant Richards, 1899). Stillman was Rome correspondent of the *Times* between 1886 and 1898 and, being very close to Crispi, was often used by him to spread official thinking. Stillman regards the Albanian roots of Crispi's family as important and compares him to Skanderberg, fifteenth-century Albanian national hero and hammer of the Turks: "To those who know the race of Skander Beg, its intellectual force, tenacity, craftiness, and curious mixture of passionless temperament with volcanic temper; cold calculating and deliberate when something has to be planned, and patient and tenacious in the carrying out of the plan; faithful to death where faith is due; honest as day where personal fidelity demands it, and crafty as a red Indian where an enemy is to be guarded against, the character of Crispi will be the cropping out of the typical individuality of the race. The roots of his nature were Skipetar, and his training Sicilian, the Italian temperament has nothing to do with either, though the southern sun and its quickening have probably their share of the result," pp. 23–24.

22. E. Ragionieri, *La storia politica e sociale, Storia d'Italia*, vol. 4, tomo 3 (Turin, Einaudi, 1976), p. 1814.

23. A. C. Jemolo, *Francesco Crispi* (Florence, Le Monnier, 1970), p. 99.

24. See Fonzi, *Crispi e lo "stato di Milano."*

25. A. Guiccioli, "Diario del 1892," *Nuova Antologia*, 1626, December 16, 1939, 364–381 (p. 370). Guiccioli, born in Venice in 1843, was a conservative diplomat, politician, and civil servant from one of the country's patrician families who came to have a "profound aversion for democratic and parliamentary institutions," M. Casella, "Il marchese Alessandro Guiccioli, parlamentare, prefetto e diplomatico dell'Italia postunitaria," *Archivio Storico Italiano*, 2 (1994), 317–396 (p. 331). On the radical doubts expressed even by Italian liberals about the parliamentary system, see A. M. Banti, "Retoriche e idiomi: l'antiparlamentarismo nell'Italia di fine Ottocento," *Storica*, I, 3 (1995), 7–41, and *Storia della borghesia italiana. L'età liberale* (Rome, Donzelli, 1996), pp. 237–270.

26. See S. Sighele, *Contro il parlamentarismo*, first published 1895, reprinted in appendix to *La delinquenza settaria* (Milan, Treves, 1897), pp. 229–274. The essay attempts to solve the riddle of the Italian parliament, namely that "party discipline is missing or weak where it would be needed, and yet it can be found in a dubious, camorristic form," p. 231. Sighele's antiparliamentarism was part of a highly individual political profile: he became a forthright irredentist and presided over the first conference of the Italian Nationalist Association in 1911, yet he also had sympathies with Enrico Ferri's brand of socialism and there were strong liberal influences on his thought. Yet many aspects of *Contro il parlamentarismo* relate closely to themes in the wider antiparliamentary culture of Umbertian Italy. See E. Landolfi, *Scipio Sighele. Un giobertiano tra democrazia nazionale e socialismo tricolore* (Rome, Volpe, 1981). Under the

pseudonym of "Sigma," Sighele also wrote a crime column for the *Illustrazione Italiana*. There are some useful observations on Sighele's crowd theory in D. Pick, *Faces of Degeneration: a European disorder, c. 1848–c. 1918* (Cambridge, Cambridge University Press, 1989), pp. 93–94 and 121–122.

27. P. Villari, "Dove andiamo?," *Nuova Antologia*, November 1, 1893, 5–24 (p. 8). Niceforo later repeats the argument Villari is criticizing in *L'Italia barbara contemporanea*. The "spagnolismo" ("Spanishry," or "Spanish practices") typical of the South has, through parliament, made the whole country backward and southern (p. 304). As Angelo Majorana observed in his *Del parlamentarismo* published by Loescher in Rome in 1885, Spain had become a byword for the corruption of parliamentary institutions in the Latin countries. The term "spagnolismo" also frequently connoted quasi-feudal Bourbon misrule that Niceforo associates with the governments of his time: "Bourbonism and misgovernment made Southern Italy barbaric; current governments are destroying and killing the whole of Italy" (*op. cit,* p. 304).

28. See A. Briganti, *Il parlamento italiano nel romanzo italiano del secondo ottocento* (Florence, Le Monnier, 1972).

29. A. Bizzoni, *L'Onorevole* (Milan, Sonzogno, 1895), p. 89.

30. See the discussion of Fogazzaro's politics in Salinari, *Miti e coscienza*, p. 196 ff.

31. A. Fogazzaro, *Daniele Cortis* (Milan, Mondadori, 1980), p. 52.

32. P. Turiello, "Il secolo XIX," in *Il secolo XIX ed altri scritti di politica internazionale e coloniale* (Bologna, Zanichelli, 1944), pp. 3–105 (pp. 53–56). Turiello's arguments are a development of ideas he put forward as early as 1881 in *Governo e governati in Italia* (Turin, Einaudi, 1980).

33. Gabriele D'Annunzio, *Le vergini delle rocce* (Milan, Mondadori, 1978), pp. 57 and 89.

34. "In the same individual,—Siculan fibre, Italian soul—the revolutionary and the Statesman were fused without cancelling each other out," G. Arcoleo, "Francesco Crispi: oratore," *L'Eloquenza*, 1912, 1–2 (1–12), p. 7.

35. G. Siculo, *Francesco Crispi a Torino* (Turin, Casanova, 1887), p. 31 (my emphasis).

36. G. Pieragnoli, *Francesco Crispi* (Rome, Pasqualini, 1887), p. 8. The book is part of a series of political profiles; it gives a very favorable impression of Crispi.

37. C. Rosani, *A S.E. Francesco Crispi Presidente del Consiglio* (privately published in Milan, 1894[?]), pp. 5–6, 7.

38. G. d'Annunzio, *Tutte le opere. Tragedie, sogni e misteri,* 1 (Milan, Mondadori, 1968), pp. 341–461 (p. 400).

39. Some of the less inhibited critics of Crispi are N. Morelli, *Gli orrori e le turpitudini del governo Crispi* (Rome, Ciotola, 1890); G. Brandini, *La Crispiade o Doncicceide ossia le glorie di don Ciccio il grande* (Rome, Tipografia degli operai, 1894); "Dottor Calce," *Italia o Crispalia?* (Sandrio, Quadrio, 1895); and N. V. Colella, *L'ombra di Cavour* (Bari, Fusco, 1890).

The last of these, a satirical dialogue in verse between Crispi and Cavour's ghost, is unequivocal in its references to "this Pluto with a Sicilian face" (p. 18) and his "Moslem despotism" (p. 25). "Dottor" [Giuseppe] Calce, eccentric propagator of his own brand of philosophical-literary-scientific-mystical thought, does not conceal his ethnocentric contempt for "Allah Caesar Crispi" (p. 12): "God and Crispi are colleagues; God's only advantage is his age . . . In fact, Crispi invokes him, as do his Neapolitan compatriots when they are in danger of shipwreck. And, after the panic has subsided, they mock him as they eat their maccheroni" (p. 17).

40. *Illustrazione Italiana,* January 13, 1895, p. 19.

41. B. Galletti, *L'attualità e l'onorevole Francesco Crispi* (Palermo, Spinnato, 1890), pp. 42–3.

42. For one of Crispi's critics who sees him as over-imaginative, see the portrait by Matilde Serao in *Il Mattino,* January 10–11, 1894, which describes him as a "novelist," endowed with an "unbridled imagination" and living in his own fictional world. The quotation is from V. Riccio, *I meridionali alla camera,* vol. 1 (Turin, Roux, 1888), pp. 1–2.

43. Riccio, pp. xiii, 5. See also F. Narjoux, *Francesco Crispi—l'homme public, l'homme privé* (Paris, Savine, 1890). Narjoux's book is an attempt from France to rectify Gallic "misunderstandings" of Crispi: "The Sicilian . . . is noble and dignified; he has Arab blood in his veins. His pride is extreme, he likes grandeur, titles, things that satisfy his self-esteem; he would like to be first in everything. Crispi is Sicilian," p. 295.

44. A. Oriani, *Punte secche, Opera omnia,* Vol. XXIII (Bologna, Cappelli, 1934), pp. 108–109.

45. D. Farini, *Diario di fine secolo,* 2 vols. (Rome, Bardi, 1961), pp. 176–177. Guiccioli is of course commenting on the formation of Crispi's government at the end of 1893.

46. The quotation is from Guiccioli's diary on September 14, 1889 after a stone thrown from the crowd had hit Crispi on the head in Naples: "These attacks are the product of wicked propaganda against the most elevated principles and against the men who personify them," A. Guiccioli, "Diario del 1889," *Nuova Antologia,* December 1, 1938 (1601), 273–295 (p. 289).

47. Sergio Romano has observed that "In theory nothing would prevent Northern Italian newspapers from using Crispi's *sicilianità* as material for satire. However, regional references are rare, at least in the best cartoons. One is led to believe that the artists as well obeyed what amounted to the new state's code of honor decreeing that the peninsula's inhabitants were 'Italians' first of all, and that any allusion to their specific regional identity was unpatriotic," S. Romano, *Crispi* (Milan, Bompiani, 1986), p. 282. Romano's case needs some elaboration and qualification. It would be a mistake, as I hope to have made clear, to think that only in Northern Italy was Crispi likely to be conceived of in terms that today would be thought prejudiced. It is also wrong to assume that such notions were always negatively connoted in any straightforward way. For some interesting but unsystematic observations on

satirical representations of Crispi, see V. Tedesco, *La stampa satirica in Italia 1860–1914* (Milan, Franco Angeli, 1991), pp. 99–106, and pp. 120–125.

48. The image of Crispi is one which, according to Romano (*op cit*), has its origins in the French press. For example, the Bolognese *La Rana* produced twin cartoons entitled "The miracle of the pistol," which illustrate contrasting public attitudes to Crispi as first a brigand, his foot resting on the severed head of Liberty, and then an angel floating on a cloud of popularity. The accompanying text accounts for the transformation with reference to a recent assassination attempt. And while associations with the South are made via Crispi's superstitiousness, the commentator's license is earned by objections to such "exaggerations" and an affirmation of support for Crispi as "the only possible man for government in the current predicament," *La Rana,* June 22–23 1894. The most frequent themes in caricatures of Crispi are an ancient Roman setting or variations on his admiration for Bismarck. In the case of the latter, many cartoons play on the physical resemblance between the two statesmen. John Grand-Carteret produced a collection of *Crispi, Bismarck et la Triple Alliance en caricatures* (Paris, Delagrave, 1891), in which he makes well-informed comments on the background to the illustrations. He identifies a comic contrast in the subtext of Crispi-Bismarck comparisons: "Crispi is Italian mixed with Arab, just as Bismarck is a German mixed with Borussian. From a racial point of view, the former is from the extreme South, the latter from the extreme North," p. 64. If Grand-Carteret is right, even when it is not specifically mentioned, Crispi's *sicilianità* lurks in the *déjà-lu* of cartoon and written portrayals of him.

49. See E. W. Lane, *An Account of the Manners and Customs of the Modern Egyptians* (London, J. Murray, 1860), pp. 451–456. See also the entry under "Dawsa" in *The Encyclopaedia of Islam,* new edition, vol. 2 (Leiden, Brill, 1965), pp. 181–182. My thanks are due to Simonetta Calderini of SOAS for this information.

50. "Il ritorno del tappeto dalla Mecca, dipinto da Teja." Originally published in *Il Pasquino,* October 23, 1887. Reproduced here from A. Ferrero (ed.), *Caricature di Teja (dal Pasquino)* (Turin, Roux & Viarengo, 1900), p. 284. The caption reads, "Faith is a fine thing, as long as it does not reach such a point of self-abnegation." Ferrero, commenting on the cartoon, writes, "With the death of Depretis, one star has dimmed, but another has begun to shine: Crispi. In Parliament and in the country today, he finds before him the same submissiveness that was once experienced by Depretis. Everyone gathers faithfully round him, everyone bows before him. . . . Faith is a good thing, Teja is saying, but it should not become fanaticism which leads to self-abnegating servility and suicide as it does with the Moslems."

51. "La visite des Marocains a Crispi." Originally published in *Il Fischietto,* January 21, 1890. Reproduced here from Grand-Carteret, *Crispi, Bismarck et la Triple Alliance,* p. 217. Grand-Carteret's translation of the accompanying text is as follows: "The Rome newspapers report that Crispi gave a splendid and extremely courteous reception to the Maroccan delegation. He led his

illustrious visitors through the galleries of his historical Museum, and gave them the most detailed explanation of each object he has preserved there, from Garibaldi's red shirt (1860) to Bismarck's greatcoat. Then, with his large horn-shaped coral amulet flashing in their eyes, he said, 'Here, gentlemen, is the secret of my great power, my talisman against my enemies, . . . I show it sometimes, but I am never without it.' At that point, the astonished ambassadors cried out, 'May Allah keep it safe for you for a long time to come!'" Grand-Carteret points out that the large number of elephant tusks represent Italy's African power and that the statue of three Graces is yet another reference to Crispi's three wives.

52. For Ferrero, Crispi also has a very active imagination, which is far more inclined to be "fictitious" than "realistic." Like a poet, his thought oscillates between extremes. In him, passion is stronger than reason. He is mentally juvenile. See Ferrero, *Il fenomeno Crispi e la crisi italiana*, pp. 11–21.

53. Ferrero, pp. 28–35. The concept of the "type" obviously had strong racial connotations. Ferrero argues that "with his policy of surprises, with the passion he brings to everything, with his gigantic personal pride, with the impulsive audacity that comes over him sometimes, and with the ostentatiousness of his private life which is so distinct from most people's habits, Crispi grabs the crowd's crude imagination and can easily appear to be a superior and providential man" (p. 38).

54. Siculo, *Francesco Crispi a Torino*, p. 35. Siculo was the pseudonym of a "distinguished politician" according to *Il Secolo XIX*, October 24, 1887.

55. C. Del Balzo, *Le ostriche* (Milan, Aliprandi, 1901), pp. 198, 190. The novel was part of a series, *I deviati*, by the same author. Del Balzo also contributed frequently to the *Illustrazione Italiana*. His articles on Naples, written very much in the key of the picturesque, were published in 1884 as *Napoli e i napoletani* (Rome, Edizioni dell'Ateneo, 1972). He was born in the province of Naples in 1853.

56. Quotations from L. Fortis, *Francesco Crispi* (Rome, Voghera, 1895), pp. 8 and 5. Fortis, born in 1824 in Trieste, wrote the "Conversazioni" of "Doctor Veritas," which appeared in the *Illustrazione Italiana* and later in *Vita Italiana*.

57. The pseudonymous "Dottor Calce" also dwells on Crispi's power over the masses, who are won over "with the undue psychological influence of imposture." His particular achievement is to have appropriated for large-scale daily use the "the modern system of hypnotic suggestion," *Italia o Crispalia?*, pp. 23, 19.

58. E. Di Natale, *A Francesco Crispi—Canto politico* (Siracuse, Norcia, 1892), pp. 4–5. Di Natale was a local literary figure in Siracuse, and the author of a series of commemorative poems and speeches.

59. Contemplating the surrounding countryside from the summit he asserts, "The people alone, with its melancholy song, has sculpted the beauties of this its enchanted Italy," Fucini, *Napoli a occhio nudo* (Turin, Einaudi, 1976), p. 108.

60. The following extract is from a character sketch by Ruggero Bonghi, a prominent politician from the southern Right: "Normally he is in control of himself. Yet on occasion he lets his real nature win out: he is like a volcano which, in tranquil periods, builds up fire in its womb, and then suddenly bursts into flame, burning the orchards and woods which it had allowed to sprout and flourish on its slopes," "Francesco Crispi," first published in *La Tribuna Illustrata,* February 1893 and reproduced in R. Bonghi, *Ritratti e profili di contemporanei,* vol. 1 (Florence, Le Monnier, 1935), pp. 335–339 (p. 337). Vincenzo Riccio has doubts about Crispi's temperament: "I hope for his sake that, with his willpower, he is able to subdue his hasty temperament in just the same way (to use a fine image of his) that the snow lies white and peaceful on the summit of Mount Etna while the fiery matter boils within its bosom" (Riccio, p. 139). See also Salvatore Barzilai's description of "the cutting words brought to his mouth by his blood which boils like the lava of Mount Etna," *Vita parlamentare* (Rome, Nazionale, 1912), p. 43. Barzilai was a Triestine journalist Crispi elected to parliament in 1890 under the banner of the extreme Left.

61. Fortis, p. 11. See also: "His faith in himself reaches the point of superstition (he is not a southerner for nothing), as is proved by the coral amulet he carries on his watch-chain" (p. 12).

62. See the stimulating pages on *crispismo* in Lanaro, *Nazione e lavoro,* especially pp. 190–217, and "Il Plutarco italiano," pp. 553–563.

63. Lanaro, "Il Plutarco italiano," p. 554. Christopher Duggan argues that a project of "national education" had been the element of continuity in Crispi's career since unification: C. Duggan, "Francesco Crispi, 'political education' and the problem of Italian national consciousness, 1860–96," *Journal of Modern Italian Studies,* 2, 2 (1997), 141–66.

64. "Crispi was the one to reassert that the 'bourgeoisie' still had every right to be the sole, true protagonist of the nation's political life. On this basis he managed to gather a bloc around him which overcame parliamentary divisions and enabled him to carry out most of a daring and coherent policy programme which tackled every aspect of the crisis," G. Manacorda, *Crisi economica e lotta politica in Italia 1892–1896* (Turin, Einaudi, 1968), p. 110.

65. In this very limited sense, Crispi's *sicilianità* would echo the way in which, according to some readings, he was part of a European trend in the age of Imperialism for "outsiders," leaders from the ranks of democratic politics, to enact the policies of the ruling class. See, for example, Ragionieri, *La storia politica e sociale,* p. 1753.

66. On Dogali see R. Battaglia, *La prima guerra d'Africa* (Turin, Einaudi, 1973), p. 262. On Aigues Mortes see R. Paris, "L'Italia fuori d'Italia," in *Storia d'Italia,* vol. IV, *Dall'Unità a oggi,* 1 (Turin, Einaudi, 1975), pp. 509–818 (pp. 535–541).

67. Fulvio Cammarano refers to the "the psychological rather than political feeling" in the public mood surrounding Crispi's succession to Depretis in 1887, *Il progresso moderato,* p. 36. Francesco Brancato argues that the extra-

ordinary political tension generated by the battles between Crispi and his radical enemies during his second period in office cannot be understood without "a whole psychological context," *Storia del parlamento italiano,* vol. X, p. 69. Manacorda writes powerfully about a widespread crisis in the forty days between the fall of Giolitti and the declaration of the "state of siege" in Sicily at the end of 1893: "a moral crisis, a sense of bewilderment and guilt, the anxious search for a way out," Manacorda, *Crisi economica e lotta politica,* p. 106.

68. The quotation is from the *Illustrazione Italiana,* January 14, 1894, p. 18, referring to the Sicilian *Fasci.*

69. Manacorda, *Crisi economica e lotta politica.* G. Manacorda, "Crispi e la legge agraria per la Sicilia," in *Il movimento reale e la coscienza inquieta. L'Italia liberale e il socialismo e altri scritti tra storia e memoria* (Milan, Franco Angeli, 1992), pp. 15–84.

Conclusion

1. See, for example, E. Gentile, *L'Italia giolittiana* (Bologna, Il Mulino, 1977).

2. See the accounts in: A. Galante Garrone, "Prefazione," in U. Zanotti-Bianco, *Carteggio 1906–18* (Rome-Bari, Laterza, 1987), pp. vii–xxiv; P. Amato, "Zanotti-Bianco e l'associazionismo democratico nel Mezzogiorno (1910–63)," in P. Amato (ed.), *Umberto Zanotti-Bianco meridionalista militante* (Venice, Marsilio, 1981), pp. 1–52; and U. Zanotti-Bianco, "Una piaga secolare del Mezzogiorno: la malaria," in *Meridione e meridionalisti,* (Rome, Collezione Meridionale, 1964), pp. 131–160.

3. L. Pirandello, *I vecchi e i giovani* (Milan, Mondadori, 1967), p. 441.

4. See, for example, M. Isnenghi, *Il mito della grande guerra* (Bologna, Il Mulino, 1989), pp. 398–404.

5. A. Soffici,"Diario napoletano," in *La giostra dei sensi,* fourth edition (Florence, Vallecchi, 1943), pp. 63, 52.

6. See, from the growing literature on the League, R. Biorcio, "La Lega come attore politico: dal federalismo al populismo regionalista," in R. Mannheimer (ed.), *La Lega Lombarda* (Rome, Feltrinelli, 1991), pp. 34–82; A. Cento Bull, "The Lega Lombarda. A new political sub-culture for Lombardy's localized industries," *The Italianist,* 12 (1992), 179–183, "The politics of industrial districts in Lombardy: replacing Christian Democracy with the Northern League," *The Italianist,* 13 (1993), 209–229, and "Ethnicity, racism and the Northern League," in C. Levy (ed.), *Italian Regionalism. History, Identity and Politics* (Oxford, Berg, 1996); I. Diamanti, *La Lega. Geografia, storia e sociologia di un nuovo soggetto politico* (Rome, Donzelli, 1993).

7. I. Diamanti, "La Lega, imprenditore politico della crisi. Origini, crescita e successo delle leghe autonomiste in Italia," *Meridiana,* 16 (1993), 99–133.

8. Quoted in *La Repubblica,* April 7, 1992.

9. E. Said, *Orientalism* (London, Penguin, 1985), p. 103.

10. Quoted in L. Costantini, *Dentro la Lega. Come nasce, come cresce, come comunica* (Rome, Koinè, 1994), p. 155.

11. See Biorcio: "The Lombard League thus found itself dealing with problems entirely analogous to those which emerged during the processes which brought about the construction of nation-states" (p. 67).

12. For further considerations on the Lega in relation to the history of stereotypes of the Mezzogiorno, see my "The South as Other: From Liberal Italy to the Lega Nord," in A. Cento Bull and A. Giorgio (eds.), *Culture and Society in Southern Italy. Past and Present,* supplement to *The Italianist,* 14 (1994), 124–140.

13. A. M. Banti, *Storia della borghesia italiana. L'età liberale* (Rome, Donzelli, 1996), pp. 213–236.

Bibliography

Adorni, D. "Lettere ai potenti: i siciliani che scrivevano a Crispi e a Rudinì (1887–1898)," *Studi Storici,* 2 (1994), 327–403.

Alatri, P. "Le condizioni dell'Italia meridionale in un rapporto di Diomede Pantaleoni a Marco Minghetti (1861)," *Movimento Operaio,* 5–6 (1953), 750–92.

Albanese, A. "Crimini e criminalità in Terra di Bari nell'età della Restaurazione (1818–1835). Le comitive armate," in A. Massafra (ed.) *Il Mezzogiorno preunitario. Economia, società e istituzioni.* Bari, Dedalo, 1988, pp. 1055–1068.

Alighieri, D. *The Divine Comedy,* translated and with a commentary by C. S. Singleton. Princeton, Princeton University Press, 1977.

Alvazzi del Frate, P. "Giustizia militare e brigantaggio. Il tribunale di guerra di Gaeta (1863–5)," in *Rassegna Storica del Risorgimento,* IV (1985), 447–464.

Amato, P. "Zanotti-Bianco e l'associazionismo democratico nel Mezzogiorno (1910–63)," in P. Amato (ed.) *Umberto Zanotti-Bianco meridionalista militante.* Venice, Marsilio, 1981, pp. 1–52.

Anderson, B. *Imagined Communities. Reflections on the Origin and Spread of Nationalism,* revised edition. London, Verso, 1991.

Arcoleo, G. *Francesco Crispi.* Milan, Treves, 1905.

Arcoleo, G. "Francesco Crispi: oratore," *L'Eloquenza,* 1912, 1–2, (1–12).

Arcoleo, G. *Opere,* I, *Studii e profili.* Milan, Mondadori, 1929.

Artom, E. "Il Conte di Cavour e la questione napoletana" in B. Caizzi (ed.) *Antologia della questione meridionale.* Milan, Edizioni di Comunità, 1955, pp. 251–263.

Asor Rosa, A. *La cultura* in *Storia d'Italia,* Vol. IV, *Dall'Unità a oggi,* 2. Turin, Einaudi, 1975.

Asor Rosa, A. *Scrittori e popolo. Il populismo nella letteratura italiana contemporanea,* second edition. Turin, Einaudi, 1988.

Atti Parlamentari, Sessione del 1863, Discussioni, August 1, 1863.

Autuori, M. "Storia sociale della banda Capozzoli (1817–1827): lotte municipali e brigantaggio," in A. Massafra (ed.) *Il Mezzogiorno preunitario. Economia, società e istituzioni.* Bari, Dedalo, 1988, pp. 1127–1141.

Banti, A. M. "Retoriche e idiomi: l'antiparlamentarismo nell'Italia di fine Ottocento," *Storica,* I, 3 (1995), 7–41.

Banti, A. M. *Storia della borghesia italiana. L'età liberale.* Rome, Donzelli, 1996.

Banti, A. M. "Comunità immaginarie," *Storica,* 6, 1996, 189–194.

F. Barbagallo, "Introduzione," in P. Villari, *Le lettere meridionali ed altri scritti sulla questione sociale in Italia.* Naples, Guida, 1979, pp. 5–19.

Barbagli, M. *Disoccupazione intellettuale e sistema scolastico in Italia (1859–1973).* Bologna, Il Mulino, 1974.

Barbiera, R. *Il salotto della contessa Maffei.* Milan, Garzanti, 1943.

Barzilai, S. *Vita parlamentare.* Rome, Nazionale, 1912.

Battacchi, M. W. *Meridionali e settentrionali nella struttura del pregiudizio etnico in Italia,* second edition. Bologna, Il Mulino, 1972.

Battaglia, R. *Risorgimento e Resistenza.* Rome, Editori Riuniti, 1964.

Battaglia, R. *La prima guerra d'Africa.* Turin, Einaudi, 1973.

Bernardini, N. (ed.) *Guida della stampa periodica italiana.* Lecce, Tipografia Editrice Salentina, 1890.

Bertelli, C. and G. Bollati. *Storia d'Italia, Annali* 2, "L'immagine fotografica." Turin, Einaudi, 1979.

Bertoni Jovine, D. *Storia dell'educazione popolare in Italia.* Bari, Laterza, 1965.

Bevilacqua, P. *Breve storia dell'Italia meridionale dall'Ottocento a oggi.* Rome, Donzelli, 1993.

Bevilacqua, P. "New and old in the southern question," *Modern Italy,* 1, 2 (1996), 81–92.

Bevilacqua, P. "A reply to Anna Bull," *Modern Italy,* 2, 1/2, (1997), 77–80.

Bhabha, H. *The Location of Culture.* London, Routledge, 1994.

Bianco di Saint Jorioz, A. *Il brigantaggio alla frontiera pontificia, 1860–63.* Milan, Daelli, 1864.

Biorcio, R. "La Lega come attore politico: dal federalismo al populismo regionalista," in R. Mannheimer (ed.) *La Lega Lombarda.* Rome, Feltrinelli, 1991, pp. 34–82.

Bixio, N. *Epistolario,* Vol. II (1861–5). Rome, Vittoriano, 1942.

Bizzoni, A. *L'Onorevole.* Milan, Sonzogno, 1895.

Blok, A. "The Peasant and the Brigand: Social Banditry Reconsidered," in *Comparative Studies in Society and History,* 14, 4 (1972), 494–503.

Blok, A. *The Mafia of a Sicilian Village, 1860–1960. A Study of Violent Peasant Entrepreneurs.* Cambridge, Polity Press, 1988.

Bocca, G. *L'inferno. Profondo sud, male oscuro.* Milan, Mondadori, 1992.

Bollati, G. "L'italiano," in R. Romano and C. Vivanti (eds.) *Storia d'Italia, I caratteri originali,* Vol. II, 951–1022. Turin, Einaudi, 1972.

Bollati, G. "Il modo di vedere italiano (note su fotografia e storia)," in *L'italiano. Il carattere nazionale come storia e come invenzione.* Turin, Einaudi, 1983, pp. 124–178.

Bonetti, M. *Storia dell'editoria italiana.* Rome, Gazzetta del Libro, 1960.

Bonghi, R. *Ritratti e profili di contemporanei,* Vol. 1. Florence, Le Monnier, 1935.

Bonini, F. "Il mito Crispi nella propaganda fascista," *Rivista di Storia Contemporanea,* 4 (1981), 548–574.

Borgese, M. *La contessa Lara. Una vita di passione e di poesia nell'Ottocento italiano.* Milan, Treves, 1938.

Boswell, J. *Life of Johnson,* edited by G. Birkbeck Hill, Vol. II (1765–1776). Oxford, Clarendon, 1887.

Bourelly, G. *Brigantaggio nelle zone militari di Melfi e Lacedonia dal 1860 al 1865.* Naples, Mea, 1865.

Brandini, G. *La Crispiade o Doncicceide ossia le glorie di don Ciccio il grande.* Rome, Tipografia degli operai, 1894.

Briganti, A. *Il parlamento italiano nel romanzo italiano del secondo ottocento.* Florence, Le Monnier, 1972.

Brunello, P. *Ribelli, questuanti e banditi. Proteste contadine in Veneto e Friuli 1814–1866.* Venice, Marsilio, 1981.

Buffa di Perrero, C. *Biografia del Conte Gustavo Mazé de la Roche.* Turin, Bocca, 1888.

Buttà, G. *Un viaggio da Boccadifalco a Gaeta. Memorie della rivoluzione del 1860 al 1861.* (1875) Naples, Benso, 1966.

Cafagna, L. "Italy 1830–1914," in C. Cipolla (ed.) *The Fontana Economic History of Europe,* Vol. IV, *The Emergence of Industrial Societies,* Part One. London, Collins/Fontana, 1973, pp. 279–328.

Caiazza, A. *La banda Manzo.* Naples, Tempi Moderni, 1984.

Candeloro, G. *Storia dell'Italia moderna,* Vol. V, *La costruzione dello stato unitario, 1860–1871.* Milan, Feltrinelli, 1968.

Carcani, F. *Sul brigantaggio—osservazioni.* Trani, Cannone, 1863.

Carlisle, J. *John Stuart Mill and the Writing of Character.* Athens-London, University of Georgia Press, 1991.

Carlucci, P. "La 'Rassegna Settimanale' (1878–1882). Il percorso originale di una rivista militante," in M. M. Augello *et al.* (eds.) *Le riviste di economia in Italia (1700–1900). Dai giornali scientifico-letterari ai periodici specialistici.* Milan, Franco Angeli, 1996, pp. 443–470.

Carocci, G. "La caduta della destra," *Belfagor,* January 31, 1955, 37–69.

Casella, M. "Il marchese Alessandro Guiccioli, parlamentare, prefetto e diplomatico dell'Italia postunitaria," *Archivio Storico Italiano,* 2 (1994), 317–396.

Casulli, A. *Giorgio Arcoleo,* second edition. Rome, Voghera, 1914.

Cavalieri, E. "Introduzione alla seconda edizione," in L. Franchetti and S. Sonnino, *Inchiesta in Sicilia,* Vol. I. Florence, Vallecchi, 1974, pp. vii-xlix.

Cavour, C. *Carteggi: la liberazione del Mezzogiorno e la formazione del Regno d'Italia,* Vol. III (October-November 1860). Bologna, Zanichelli, 1952.

Cento Bull, A. "The Lega Lombarda. A new political sub-culture for Lombardy's localized industries," *The Italianist,* 12 (1992), 179–183.

Cento Bull, A. "The politics of industrial districts in Lombardy: replacing Christian Democracy with the Northern League," *The Italianist,* 13 (1993), 209–229.

Cento Bull, A. "Ethnicity, racism and the Northern League," in C. Levy (ed.) *Italian Regionalism. History, Identity and Politics.* Oxford, Berg, 1996.

Cento Bull, A. "The South, the state and economic development: remarks on Piero Bevilacqua's 'Old and new in the southern question,'" *Modern Italy,* 2, 1/2, (1997), 72–76.

Cesari, C. *Il brigantaggio e l'opera dell'esercito italiano dal 1860 al 1870.* Rome, Ausonia, 1920.

Chabod, F. *Storia della politica estera italiana dal 1870 al 1896,* Vol. I, *Le premesse.* Bari, Laterza, 1951.

Cicalese, M. L. *Note per un profilo di Pasquale Villari.* Rome, Istituto Storico Italiano per l'Età Moderna e Contemporanea, 1979.

Ciuffoletti, Z. "Nota storica" in L. Franchetti and S. Sonnino, *Inchiesta in Sicilia.* Florence, Vallecchi, 1974, Vol. II, pp. 281–343.

Clifford, J. "On Orientalism," in *The Predicament of Culture. Twentieth Century Ethnography, Literature, and Art.* Cambridge, Mass., Harvard University Press, 1988, pp. 255–276.

Codice penale militare per gli stati di S.M. il Re di Sardegna. Turin, Fodratti, 1859.

Colapietra, R. (ed.) *Storia del parlamento italiano,* Vol. VIII, *La Sinistra al potere.* Palermo, Flaccovio, 1975.

Colella, N. V. *L'ombra di Cavour.* Bari, Fusco, 1890.

"Il concetto storico spaziale di regione: una identificazione controversa," debate between various authors including Immanuel Wallerstein, *Passato e Presente,* 9, 1985, 13–37.

Contessa Lara, *E ancora versi.* Florence, Sersale, 1886.

Contessa Lara, "Un'omicida," in *Storie d'amore e di dolore,* Milan, Chiesa & Guindani, 1893, pp. 251–282.

Contessa Lara, *L'innamorata.* Rome, Il Sigillo, 1981.

Copley, S. and P. Garside, "Introduction" in S. Copley and P. Garside (eds.) *The Politics of the Picturesque. Literature, landscape and aesthetics since 1770.* Cambridge, Cambridge University Press, 1994, pp. 1–12.

Corselli, M. "Un esempio di ideologismo nella questione meridionale: l'inchiesta di Franchetti e Sonnino," *Nuovi Quaderni del Meridione,* 51–2 (July-December 1975), 17–35.

Costantini, L. *Dentro la Lega. Come nasce, come cresce, come comunica.* Rome, Koinè, 1994.

Costantini, P. *Silvio Spaventa e la repressione del brigantaggio.* Pescara, Attraverso l'Abruzzo, 1960.

Craveri, P. "Un nuovo meridionalismo," *La Rivista dei Libri,* 1, 1993, 11–13.

Crispi, F. "A Torino," in *Scritti e discorsi politici (1849–1890).* Rome, Unione Cooperativa Editrice, 1890, pp. 695–712.

Crispi, F. "Crispi Presidente della Camera," in *Discorsi parlamentari di Francesco Crispi,* Vol. 2. Rome, Tipografia della Camera, 1915, pp. 287–288.

Croce, B. "La contessa Lara—Annie Vivanti," in *La letteratura della nuova Italia. Saggi critici,* Vol. II. Bari, Laterza, 1914, pp. 315–333.

D'Annunzio, G. *Tutte le opere. Tragedie, sogni e misteri,* 1. Milan, Mondadori, 1968.

D'Annunzio, G. *Le vergini delle rocce.* Milan, Mondadori, 1978.

Davis, J. A. *Conflict and Control. Law and Order in Nineteenth-Century Italy.* London, Macmillan, 1988.

Davis, J. A. "Changing perspectives on Italy's 'southern problem,'" in C. Levy (ed.) *Italian Regionalism. History, Identity and Politics.* Oxford, Berg, 1996, pp. 53–68.

De Jaco, A., ed. *Il brigantaggio meridionale: cronaca inedita dell'unità d'Italia.* Rome, Editori Riuniti, 1969.

Del Balzo, C. *Le ostriche.* Milan, Aliprandi, 1901.

Del Balzo, C. *Napoli e i napoletani.* Rome, Edizioni dell'Ateneo, 1972.

Della Rocca, E. *The Autobiography of a Veteran.* London, Unwin, 1899.

De Marchi, E. *Demetrio Pianelli.* Milan, Mondadori, 1979.

De Mattei, R. "L'inchiesta siciliana di Franchetti e Sonnino," *Annali del Mezzogiorno,* Vol. III (1963), 113–147.

Derrida, J. "Signature Event Context," in *Margins of Philosophy.* Brighton, Harvester, 1982, pp. 307–330.

Derrida, J. "Racism's Last Word," in H. L. Gates Jr. (ed.) *"Race," Writing, and Difference.* Chicago, Chicago University Press, 1986, pp. 329–338.

De Ruggieri, N. "Indagine antropologica su la personalità del brigante Giuseppe Nicola Summa, detto Ninco-Nanco," in *Archivio storico per la Calabria e la Lucania,* XLII (1975), 231–233.

De Seta, C. "L'Italia nello specchio del Grand Tour," in C. De Seta (ed.) *Storia d'Italia, Annali* 5, "Il paesaggio." Turin, Einaudi, 1982, pp. 125–263.

Diamanti, I. *La Lega. Geografia, storia e sociologia di un nuovo soggetto politico.* Rome, Donzelli, 1993.

Diamanti, I. "La Lega, imprenditore politico della crisi. Origini, crescita e successo delle leghe autonomiste in Italia," *Meridiana,* 16 (1993), 99–133.

Dickie, J. "The South as Other: From Liberal Italy to the Lega Nord," in A. Cento Bull and A. Giorgio (eds.) *Culture and Society in Southern Italy. Past and Present,* supplement to *The Italianist,* 14 (1994), 124–140.

Dickie, J. "*La macchina da scrivere:* the Victor Emmanuel monument and Italian nationalism," *The Italianist,* 14 (1994), 261–285.

Dickie, J. "Imagined Italies," in D. Forgacs and R. Lumley (eds.) *Italian Cultural Studies. An Introduction.* Oxford, Oxford University Press, 1996, pp. 19–33.

Dickie, J. "Many Souths: many stereotypes," *Modern Italy,* 4 (1) 1999, 79–86.

Di Natale, E. *A Francesco Crispi—Canto politico.* Siracuse, Norcia, 1892.

Donzelli, C. "Mezzogiorno tra 'questione' e purgatorio. Opinione comune, immagine scientifica, strategie di ricerca," *Meridiana,* 9, 1990, 13–53.

Doria, G. *Per la storia del brigantaggio nelle province meridionali.* Naples, extract from *Archivio Storico per le Province Napoletane,* 1931.

"Dottor Calce," *Italia o Crispalia?* Sandrio, Quadrio, 1895.

Douglas, M. *Purity and Danger.* London, ARK, 1984.

Duggan, C. *Fascism and the Mafia.* New Haven, Yale University Press, 1989.

Duggan, C. "Francesco Crispi, 'political education' and the problem of Italian national consciousness, 1860–96," *Journal of Modern Italian Studies,* 2, 2 (1997), 141–66.

Dumas, A. père. *Cento anni di brigantaggio nelle province meridionali d'Italia,* translated by E. Torelli. Naples, De Marco, 1863.

Eco, U. "La struttura del cattivo gusto," in *Apocalittici e integrati.* Milan, Bompiani, 1964, pp. 65–129.

Encyclopaedia of Islam, new edition, Vol. 2. Leiden, Brill, 1965.

Falzone, G. "La Sicilia di Crispi," *Rassegna Storica Toscana,* XVI, 1 (1970), 25–35.

Farini, D. *Diario di fine secolo,* 2 vols. Rome, Bardi, 1961.

Feld, M. D. *The Structure of Violence: Armed Forces as Social Systems.* Beverly Hills/London, Sage, 1977.

Ferrero, A., ed. *Caricature di Teja (dal Pasquino).* Turin, Roux & Viarengo, 1900.

Ferrero, G. *Il fenomeno Crispi e la crisi italiana.* Turin, Roux and Frassati, 1894.

Finley, M. I., D. Mack Smith, and C. Duggan. *A History of Sicily.* London, Chatto and Windus, 1986.

Fiume, G. "Bandits, violence and the organization of power in Sicily in the early nineteenth century," in J. A. Davis and P. Ginsborg (eds.) *Society and Politics in the Age of the Risorgimento. Essays in honour of Denis Mack Smith.* Cambridge, Cambridge University Press, 1991, pp. 70–91.

Fogazzaro, A. *Daniele Cortis.* Milan, Mondadori, 1980.

Fonzi, F. *Crispi e lo "stato di Milano."* Milan, Giuffré, 1965.

Forgacs, D. *Italian Culture in the Industrial Era 1880–1980. Cultural industries, politics and the public.* Manchester, Manchester University Press, 1990.

Fortis, L. *Francesco Crispi.* Rome, Voghera, 1895.

Foucault, M. *Surveiller et punir. Naissance de la prison.* Paris, Gallimard, 1975.

Franchetti, L. *Mezzogiorno e colonie.* Florence, La Nuova Italia, 1950, pp. 3–152.

Franchetti, L. *Condizioni politiche e amministrative della Sicilia,* Vol. I of L. Franchetti and S. Sonnino, *Inchiesta in Sicilia.* Florence, Vallecchi, 1974.

Franchetti, L. *Politica e mafia in Sicilia. Gli inediti del 1876.* Naples, Bibliopolis, 1995.

Franchini, S. "Moda e catechismo civile nei giornali delle signore italiane," in S. Soldani and G. Turi (eds.) *Fare gli italiani. Scuola e cultura nell'Italia contemporanea,* Vol. 1, *La nascita dello Stato nazionale.* Bologna, Il Mulino, 1993, pp. 341–383.

Franzina, E. *La transizione dolce. Storie del Veneto tra '800 e '900.* Verona, Cierre, 1991.

Freud, S. "On fetishism," in *On Sexuality.* Harmondsworth, Penguin, 1977, pp. 345–357.

Fucini, R. *Napoli a occhio nudo.* Turin, Einaudi, 1976.

Galante Garrone, A. "Prefazione," in U. Zanotti-Bianco, *Carteggio 1906–18.* Rome-Bari, Laterza, 1987, pp. vii–xxiv.

Galasso, G. "Le forme del potere, classi e gerarchie sociali," in *Storia d'Italia,* Vol. I, *I caratteri originali.* Turin, Einaudi, 1972, pp. 401–599.

Galasso, G. "Lo stereotipo del napoletano e le sue variazioni regionali," in *L'altra Europa. Per un'antropologia storica del Mezzogiorno d'Italia.* Milan, Mondadori, 1982.

Galletti, B. *L'attualità e l'onorevole Francesco Crispi.* Palermo, Spinnato, 1890.

Gallie, W. B. "Essentially contested concepts," *Proceedings of the Aristotelian Society,* Vol. LVI, 1955–6, 167–199.

Gambetta, D. *The Sicilian Mafia: The Business of Private Protection.* Cambridge, Mass., Harvard University Press, 1993.

Gambetta, D., S. Lupo, P. Pezzino, and N. Tranfaglia "La mafia e la sua storia. Radici locali e dimensione internazionale," *Passato e Presente,* 31 (1994), 19–40.

Gambi, L. "Le 'regioni' italiane come problema storico," *Quaderni Storici,* 34, 1977, 275–298.

Gargiulo, L. *Relazione sulla vera sorgente del brigantaggio.* Naples, De Angelis, 1863.

Gates, H. L. Jr. "Introduction: Writing 'Race' and the Difference It Makes," in Gates, H. L. Jr. (ed.) *"Race," Writing, and Difference.* Chicago, Chicago University Press, 1986, pp. 1–20.

Gatto, S. "Attualità di un'inchiesta del 1876 sulla Sicilia," *Belfagor,* March 31, 1950 (229–233).

Gellner, E. *Nations and Nationalism.* Oxford, Blackwell, 1983.

Gentile, E. *L'Italia giolittiana.* Bologna, Il Mulino, 1977.

Giarrizzo, G. "Introduzione," in M. Aymard and G. Giarrizzo (eds.) *Storia d'Italia. Le regioni dall'Unità a oggi. La Sicilia.* Turin, Einaudi, 1987, pp. XIX-LVII.

Gibellini, V. "Esercito italiano (1861–70): la lotta al brigantaggio," in *Rivista Militare,* 105, 2, (1982), 123–26.

Giddens, A. *The Nation-State and Violence,* Vol. II of *A Contemporary Critique of Historical Materialism.* Cambridge, Polity, 1985.

Gigli Marchetti, A. "Lo stato e i caratteri dell'industria tipografica," in *I tre anelli. Mutualità, resistenza, cooperazione dei tipografi milanesi (1860–1925).* Milan, Franco Angeli, 1983, pp. 9–33.

Gilman, S. L. *Difference and Pathology: Stereotypes of Sexuality, Race, and Madness.* Ithaca, Cornell University Press, 1985.

Ginsborg, P. "After the Revolution: bandits on the plains of the Po 1848–54," in J. A. Davis and P. Ginsborg (eds.) *Society and Politics in the Age of the Risorgimento. Essays in Honour of Denis Mack Smith.* Cambridge, Cambridge University Press, 1991, pp. 128–151.

Gooch, J. *Army, State and Society in Italy, 1870–1915.* Basingstoke, Macmillan, 1989.

Govone, G. "Memoria sulle cause del brigantaggio," in U. Govone, *Il generale Giuseppe Govone. Frammenti di memorie.* Turin, Casanova, 1902, pp. 393–408.

Gramsci, A. *Il Risorgimento.* Rome, Riuniti, 1975.

Grand-Carteret, J. *Crispi, Bismarck et la Triple Alliance en caricatures.* Paris, Delagrave, 1891.

Gribaudi, G. "Images of the South: the Mezzogiorno as seen by insiders and outsiders," in R. Lumley and J. Morris (eds.) *The New History of the Italian South. The Mezzogiorno Revisited.* Exeter, Exeter University Press, 1997, pp. 83–113.

Grillandi, M. *Francesco Crispi.* Turin, UTET, 1969.

Grillandi, M. *Emilio Treves.* Turin, UTET, 1977.

Guarnieri, A. *Otto anni di storia militare in Italia.* Florence, Galletti, 1868.

Guiccioli, A. "Diario del 1889," *Nuova Antologia,* 1601, December 1, 1938, 273–295.

Guiccioli, A. "Diario del 1892," *Nuova Antologia,* 1626, December 16, 1939, 364–381.

Hobsbawm, E. J. *Bandits.* London, Pelican, 1972.

Hobsbawm, E. J. "Social Bandits: Reply," *Comparative Studies in Society and History,* 14, 4, (1972), 503–505.

Hobsbawm, E. J. *Nations and Nationalism since 1780: Programme, myth, reality.* Cambridge, Cambridge University Press, 1990.

Hughes, S. C. *Crime, Disorder and the Risorgimento: The Politics of Policing in Bologna.* Cambridge, Cambridge University Press, 1994.

Isnenghi, M. *Il mito della grande guerra.* Bologna, Il Mulino, 1989.

Jannazzo, A. "Introduzione" in L. Franchetti, *Politica e mafia in Sicilia. Gli inediti del 1876.* Naples, Bibliopolis, 1995, pp. 9–25.

Jemolo, A. C. *Francesco Crispi.* Florence, Le Monnier, 1970.

Jenkins, R. *Social Identity.* London, Routledge, 1996.

Kemp, T. *Industrialisation in Nineteenth-Century Europe.* London, Longman, 1969.

La Marmora, A. *Carteggi.* Turin, Chiantore, 1928.

Lanaro, S. *Nazione e lavoro. Saggio sulla cultura borghese in Italia, 1870–1925.* Venice, Marsilio, 1979.

Lanaro, S. "Il Plutarco italiano: l'istruzione del 'popolo' dopo l'Unità," in C. Vivanti (ed.) *Storia d'Italia,* Annali 4, *Intellettuali e potere.* Turin, Einaudi, 1981, pp. 553–587.

Lanaro, S. *L'Italia nuova.* Turin, Einaudi, 1988.

Lanaro, S. "Le élites settentrionali e la storia italiana," *Meridiana,* 16, 1993, 19–39.

Landolfi, E. *Scipio Sighele. Un giobertiano tra democrazia nazionale e socialismo tricolore.* Rome, Volpe, 1981.

Lane, E. W. *An Account of the Manners and Customs of the Modern Egyptians.* London, J. Murray, 1860.

Lévi-Strauss, C. *Le totémisme aujourd'hui.* Paris, Presses Universitaires, 1962.

Levra, U. "Il Risorgimento nazional-popolare di Crispi," in *Fare gli Italiani. Memoria e celebrazione del Risorgimento.* Turin, Comitato di Torino dell'Istituto per la Storia del Risorgimento Italiano, 1992, pp. 299–386.

Levy, C., (ed.) *Italian Regionalism: History, Identity and Politics.* Oxford, Berg, 1996.

Lumley, R. and J. Morris, (eds.) *The New History of the Italian South: The Mezzogiorno Revisited.* Exeter, Exeter University Press, 1997.

Lupo, S. *Il giardino degli aranci. Il mondo degli agrumi nella storia del Mezzogiorno.* Venice, Marsilio, 1990.

Lupo, S. *Storia della mafia dalle origini ai nostri giorni.* Rome, Donzelli, 1993.

Lupo, S. *Storia della mafia dalle origini ai giorni nostri,* revised edition. Rome, Donzelli, 1997.

Lyttelton, A. *et al.* "Élites, famiglie, strategie imprenditoriali: Macry e Banti sull'Ottocento italiano," *Meridiana,* 6, 1989, 231–259.

Lyttelton, A. "The middle classes in Liberal Italy," in J. A. Davis and P. Ginsborg (eds.) *Society and Politics in the Age of the Risorgimento. Essays in honour of Denis Mack Smith.* Cambridge, Cambridge University Press, 1991, pp. 217–250.

Lyttelton, A. "A new past for the Mezzogiorno," *TLS,* 4618, October 4, 1991, 14–15.

Mack Smith, D. *Italy—A Modern History.* Michigan, University of Michigan Press, 1959.

Mack Smith, D. "Regionalism," in E. R. Tannenbaum and E. P. Noether (eds.) *Modern Italy. A Topical History Since 1861.* New York, New York University Press, 1974, pp. 125–146.

Macry, P. "La Napoli dei dotti. Lettori, libri e biblioteche di una ex-capitale (1870–1900)," *Meridiana,* 4 (1988), 131–161.

Maffei, A. *Brigand Life in Italy: A History of Bourbonist Reaction.* London, Hurst and Blackett, 1865.

Majorana, A. *Del parlamentarismo.* Rome, Loescher, 1885.

Manacorda, G. *Crisi economica e lotta politica in Italia 1892–1896*. Turin, Einaudi, 1968.

Manacorda, G. "Crispi e la legge agraria per la Sicilia," in *Il movimento reale e la coscienza inquieta. L'Italia liberale e il socialismo e altri scritti tra storia e memoria*. Milan, Franco Angeli, 1992, pp. 15–84.

Marino, G. C. *L'opposizione mafiosa (1870–1882). Baroni e mafia contro lo stato liberale*. Palermo, Flaccovio, 1964.

Marino, R. "Nuova borghesia e amministrazione locale nelle cronache giudiziarie del principato Citra," in A. Massafra (ed.) *Il Mezzogiorno preunitario. Economia, società e istituzioni*. Bari, Dedalo, 1988, pp. 1087–1101.

Marmo, M. "Le ragioni della mafia: due recenti letture di storia politica e sociologia economica," *Quaderni Storici*, 88 (1995), 195–212.

Martucci, R. *Emergenza e tutela dell'ordine pubblico nell'Italia liberale*. Bologna, Il Mulino, 1980.

Massafra, A. (ed.) *Il Mezzogiorno preunitario. Economia, società e istituzioni*. Bari, Dedalo, 1988.

Massari, G. "Relazione della commissione d'inchiesta del deputato Massari letta alla camera nella tornata segreta del 3 maggio 1863," in T. Pedìo, *Inchiesta sul brigantaggio*. Manduria, Lacaita, 1983, pp. 105–229.

Mazzamuto, P. "La Sicilia di Franchetti e Sonnino e i suoi stereotipi socio-letterari," *Nuovi Quaderni del Meridione*, 51–2, 1975, 36–67.

Mediolanum, 4 vols. Milan, Vallardi, 1881.

Meriggi, M. "The Italian 'Borghesia,'" in J. Kocka and A. Mitchell (eds.) *Bourgeois Society in Nineteenth-Century Europe*. Oxford, Berg, 1993, pp. 423–438.

Meriggi, M. *Breve storia dell'Italia settentrionale dall'Ottocento a oggi*. Rome, Donzelli, 1996.

Milani, M. *La repressione dell'ultimo brigantaggio nelle Calabrie, 1868–9*. Pavia, Biblioteca pavese di storia patria, 1952.

Mill, J. S. *A System of Logic Ratiocinative and Inductive. Being a Connected View of the Principles of Evidence and the Methods of Scientific Investigation, Collected Works of John Stuart Mill*, Vol. VIII, edited by J. M. Robson. Toronto, University of Toronto Press, 1974.

Moe, N. *Representing the South in Post-Unification Italy, c. 1860–1880*. Johns Hopkins University Doctoral Thesis, 1994.

Molfese, F. *Storia del brigantaggio dopo l'Unità*. Milan, Feltrinelli, 1964.

Molfese, F. "Il brigantaggio nel Mezzogiorno dopo l'Unità d'Italia," *Archivio Storico per la Calabria e la Lucania*, XLII (1975), 99–136.

Molfese, F. "La repressione del brigantaggio post-unitario nel mezzogiorno continentale (1860–70)," *Archivio Storico per le Province Napoletane*, CI (1983), 33–64.

Monnier, M. *Notizie storiche sul brigantaggio nelle provincie napoletane dai tempi di Frà Diavolo sino ai giorni nostri*. Florence, Barbèra, 1862.

Monnier, M. *Histoire du brigandage dans l'Italie méridionale*. Paris, Lévy, 1862.

Montagu, A. *Man's Most Dangerous Myth: The Fallacy of Race*. Cleveland, Meridian, 1964.

Morelli, N. *Gli orrori e le turpitudini del governo Crispi.* Rome, Ciotola, 1890.

Moretti, M. "Preliminari ad uno studio su Pasquale Villari," *Giornale Critico della Filosofia Italiana,* V serie, LIX (LXI), fascicolo 1–4 (1980), 190–232.

Moretti, M. "La storiografia italiana e la cultura del secondo ottocento. Preliminari ad uno studio su Pasquale Villari," *Giornale Critico della Filosofia Italiana,* V serie, LX, fascicolo 3 (1981), 300–372.

Morris, J. "Challenging *meridionalismo:* constructing a new history for Southern Italy," in R. Lumley and J. Morris (eds.) *The New History of the Italian South. The Mezzogiorno Revisited.* Exeter, Exeter University Press, 1997, pp. 1–19.

Mozzillo, A. *Viaggiatori stranieri nel Sud.* Milan, Edizioni di comunità, 1964.

Musella, L. *Individui, amici, clienti. Relazioni personali e circuiti politici in Italia meridionale tra Otto e Novecento.* Bologna, Il Mulino, 1994.

Narjoux, F. *Francesco Crispi—l'homme public, l'homme privé.* Paris, Savine, 1890.

Niceforo, A. *L'Italia barbara contemporanea (Studi ed appunti).* Sandron, Milan-Palermo, 1898.

Nozzoli, A. "La letteratura femminile in Italia tra Ottocento e Novecento," in *Tabù e coscienza. La condizione femminile nella letteratura italiana del Novecento.* Florence, La Nuova Italia, 1978, pp. 1–40.

Oriani, A. *Punte secche, Opera omnia,* Vol. XXIII. Bologna, Cappelli, 1934.

Padula, V. *Il brigantaggio in Calabria (1864–5).* Rome, Carlo M. Padula, 1981.

Pantaleoni, D. "Le ultime elezioni politiche in Italia," *Nuova Antologia,* 12 (1874), 928–944.

Paris, R. "L'Italia fuori d'Italia," in *Storia d'Italia,* Vol. IV, *Dall'Unità a oggi,* 1. Turin, Einaudi, 1975, pp. 509–818.

Pasolini dall'Onda, P. *Giuseppe Pasolini 1815–1876—Memorie raccolte da suo figlio,* Vol. II. Turin, Bocca, 1915.

Pearton, M. *The Knowledgeable State: Diplomacy, War and Technology since 1830.* London, Burnett, 1982.

Pellegrino, B. *Vescovi "borbonici" e stato "liberale" (1860–61).* Rome-Bari, Laterza, 1992.

Pemble, J. *The Mediterranean Passion. Victorians and Edwardians in the South.* Oxford, Oxford University Press, 1988.

Petrusewicz, M. *Latifondo. Economia morale e vita materiale in una periferia dell'Ottocento.* Venice, Marsilio, 1989.

Petrusewicz, M. "The demise of *latifondismo,*" in R. Lumley and J. Morris (eds.) *The New History of the Italian South. The Mezzogiorno Revisited.* Exeter, Exeter University Press, 1997, pp. 20–41.

Petrusewicz, M. *Come il meridione divenne una Questione. Rappresentazioni del Sud prima e dopo il Quarantotto.* Catanzaro, Rubbettino, 1998.

Pezzino, P. "Stato, violenza, società. Nascita e sviluppo del paradigma mafioso," in M. Aymard and G. Giarrizzo (eds.) *Storia d'Italia. Le regioni dall'Unità a oggi. La Sicilia.* Turin, Einaudi, 1987, pp. 903–982.

Pezzino, P. "Nota introduttiva" in L. Franchetti, *Condizioni politiche e amministrative della Sicilia.* Rome, Meridiana, 1992, pp. xii-xx.

Pick, D. *Faces of Degeneration: A European disorder, c. 1848–c. 1918.* Cambridge, Cambridge University Press, 1989.

Pieragnoli, G. *Francesco Crispi.* Rome, Pasqualini, 1887.

Pieri, P. *Storia militare del Risorgimento.* Turin, Einaudi, 1962.

Pieri, P. *Le forze armate nell'età della destra.* Milan, Giuffrè, 1962.

Platania, M. "Instabilità sociale e delinquenza," in A. Massafra (ed.) *Il Mezzogiorno preunitario. Economia, società e istituzioni.* Bari, Dedalo, 1988, pp. 1069–1085.

Porciani, I. *La festa della nazione. Rappresentazione dello Stato e spazi sociali nell'Italia unita.* Bologna, Il Mulino, 1997.

Procacci, G. *Le elezioni del 1874 e l'opposizione meridionale.* Milan, Feltrinelli, 1956.

Ragionieri, E. *La storia politica e sociale, Storia d'Italia,* Vol. 4, tomo 3. Turin, Einaudi, 1976.

Recupero, A. "La Sicilia all'opposizione (1848–74)," in M. Aymard and G. Giarrizzo (eds.) *Storia d'Italia. Le regioni dall'Unità a oggi. La Sicilia.* Turin, Einaudi, 1987, pp. 39–85.

Regolamento di disciplina militare per le truppe di cavalleria ed artiglieria. Turin, Fodratti, 1840.

Renda, A., ed. *La questione meridionale.* Milan-Palermo, Sandron, 1900.

Renda, F. *I Fasci siciliani (1892–94).* Turin, Einaudi, 1977.

Renda, F. "La 'questione sociale' e i Fasci (1874–94)," in M. Aymard and G. Giarrizzo (eds.) *Storia d'Italia. Le regioni dall'Unità a oggi. La Sicilia.* Turin, Einaudi, 1987, pp. 157–188.

Riall, L. "Elite resistance to state formation: the case of Italy," in M. Fulbrook (ed.) *National Histories and European History.* London, UCL Press, 1993, pp. 46–68.

Riall, L. *The Italian Risorgimento: State, society and national unification.* Routledge, London, 1994.

Riall, L. *Sicily and the Unification of Italy: Liberal Policy and Local Power, 1859–1866.* Oxford, Oxford University Press, 1998.

Riccio, V. *I meridionali alla camera,* Vol. 1. Turin, Roux, 1888.

Riviello, R. *Cronaca potentina dal 1799 al 1882.* Potenza, Santanello, 1888.

Rochat, G., and G. Massobrio, *Breve storia dell'esercito italiano dal 1861 al 1943.* Turin, Einaudi, 1978.

Rochat, G. "La professione militare in Italia dall'Ottocento alla seconda guerra mondiale," in *L'esercito italiano in pace e in guerra. Studi di storia militare.* Milan, RARA, 1991, pp. 29–40.

Romagnoli, S. *Storia della letteratura italiana,* Vol. VIII, *Dall'Ottocento al Novecento.* Milan, Garzanti, 1968.

Romagnoli, S. "Il brigante nel romanzo storico italiano," *Archivio Storico per la Calabria e la Lucania,* XLII (1975), 176–212.

Romanelli, R. *L'Italia liberale (1860–1900).* Bologna, Il Mulino, 1979.

Romanelli, R. "Borghesi d'Italia," *Rivista dei Libri,* 1, 1993, 29–32.

Romanelli, R. "Esiste il Mezzogiorno?," *Rivista dei Libri,* 5, 1993, 26–28.

Romanelli, R. "Francesco Crispi e la riforma dello stato nella svolta del 1887," in *Il comando impossibile. Stato e società nell'Italia liberale,* second edition. Bologna, Il Mulino, 1995, pp. 279–351.

Romani, R. *L'economia politica del Risorgimento italiano.* Turin, Bollati Boringhieri, 1994.

Romano, S. *Crispi—progetto per una dittatura.* Milan, Bompiani, 1973.

Romano, S. *Crispi.* Milan, Bompiani, 1986.

Rosa, G. *Il mito della capitale morale. Letteratura e pubblicistica a Milano fra Otto e Novecento.* Milan, Edizioni di Comunità, 1982.

Rosani, C. *A S.E. Francesco Crispi Presidente del Consiglio.* Milan, 1894(?).

Saffi, A. "La commissione parlamentare d'inchiesta nelle province meridionali attraverso le lettere di Aurelio Saffi," in T. Pedìo, *Inchiesta sul brigantaggio.* Manduria, Lacaita, 1983, pp. 57–90.

Said, E. W. *Orientalism.* Harmondsworth, Penguin, 1978.

Said, E. W. *Culture and Imperialism.* London, Vintage, 1994.

Salinari, C. *Miti e coscienza del decadentismo italiano (D'Annunzio, Pascoli, Fogazzaro e Pirandello)* Milan, Feltrinelli, 1960.

Salvadori, M. L. *Il mito del buongoverno. La questione meridionale da Cavour a Gramsci.* Turin, Einaudi, 1963.

Schneider, J., and P. Schneider. *Culture and Political Economy in Western Sicily.* London, Academic Press, 1976.

Schneider, J. "Introduction: the dynamics of neo-orientalism in Italy (1848–1995)," in J. Schneider (ed.) *Italy's "Southern Question." Orientalism in one country.* Oxford-New York, Berg, 1998, pp. 1–23.

Scirocco, A. *Governo e paese nel Mezzogiorno nella crisi dell'unificazione (1860–61).* Milan, Giuffrè, 1963.

Scirocco, A. *Il mezzogiorno nell'Italia unita (1861–5).* Naples, Società Editrice Napoletana, 1979.

Scirocco, A. "Aurelio Saffi nella vita parlamentare," *Il Risorgimento,* 1 (1991), 5–33.

Scherillo, M. "Gaetano Negri alla caccia dei briganti," in G. Negri, *Opere di Gaetano Negri I—Nel presente e nel passato.* Milan, Hoepli, 1905, pp. 3–65.

Serao, M. "Francesco Crispi," *Il Mattino,* January 10–11, 1894.

Siculo, G. *Francesco Crispi a Torino.* Turin, Casanova, 1887.

Siegrist, H. "Gli avvocati nell'Italia del XIX secolo. Provenienza e matrimoni, titolo e prestigio," *Meridiana,* 14, 1992, 145–181.

Sighele, S. "Contro il parlamentarismo," in *La delinquenza settaria.* Milan, Treves, 1897, pp. 229–274.

Soffici, A. "Diario napoletano," in *La giostra dei sensi,* fourth edition. Florence, Vallecchi, 1943.

Snowden, F. M. *Naples in the Time of Cholera, 1884–1911.* Cambridge, Cambridge University Press, 1995.

Snowden, F. M. "'Fields of death': malaria in Italy, 1861–1962," *Modern Italy,* 4 (1) 1999, 25–57.

Sonnino, S. "La mezzeria in Toscana," in S. Sonnino, *Scritti e discorsi extraparlamentari,* Vol. I, *1870–1902.* Bari, Laterza, 1972, pp. 105–149.

Sonnino, S. *I contadini in Sicilia,* Vol. II of L. Franchetti and S. Sonnino, *Inchiesta in Sicilia.* Florence, Vallecchi, 1974.

Spampinato, R. "Per una storia della mafia. Interpretazioni e questioni controverse," in M. Aymard and G. Giarrizzo (eds.) *Storia d'Italia. Le regioni dall'Unità a oggi. La Sicilia.* Turin, Einaudi, 1987, pp. 881–902.

Spinella, M. "Politica e ideologia politica" in M. Spinella *et al.* (eds.) *Critica Sociale,* Vol. I. Milan, Feltrinelli, 1959, pp. ix-lxxix.

Squarciapino, G. *Roma bizantina. Società e letteratura ai tempi di Angelo Sommaruga.* Turin, Einaudi, 1950.

Stillman, W. J. *Francesco Crispi—Insurgent, Exile, Revolutionist and Statesman.* London, Grant Richards, 1899.

"Sul brigantaggio—note di un uffiziale italiano," *Rivista Contemporanea,* May 1862, 185–201.

Tagliacozzo, E. *Voci di realismo politico dopo il 1870.* Bari, Laterza, 1937.

Talamo, G. "Diversità e squilibri regionali nella cultura politica del Risorgimento," in *De Sanctis politico e altri saggi.* Rome, Editrice De Santis, 1969, pp. 115–156.

Tedesco, V. *La stampa satirica in Italia 1860–1914.* Milan, Franco Angeli, 1991.

Teti, V. *La razza maledetta. Origini del pregiudizio antimeridionale.* Rome, Manifestolibri, 1993.

Themelly, M. "Trasgressione, criminalità, comportamenti collettivi nelle province meridionali," in A. Massafra (ed.) *Il Mezzogiorno preunitario. Economia, società e istituzioni.* Bari, Dedalo, 1988, pp. 1039–1054.

Tobia, B. *Una patria per gli italiani. Spazi, itinerari, monumenti nell'Italia unita (1870–1900).* Rome-Bari, Laterza, 1991.

Torelli-Viollier, E. "Movimento librario," in *Mediolanum* III. Milan, Vallardi, 1881, pp. 341–361.

Trevellini, N. "Lungo le ferrovie meridionali," *Illustrazione Italiana,* 2 August, 1874, p. 84.

Tullio-Altan, C. *La nostra Italia. Arretratezza socioculturale, clientelismo, trasformismo e ribellismo dall'Unità ad oggi.* Milan, Feltrinelli, 1986.

Turiello, P. "Il secolo XIX," in *Il secolo XIX ed altri scritti di politica internazionale e coloniale.* Bologna, Zanichelli, 1944, pp. 3–105.

Turiello, P. *Governo e governati in Italia.* Turin, Einaudi, 1980.

Urbinati, N. *Le civili libertà. Positivismo e liberalismo nell'Italia unita.* Venice, Marsilio, 1990.

Verga, G. *Cavalleria rusticana,* in *Teatro.* Milan, Garzanti, 1987, pp. 207–29.

Vigo, G. "Gli italiani alla conquista dell'alfabeto," in S. Soldani and G. Turi (eds.) *Fare gli italiani. Scuola e cultura nell'Italia contemporanea. 1. La nascita dello Stato nazionale.* Bologna, Il Mulino, 1993, pp. 37–66.

Villari, P. *Arte, storia e filosofia. Saggi critici.* Florence, Sansoni, 1884.

Villari, P. *Le lettere meridionali ed altri scritti sulla questione sociale in Italia,* second edition. Turin, Bocca, 1885.

Villari, P. "Dove andiamo?," *Nuova Antologia,* November 1, 1893, 5–24.

Villari, P. *Le prime lettere meridionali.* Rome, La Voce, 1920.

Vivanti, C. "Lacerazioni e constrasti," in R. Romano and C. Vivanti (eds.) *Storia d'Italia,* Vol. I, *I caratteri originali.* Turin, Einaudi, 1972, pp. 867–948.

Vozzi, M. P. "La comitiva armata dei fratelli Capozzoli e la rivoluzione cilentana del 1828. Lotta politica e brigantaggio," in A. Massafra (ed.) *Il Mezzogiorno preunitario. Economia, società e istituzioni.* Bari, Dedalo, 1988, pp. 1143–1157.

Weber, E. "Of stereotypes and of the French," *Journal of Contemporary History,* 25 (2–3) 1990, 169–203.

Weber, M. *The Theory of Social and Economic Organization.* New York, Free Press of Glencoe, 1964.

Whittam, J. *The Politics of the Italian Army 1861–1918.* London, Croom Helm, 1977.

Woodward, C. V. *American Counterpoint: Slavery and Racism in the North-South Dialogue.* Boston-Toronto, Little, Brown and Co., 1964.

Woolf, S. *A History of Italy 1700–1860: The social constraints of political change.* London, Methuen, 1979.

Young, R. *White Mythologies: Writing History and the West.* London, Routledge, 1990.

Zanotti-Bianco, U. "Una piaga secolare del Mezzogiorno: la malaria," in *Meridione e meridionalisti.* Rome, Collezione Meridionale, 1964, pp. 131–60.

Zanotti-Bianco, U. *Carteggio 1906–18.* Rome-Bari, Laterza, 1987.

Zanzi, G. *Memorie di Zanzi Guglielmo Maggior Generale della Riserva sulla repressione del brigantaggio negli Abruzzi e Terra di Lavoro.* Milan, Cogliati, 1913.

Zito, N. "Le inchieste del 1875–76 in Sicilia. Appunti per un'analisi comparata," *Nuovi Quaderni del Meridione,* 51–2, 1975, 263–293.

Index